You Can
Love Again

MEG MESSER

YOU CAN LOVE AGAIN

The Tapestry of a Life,
of a War Survivor's Love Story

Outskirts Press, Inc.
Denver, Colorado

You Can Love Again
The Tapestry of a Life, of a War Survivor's Love Story

Outskirts Press, Inc.
http://www.outskirtspress.com

ISBN: 978-1-4327-6162-2

Outskirts Press and the "OP" logo are trademarks belonging to Outskirts Press, Inc.

PRINTED IN THE UNITED STATES OF AMERICA

TABLE OF CONTENTS

CHAPTER ONE

THE WAR YEARS AS SEEN
THROUGH THE EYES OF A CHILD

I grew up during World War II in the city of Berlin, Germany. We lived in a beautiful, quiet neighborhood of large one-family mansions.

There was a big wrought iron gate in front of the long driveway to our home. Our home was a red, three-story brick house with a beautiful backyard with huge shade trees and a small cement pool. In the back of our yard was a long high hedge. The path led to our private place; a swing, a sandbox, a picnic table, and the garden house with tools in it. In short our "clubhouse" was where the neighborhood met. If you had stopped at the front of the house, you would have to come to a heavy oak front door with brass knockers polished to a high sheen.

When you entered the house, there was a small foyer with hooks to hang coats and hats, and store umbrellas. This foyer opened up to a reception room with marble floors, a big fireplace, and a comfortable sitting area in front of it. There was an open Florida room full of plants blooming even in the winter.

Three doors opened from this reception area. One door opened into my mother's music room where she had her big grand piano. The room was furnished with French provincial furniture. There was a big Motorola record player in there. This was the room where my parents entertained a lot. I can still see my dainty, beautiful mother dancing with handsome young men in dashing uniforms to the nostalgic music of the forties.

My father's library opened up into her music room. It had books all the way up to the ceiling, a gigantic desk, leather furniture and oriental rugs. Next to these two rooms was a huge kitchen with a dumbwaiter on which the food from the kitchen was sent to the upstairs dining room. We had a formal dining room upstairs, two baths and three bedrooms on that floor. On the third floor we had a big attic and the maid's bedroom and bath.

My father was a well-respected scientist with a doctor's degree in chemistry and engineering. My mother was a concert pianist. I can still hear her practicing her music for several hours every day.

In the summertime she would leave the windows open, and we could hear the music carrying to the outside. She told us to listen for the Brahms lullaby. That meant it was time to come in for supper. We were raised on classical music.

My mother always had full-time help for the house. In short, at that time she lived a fairy tale life, It was wonderful, but it didn't last very long.

My brother Manfred was three years older than I, and I adored him. He called me "Dolly." In German "Pueppi," and the name stuck.

When I was five years old the war was getting really bad. The air raids on Berlin happened nightly. We slept in sweatshirts because usually the sirens would get us up in the middle of the night. My mother would get my brother, and my father would run and get me. Together, we would hurry to the basement, which was steel reinforced for extra safety.

We would spend hours down there listening to the bombs falling. They would fall from the sky with a loud whistle until they hit the ground with a horrible crash. It would make the earth tremble and blow out the windows in the houses nearby. By the loudness of the crash, we would guess how close the planes were to us.

We could also hear the constant droning of the airplanes. They sounded like hundreds of planes in the sky. We could hear the artillery shooting from the ground toward the planes.

One night our house was hit. It sounded as if the bomb was coming through the ceiling of our basement. My daddy threw himself over my body, where I was laying on the cot, to protect my body with his.

As it turned out, the bomb had only gone through to the third floor of our home. It was a phosphorous bomb, and the whole third floor was on fire. My brother and I were standing outside holding hands and sobbing as neighbors were trying to help put out the fire. I remember looking up to the top of our house where the yellow and orange flames were leaping into the black night sky. It's something I will never forget as long as I live.

The fire was put out. Our house got repaired, and we remained in Berlin for the time being. It was a horrible way to live. Hitler was a true dictator and didn't care whom he had to kill, and in what cruel manner to make an example.

My father spoke up against Hitler once at a cocktail party, supposedly among friends. The next morning the Gestapo showed up and took him with them. The Gestapo was like a secret police, and everybody was scared to death of them. Our house was quiet with fear. They interrogated my father for three days with bright lights on him day and night. Then they told him that they would let him go, but if he ever spoke against Hitler again, he would never see his family again. From that day on, our telephone was tapped, and our parents showed us when we picked up the phone, we would hear a little click and our conversation was being taped. We were told never to repeat anything we ever heard being said in our home - a tough way for small children to grow up.

Friends of my parents, officers in the service, started to realize what was going on. There were acts of Jewish persecution and cruelty also against other Germans. They tried to get away from various branches of the service because they could no longer believe in the cause for which they were fighting. They were caught, tortured, and killed in many different cruel ways.

My mother had a friend who lived next door to us. She had the most handsome husband, and a little daughter. Her mother lived with them. He was one of many officers totally disillusioned with the way things were going in Germany. He talked to his wife and told her he would be awaiting her visits in the cemetery. Soon afterwards the SS showed up at her house and told her that they knew her husband would come home soon. She was no longer allowed to leave the house, and they stationed two SS men in her home. She was told that if her husband came to the door, she was not supposed to give him any sign they were there, or her child and her mother would be killed. It was not many days when he came home looking for her. The two SS men were standing behind the door, and as he came in looking at his wife, they overpowered him. He was taken away, tortured, killed, and hung by a meat hook.

A neighbor of ours, a very friendly but quiet man, who always stopped to say hello to us children got surprised one night by the SS, a cruel branch of Hitler's favorites, as they forced their way into his house in the middle of the night.

In fear of what they would do to him, he threw himself out of a third floor window. As he hit the ground, he screamed and screamed. It woke me up out of a sound sleep, and I can still hear him.

Children play what they see. We played war. Here we lived in this beautiful suburb of Berlin with beautiful homes all around us. But for play, we collected buckets full of rocks, declared war on the neighboring street and threw rocks at each other. I got to follow the boys way in the back, out of the line of fire. I was the nurse. My brother got hit in the head with a rock, and I had to take him home to my mother. I led him screaming all the way.

War brings out the worst in people. One day my brother and I were playing outside on the street with other children when a nasty looking man came by pulling a wagon. He grabbed me and lifted me into his wagon and started to run. I was screaming. I couldn't get out; he was running too fast. My brother ran after me and grabbed the side of the wagon and dragged hard enough that it slowed down, and I could jump out. We ran up our long driveway to our house.

From that day on, we were not allowed outside our property, and the big wrought iron gate was always closed.

I was such a nervous child that I was sent to my beloved Uncle Fritz and Aunt Pia's for a vacation in the city of Stuttgart, which had not been bombed yet. I looked so forward to my visit.

Aunt Pia always cooked the most delicious meals. She made homemade noodles with the greatest gravy ever tasted by children from Berlin, and whole sheets of cakes covered with the most delicious fruit, and topped with whipping cream.

I played ball out in the street, in front of the house with the neighbor children, running and screaming like a mad person I had a wonderful time.

I had been there for three days when Stuttgart was bombed for the first time. The sirens went off, and I was out of bed before my aunt even made it to my room. "Put your clothes on, darling!

We are going to the bomb shelter!" We headed out of the house. Within minutes we were on our way. My uncle stayed behind. He always looked after old people and made sure the neighbors had their black curtains in front of their windows so no light was showing. We grew up in total darkness at night. This night was no different. There were no stars in the sky; there were no streetlights on; and all the windows of the houses had their black curtains drawn. All of this was supposed to protect us a little bit from being hit. Eventually we got bombed anyway. They got us sooner or later. Darkness in our young lives meant danger. For the rest of my life, I never got over the fear of darkness. To this day, I have at least three night lights in the house on before I go to sleep.

My aunt and I had gone about three blocks. We had three more to go when we heard the bombers in the sky, and the steady humming of hundreds of planes. All of a sudden, the artillery sent lights up from the ground. We called them "Christmas trees." They were like fireworks, only they stayed in the sky much longer, and really had it lit up. As we were running for our lives, we could now see the bombers like tiny slivers in the sky making this scary humming noise that I so dreaded. The planes started to drop their bombs, and the artillery started to shoot at them.

The bombs whistled from the sky, and landed with a crash. The noise was like something straight out of hell. We ran as fast as we could with my aunt holding my hand. We were in a suburb on a mountain outside the city of Stuttgart, and we could see the whole spectacle.

We finally got to the shelter. It was drilled right into a mountain. We banged on the huge, heavy door which was instantly opened for us. The shelter was full of several hundred people who sat on wooden benches.

The massive door closed behind us and the noise instantly faded. My aunt and I sat on a wooden bench with our backs against the rock. I can still feel it. Whenever a bomb hit, the mountain would tremble slightly.

I did not have much experience with prayer. The power of prayer became very evident to me that night. My Aunt Pia was a devout Catholic. She took out her rosary and started to pray out loud. Each little pearl was a prayer. I asked her, "Who are you praying to?" She said, "The Mother Mary. She will watch over us." I asked her, "Over me too?'She said, "Oh yes!" and put her arm around me and continued to pray. "She will protect us both." I was no longer afraid.

Two and one-half hours went by, and it got quiet outside. We were told we could not leave the mountain yet because mines had been dropped, and they first had to find out where we could walk safely. After another hour or so, we were allowed to leave the shelter in single file, following the footsteps of the person in front of us. One wrong step, and we could have been blown up. I truly do not remember being afraid because someone was guiding us - the power of prayer!

We finally departed Berlin. We went to our summer house

east of Berlin in the state of Mecklenburg at a beautiful lake. The town we lived in was called Fuerstenberg, which means "The Duke's Mountain." That is where the Queen Charlotte came from. This later became East Germany.

We spent a lovely summer there - my mother, my brother and I. My dad drifted kind of in and out like he had always done, still supervising his laboratories, one in Munich, one in Darmstadt, and one in Prague. He couldn't just walk away from his job. He was a very handsome man; tall, blond hair, brown eyes, and a lot of fun. One day he showed up unexpectedly, with a huge spear over his shoulder. For my brother, he had a birdcage hanging off that spear, and a little kennel in his other hand with a tiny, miniature Spitz in it for me.

He had such a sense of humor. Our squeals of delight could be heard all the way down the street. My mother, who struggled with dwindling food supplies was not quite as delighted as we were. I was so in love with my little dog. I carried him everywhere I went. I named him, "Hansie."

Hansie was the light of my life. Just like everything else, things went bad for Hansie and me too. My tiny snow white doggie got sick. We took him to the vet. The bad news was that Hansie had distemper. The vet had no medications. There were no medicines to be had. None. After a couple of weeks when he could not get better, he had to be put to sleep. Even writing this, after all this time, I have to fight the tears.

Our property was right at the water, and we had an old rowboat down there. One day my brother said, "Come on Dolly, let's go for a little boat trip on the lake." I looked at the boat. It didn't look all that safe to me. It had an awful lot of water in it. I pointed this out to my brother.

He said, 'No problem. I row; you bail." He gave me a big empty can for that purpose. We both hopped into the boat, and off we went. It was a pretty big, beautiful lake, and on the opposite side from us, you could go through locks from our lake into another one. When you entered the locks, they would close them with big gates and equalize the water from the level of the first lake into the next lake. By then our boat was taking on so much water that my brother had to take over the bailing, and I kind of took over rowing. It was very exciting.

After a while, we decided to turn around and return home. My brother went back to rowing, and I had to bail like crazy. We had taken quite a trip with the sun shining on the water. It was beautiful, but we felt it was time to return home.

When we came back, my mother said, "Where have you been? You've been gone quite a while."

"Oh," we said. "We have just been rowing a little bit." "You children, be careful," my mother said. I think she had momentarily forgotten that my brother could swim, but I couldn't swim. We were nine and twelve then. When you have lived through as many air raids as we had, a leaky rowboat didn't seem so dangerous.

One day my brother decided to teach me how to swim. We went down to the lake. He informed me that he had found a long bean pole, and by hanging on to one end of it with one hand, and him hanging on to the other it would aid me to learn to swim. When he had me in the water, hanging on to the bean pole, (naturally scared to death) he told me he would let go now, and I should kick my legs as fast as I could. Naturally, I went under and swallowed water. When I came up, I was sputtering and coughing and screaming at him to help me as he stood there, doubling over with laughter. I was scared and hysterical. When he finally went in the water and pulled me out, he said, "Don't tell Mutti! Don't tell Mutti!"

We still went to school in Fuerstenberg. It was a tiny town. We lived right on Main Street, and the school was on the other side of Main Street. One day when we were in school, we heard the alarm. The principal announced that we had a warning that planes were going to cross over our town on the way to Berlin. We had never been bombed there, so he told all the children to run on home. I was a fast runner, and was out of the schoolyard in no time at all. All of a sudden, the planes started diving down on us children, and opened machine gunfire on us. All the children turned and ran back into the schoolhouse, but I was too far out. So, the only thing I could do was stand under this tiny, little tree. I had a little brown coat on with a hood. I told myself that if I stand very still my coat will blend in with the brown tree trunk, and they might not see me. I was never so afraid in my life. The airplanes were gone just as fast as they had come.

Maybe from way up high they could not tell whether we were adults or children. On my way home, I really questioned the hearts of people. Over and over again I thought, "But we were only children!'"

This is where the Russian Army was headed. As they came closer and closer, the refugees started coming. These were our farm people, the big land owners east of Berlin. They walked down our main street, and broke down in front of our house from exhaustion, or they rode in covered wagons, and the horses lay down in the street because they could walk no further. My mother and the neighborhood women cooked soup for them, and shared what little we had. The men brought hay and watered the horses. After they rested, they went on. No one wanted to be where the Russian Army was coming because of the terrible things they had heard about their soldiers and what they did to women, little girls, and old men.

When we could hear the artillery day and night, and the Russians were only 30 miles away, we joined the trail of refugees. We heard that there was one last train leaving from the next town.

Hitler had confiscated all cars, so everyone was walking. We left with clothes that weren't warm enough, and shoes which had holes in their soles. Each one of us carried a suitcase. I carried a little leather case which I kept for many years afterwards.

When we got to the next town, the train station was totally overcrowded with people - hundreds of them waiting for the train. When the train came rolling in, it had so many people on it that my daddy knew that I was too frail to get through all those people and onto the train. So he picked me up and simply handed me through one of those train windows to people inside. They reached for me and gently lowered me to the floor while my father, my mother, and my brother fought their way into the train. I was terrified until we were reunited.

We went from town to town, hotel to hotel. We were home-less, but thank heavens my father had the funds to put us up in hotels!

Our next stop was the city of Hamburg, a big port city. We stayed for one night in the city in the Hotel Atlantic, a four star hotel. Sure enough, in the night the alarm sounded, and we ran from the fourth floor to the basement bomb shelter. It was pretty much a narrow hallway with benches all along the wall. We sat there for hours and waited until the alarm rang all clear. There was a woman sitting next to me. She had something to say all the time. Among other things she said, "Look at all those pipes running along the ceiling above us. I am sure some of them are gas lines, and if they get hit we will be dead anyway." I was fully awake and stared at those pipes.

Remember how children hear everything, and understand a lot more than we think.

When it was over, we went back to bed and slept. The next morning, I remember standing in front of the hotel near the street, watching trucks from the zoo drive by loaded with dead animals. They were charred. Then more trucks came by, and my brother said, "Those are not animals. Those are people." They had burned the zoo down, and more than three-fourths of the city of Hamburg. Again we had been lucky. After that, I did not remember anything. It was too much for me, and my memory shut down to protect me from permanent harm. I was nine years old.

We ended up north of Hamburg in a little town called Glueckstadt. This was the town I was born in nine years ago. The name of the town means, "Happiness Town." My father put us up in a nice little hotel on the shores of the North Sea. We ran on the dunes with the strong north wind pulling on our hair. This was a happy time.

One day the English soldiers arrived with big tanks. We all stood along the street and cheered. The war was over. Our life under tyranny had come to an end. People cried with joy, and so did I, as I was jumping up and down happily.

There was no room for the officers of the English battalion that came into this little town. So they made the hotel their headquarters. We all had to move into the jail across the street. It was a real jail built with big rocks and tiny barred windows way up high. There were about seven or eight families. We all had to sleep on the floor. One woman cried hysterically. Someone had killed them self in the cell that had been assigned to her and her daughter. We had to stay there for six weeks. Then the English soldiers decided to share the hotel with us. Each family got one room, which was a great improvement from the jail.

The English soldiers were kind to us. Most of them were so young. They would save their chocolate rations for us, a treat we had not had in years. My brother and I were given an orange to share, and to the horror of our mother, we ate the whole thing, peelings and all.

As for the city of Stuttgart after the war, the people of Stuttgart hauled all the rubble away and built a huge mountain out of it outside the city. They called it "Old Stuttgart," as a memorial to what war can do. They planted a park on that mountain, and put a huge cross on top of it. You could see it for miles away. Then they proceeded to rebuild the city and their lives.

CHAPTER TWO

GROWING UP DURING THE AFTERMATH OF WORLD WAR II

Within three months of our liberation by the English army, our father showed up in Glueckstadt in a black limousine, accompanied by an American CIC man who had gotten him across all the borders of the various armies to be reunited with us, and to bring us to the American sector. My father had left us right after he had taken us to Glueckstadt, and had settled us down. He had left to check on his laboratories in Munich, Prague, and Darmstadt. So here he was in all his glory, a tall slender man with light blond hair and laughing brown eyes.

We were so glad to see him. A day or so later, we were packed up to return with him and the CIC officer to the American sector. To be exact, near Frankfht where he had negotiated with some American officials about some of his patents. Frankfurt was leveled by air raids too, and there were no places to live. We finally settled in a tiny little town, at the foot of a range of mountains called the Odenwald between Frankfurt and Heidelberg. We were to spend several years there, and I do not look back to this time with fondness. To find us a place to live, the Americans told a very wealthy family with a beautiful house to double up in their house and make room for us. Needless to say, we were not very welcome, but this was still like wartime, and this family could easily have been evicted. It was my mother who had said that we could share the space of this house. These people had not been touched by war at all since the town was so small, and had never been bombed.

Some people had come to this picturesque little village from nearby cities, but the majority of the people were villagers whose families had lived there forever. It was a typical old European village with little houses so old that some were crooked. They were built with brick or stone a long time ago, and I am sure they will withstand several more hundred years.

There was a castle on the top of the highest hill with a high stone wall around it. The oldest houses were tucked close around the outside wall of the castle. In times of feuding or war, the villagers all found refuge inside the castle walls.

Finally, during the war with Napoleon, the castle got partially burned down. It was still a thing of beauty, even though all the doors and windows were gone. Parts of the castle were restored so a family could live there and take care of the castle. There was a restaurant there, a souvenir shop, and "The Tower." You could climb up the never-ending circular stairs to the top of the observation tower. From there you could look over many wooded mountains, the little village below, and many vineyards.

The farmers planted vineyards on the lower hills. The grapes that grew there made wonderful wine. That was their biggest source of income. You could also see where the original old village ended and newer houses had been built as time went by.

The main street in this town had cobblestones, and on the bed of the cobblestones flowed the prettiest clear creek all the way down Main Street through the town where it went underground and reappeared at other locations.

There were shops on both sides of the street, and you could cross over the occasional little bridge. The baker was there, the butcher shop, the delicatessen, the store for fresh milk, a store for vegetables and fruits, the shoemaker and repair, a bookstore, and a hairdresser.

When we came to the end of the street, there was a busy highway which connected cities and towns all the way from Frankfurt to Heidelberg. There also was a train running parallel to the highway along the mountain road.

There was hardly any food in the stores, but the Americans provided us with many items that could not be bought in the stores yet.

I think we lived in that house for nearly a year. My poor brother had gotten sick, and spent a lot of time in bed with a low-grade fever, until he was finally diagnosed with a light case of TB. I loved my brother so much, and could not stand to see him sick.

The doctor suggested we send him to a more elevated area. He said that mountain air and decent food was the best for him. We still had not seen any butter or dairy products. It was clearly from malnutrition. In one way Manfred, my brother, was lucky because it was decided that he should go to Uncle Fritz and Aunt Pia's to spend some time there until he was well, and we loved them. I remember crying bitterly when he left. I loved him so, and he had always been with me. The day we took him to the train station, and when he took me in his arms, I just clung to him and sobbed into his shoulder.

It was very hard to be without my brother. I missed him terribly. School was difficult. I could not make any friends at first. I seemed to be different from most of the other kids. They called me a "City Slicker." I did have one girlfriend, though. Her name was Helga. Once we were walking in the street to her house, which was not far, when a young blond man stopped us. He was quite handsome. He said, "Excuse me young ladies, may I ask you a question? He was so nice, so we said, "Of course." He said, "My name is Ernst, and I live in the white house on top of the hill there.

May I know your names?" We both told him our names, Helga and Margret. "It is so nice to meet you," he said. "I wanted to ask Margret if she would let me paint her. She has such an interesting face, and when I have finished the picture, she can give it to her parents for Christmas." I was quite surprised, and told him I had to ask my parents. My daddy was home that evening, so I asked both my parents. They said they would like to meet Ernst. I should invite him to the house the next time I saw him. A few days went by, and then I was able to extend the invitation to him. My parents met him, and they liked each other and became friends. He took them to his house, where he lived with his parents and had a big studio. He had just returned from the war at the Russian front where he had been shot in the right arm, which was just starting to heal well enough to start painting again.

We soon got started on the picture. I came to his house and had to sit very still and quietly on the chair after he showed me how to pose. I didn't mind posing after the topsy-turvy life of ours.

It was very peaceful.

It took several sittings, and always we had a little talking time in between, which I enjoyed very much. My mother stopped by several times. She and Ernst seemed to enjoy each other's company.

The picture turned out great. It was as good as a photograph. Ernst framed it for me with a homemade frame, and wrapped it. I presented it to my parents at Christmas. They were overwhelmed, and could hardly believe it. I was so excited. Everybody thanked Ernst so much. I still have this picture hanging in my foyer. My big, dark brown eyes look haunted, and seem to follow me as I walk by.

We had moved, and lived outside the town. A long winding road weaved up a mountain. On my way from school I passed the church and the cemetery. After that, the road wound upwards some more. I could see the whole little village below me; the little houses with their red shingle roofs, their little gardens and picket fences, and even stone walks. It was a beautiful view. On top of the mountain was a property with a beautiful main house in which an American officer and his wife lived with a full-time maid. On the other end of the property was a smaller house and a barn where the owner lived. I am sure they were evicted by the American army to make room for the officer and his wife. I remember the lady who owned the property. Her name was Mrs. Harris, and she was a former soloist from the opera in Berlin. She seemed very interesting, but she had a tough look about her. She lived in the upstairs apartment with her husband, who was in a wheelchair, and his sister. They were actually quite nice to us.

My mother and I pretty much lived there alone in the downstairs apartment. My father had moved to Darmstadt, a city close to us, trying to find a reasonable place to start work on inventions again. He came home less and less. He now had an old car, but the tires were so bad that he had to take a mechanic along to visit us because they had to change the tires several times on the way. One still couldn't even buy new tires even if the money was there.

I remember my father saying that his mechanic broke into tears when they fixed the tire for the fourth time and said, "Oh no, Dr. Messer. Not again!"

My parents seemed to grow apart. My father tried so hard to pick up the pieces, but nothing seemed to work for him. When he visited us, he usually returned to Darmstadt the same day. I missed him.

Times were so tough; we hardly had anything to eat. There was hardly any income. My mother practiced her piano, which was rented, every day in order not to lose her skill.

But there were no opportunities to perform. Germany was totally torn up, and the cities were leveled. My mother tried to get food for us.

One day she said, "Dolly, I heard they have a black market in the big high school on Mountain Road. I want to try to sell some of my gold jewelry there, and try to get some food for it. We have to start eating better. We are about starved." She said, "Please come with me. I am kind of worried to go alone."

I said, "Sure." I was probably eleven or twelve at that time. My mother was in her late thirties, and very beautiful. She honestly looked very young, and like a movie star. She was very petite, with dark hair and green eyes. She wore her hair shoulder length, and even though we were so, so poor, she always looked very stylish, a little shabby, but stylish.

We set out to walk to the high school in the next town along "Mountain Road." We had to walk about three miles. No one had cars. Hitler had taken everybody's cars to serve in the war. It took us close to two hours before we found the school. There were quite a few adults hanging around, dressed quite shabbily, just like the rest of us. I saw no children anywhere. My mother, who was holding my hand tightly, stopped in front of an older man and asked if she could speak to him.

He said, "Of course. Come with me to my room, and we will talk." My mother's grip on my hand became even tighter. We followed him into the gloomy building. The man had gray hair, a lined face, and dark shifty eyes. We followed him, and he opened the door to a former classroom and let us into a sparsely furnished room, with a bed in the middle. The room smelled badly of cigarettes, and there were full ashtrays around the room. There were no curtains on the huge windows. It was very depressing! My mother got out a heavy gold bracelet that my father had given her once in better times.

The man just shifted his eyes all over her, and finally looked greedily at the bracelet. He said, "Let me see it." She gave it to him hesitantly. He kind of weighed it in his hands, and looked for the gold stamp on the inside. He pursed his lips. "It was very expensive," she said, "and fiom the best jeweler in Berlin." "Well," he said, "these are bad times, and it won't bring me much." My mother said, "Can you give me some food? We are practically starving." "Well, what do you want?" he said. "We would like some butter, canned milk, cocoa, and some coffee." She loved her coffee. He click his tongue and licked his lips. After a while he said, "O.K." He went to a cupboard and got out two pounds of butter, several cans of milk, a box of cocoa, and a can of coffee. He put it all in a bag and handed it to her, always looking her over. As she took the bag, he tried to grab her, but she was faster.

My mother yelled, "Dolly, the door!" I held the door open, and we both flew out the door as if the devil was after us, and he was. My mother never let go of the bag, and I hung onto her skirt tails. We ran, never to return to that place. Like in Berlin, this was called survival, only a different kind. There were no air raids.

I went to the fourth grade. All the kids, it seemed to me, were village kids. To them I was different. I was just starting to get pretty. Even though I was painfully thin, you had to notice my huge, dark eyes and my hair. I had straight bangs, and long straight chestnut hair halfway down my back.

One day my mother said, "Dolly, you are going to be very pretty some day." I said, "Just like you, Mama." She said, "Even prettier." She petted my cheek with a smile.

I had a hard time in that school. I didn't seem to make friends with the girls, except for Helga, and the boys gave me strange looks.

One time, after school a group of boys circled me and stared at me. I took my book bag and hit one of them with it, and started running. They left me alone after that.

It happened again about four months later. I was on my way home, up that winding road, climbing that mountain; past the church, past the cemetery, until I saw the village below me, and I was almost at the front gate of the large property. The same gang of boys, who threatened me before, appeared. They were all about two years older than I. They circled me again, and gave me strange looks. I was really scared, and said, "I know those Americans there. They are my friends. I will call for help."

They slowly opened their circle, and I ran for the first gate. It was actually forbidden for me, but I got away from them. I was very scared. I didn't know anything about hormones in those days, but I felt extremely threatened.

Things got worse still. My father wrote us a letter saying that he had had no income. In the letter was some money for the rent and for food, but he could not pay for the furniture he had rented for us. He was very sorry, and he would try very hard.

There was hardly any food in the stores. The next thing was that our money was declared worthless, from one day to the next. Each family received a certain amount of money per person, and then they were on their own. From one day to the next, the stores were miraculously full of food, but no one had any money to buy it. I remember buying some bread and charging it, when I saw Velveeta cheese on the shelf, one of my favorite foods. When I got home, I was yelling in excitement, "Mama, the store had Velveeta cheese on the shelf. Can we buy some?" My mother said, "Not right now, maybe later on."

What were we to do? We had lost everything, and had no source of income. A few days later, a big truck came and took all our furniture out of our little apartment. We had nothing but our blankets. I know I have to write this chapter quickly because it is extremely depressing to me.

That night we slept on the floor.

The next day my mother said, "It is time to visit my brother in Mannheim. We need help." In the morning we got up early to take the train. We really didn't have any money for the train. What little we had, we needed for food. So, my mother and I waited on the platform, and when the train came, we quickly stepped on the train, went to the third class and sat down among all the people there. When the conductor came by and asked if anyone needed to show their ticket, we just talked to each other, and ignored him. He just passed us by. It was very scary.

In Mannheirn, a pretty big industrial city, we took the street-car to my uncle's place of work. He was the top man in a large pharmaceutical wholesale company. He was so sweet to us when he saw us. Even though we were skinny and badly dressed, but clean, he was awfully nice to us. My mother told him our situation, and he was appalled when he found out about all our troubles. So they made a plan. First of all, he wrote my mother a sizable check for food. Then he called his wife, and told her that he was bringing us to lunch.

Mannheirn had been bombed severely too, and my uncle did not have his house anymore. They lived in a large plush apartment. My aunt was an attractive woman. She looked very well taken care of. She wore lovely clothes, and was cleverly made up. She had pitch black hair and smelled of good perfiune. Their two little girls were really cute too. She hugged us, and made us welcome. We had a great warm lunch. I couldn't believe how good this food was, and I practically licked my plate clean.

After dinner, my uncle and my mother withdrew into his office at home and made a plan. His company bought lots of prescription and non-prescription medicines, and then sold them to drug stores and pharmacies. My uncle wrote her letters of introduction to five or six large companies, and introduced my mother as his sister, and asked them to please consider her as a supplier to them for any kind of packaging for their pharmaceutical products.

The last step in this plan was my mother taking me along to Bavaria, South Germany, and visiting two old family friends. One had a glass factory, and the other a paper and cardboard factory. They were both happy to help her out to represent them to these big companies. They promised her money for train travel, money for meals, and money for hotels. All this was planned with my uncle, and we were both so happy.

One more thing, my uncle saw my shabby shoes that an old lady had given me and said, "Now we are going to buy little Meg some shoes." I thought I had died and gone to heaven. He took us to a fine shoe store with lots of selections and I got to pick out a pair. Already knowing that pretty shoes fall apart, I picked a very sturdy pair. They were not dainty or pretty. They were what I wanted. They were sturdy.

Uncle Robert then called his company and told them he was not coming back that day, and he drove us home. What took us two and a half hours by train, took us forty-five minutes in his comfy beautiful limousine. I felt like Cinderella.

Uncle Robert sent us another check, and we bought three beds, three chairs, and a tea cart with that money. So, when my brother would come home, we had a bed for each one of us, and three chairs to eat at the little tea cart.

My brother, Manfred was well again and got to come home. That was such a happy day. I couldn't let go of his hand. We cooked a roast, vegetables, noodles, and gravy. Things were definitely looking up.

All my life, I worshipped my Uncle Robert. He saved us! I got to meet my Uncle Robert's son from his first marriage. We saw each other quite often, and liked each other a lot. Too bad he was my cousin. I had a crush on him; my first crush. He looked just like me.

My mother started traveling. She used the money that companies were giving her for train travel and food, but she never stayed in hotels. No matter how tired she was, she brought the hotel money home for us to live on. She was very pretty, and put herself in danger traveling by train at night.

My brother commuted to my uncle's firm every morning at 6 a.m., where he did an apprenticeship, and returned home at 7 p.m. at night. He got paid a little bit of money, and shared it with us. One day he bought a radio. He was ecstatic, and I could not believe our good fortune. When it started to play music, we were just stunned, and listened in total, silent disbelief. Then, Manfred grabbed me and spun me around in our tiny living room, laughing and squealing. Our love for dance was born.

My mother, my brother, and I fell into quite a good routine. Each one of us had a job. Mutti was a saleslady. Manfred was an apprentice. My part in the whole deal was to do the shopping, the cooking, and much of the cleaning. I was now twelve years old. Besides, now I went to school and brought home decent grades.

Often at night, I would stand by an open window. I could see the village lights down below.

It was beautiful. There was a great big apple orchard below my window, and I would sing. I would let my voice carry into the night.

It sounded so pure and clear, and carried way far away. It made me feel so good. I had found my voice, and it would bless me for a lifetime.

I was now in my first year of high school. It was an all-girl's school, and right next door was an all-boy's school. All of us had lost at least one year of schooling through the war with our having to move around so much. I got along well with my classmates in high school. They were from different cities from wherever the war had brought them, and been through similar things as we had.

The school system is very different in Germany from the United States. The students who wanted to learn a trade stayed in elementary school and went on to be educated in the field that they had chosen with a practical part added on to their schooling. This was for students who either wanted to learn plumbing, carpentry, stone masonry, shoemaking, etc. They also did an apprenticeship while going to school. Students who wanted to go on to a specialized school like commerce, music, arts, or a university education, split off at this point of their school life and went to high school. That had been my choice since I was sure I wanted to be a professional singer.

My classmates and I had a lot more in common since we all had more ambitious plans for our life with a better education. The little town where I lived was called Auerbach, and the town with our school was called Bensheim. We all came from different little towns along the mountain road, and got there by different means of transportation. Some kids took the train. Some rode a bike. I was pretty close, so I walked. I wanted to ride a bike so badly, but my mother would not let me. That trip to school in the morning was pretty much fun because we ran into the same kids every day. A lot of yelling and greeting went on.

I made two really wonderful friends, one girl with whom I still have contact. Her name was Marlis, and she lived in the next village from where I lived. She was blond and blue eyed, and had a very cheerful nature. She also came from Berlin. The bad part was that their father was fighting in the war, so her mother stayed in their home with her daughter and her three sons. Her mother told me that they were in the basement when the Russians marched into Berlin. They broke into their house and found the family cowering in the basement. They stood there staring at the ten-year old daughter with her pretty blond hair and blue eyes. Her mother got so scared for her little girl that she got up and motioned the soldiers out of the basement and went upstairs with them. She got raped multiple times. Later on she had to have a hysterectomy because of it. But she saved her child!

My other girlfriend, Asta's story, was even wilder. They lived in what was later East Germany. When the Russians marched into their town, most of the men were gone too, except for the very old or the very young. They gathered all the young women, including their mother, and put them on a transport going to Siberia to work in the mines. Asta and her sister Nani were left behind alone because their father was also fighting, and they did not know where he was. Asta's sister was very cute. They hid in their basement and came out at night to beg for food from their neighbors, and got food out of people's garbage. After two or three months, their mother was returned; she was no good to the Russians. She was too tiny and weak to be useful in the mines, and she was very sick at this point.

Marlis's father was killed in the war, and Asta's father returned and went into the ministry.

Those were my two best friends. Asta even came to visit me many years later in the United States.

Most of us in that high school class had similar traumatic experiences. But we found each other, befriended each other, and though we were still hungry most of the time, we were ready to embrace life again. We had a class of really neat girls, and most of us matured quickly.

Now a wonderful thing happened. The religious group, the Quakers, helped us in our predicament. We were told to bring a little bowl and spoon to school the next day. The Quakers would feed us once daily from now on. We were really excited.

The next day I brought my little dish and spoon to school. We sat in class and studied. At twelve o'clock when the school bell rang, we were told to get our bowl, and stand in line outside to get our school meal from the Quakers. We rushed out and lined up. The first meal was hot chocolate, nice and sweet, and thickened up a tiny bit.

We found a place to sit and enjoyed this wonderful treat. There was a little bit left, and we lined up again and got a little bit more. We could hardly wait for the next day to see what we would get then.

Things were getting more interesting. We met a lot of nice boys on the way to and from school, and they would walk home with us. Some of them were pushing their bicycles next to us. We had a lot to talk about. Time flew as we were growing up fast. The girls started talking about who had their period and who didn't. We discussed who was starting to have breasts, and who was still anxiously waiting.

I started to be the class clown. We had a teacher who taught us German. She was a chubby little woman with humongous breasts, which she liked to rest on her desk. She was very romantic to the point of being mushy.

We liked her, but she was a little much. Several times I copied her, while we were waiting for her to come to our classroom. One winter's day, I stuffed my sweater with everybody's shawls. I looked huge as I sat down at her desk, resting my fake breasts in front of me, and copying her voice. I lectured my classmates about love. "Love is such a wonderful emotion. When you meet a young man who makes your face get flushed, and makes your heart race, you know that he must be the one." We were not quite at that point yet, and we thought it was hilarious. So this was one of my favorite subjects to imitate her with great drama. One time she came in when I was in the middle of my demonstration with everybody laughing. I quickly pulled all the scarves out of my sweater while she watched, and the whole class giggled hysterically.

My report card read that year: "Meg is very well liked in the school community. Her strongest talents are in music, art, and dance. We just wish she didn't always need to be the class clown, and have to entertain everyone."

Ernst, the painter, started to come and visit us in the evenings more and more often. You didn't need to be a genius to know that he was visiting my mother. He was very interesting and fun to talk too. My brother and I both liked him.

Around that time, we received a message that my father was not well - something with his heart. We hopped a train to Darmstadt, and then a bus to where he lived. I cannot remember the name of the tiny town he lived in just outside of Darmstadt. Darmstadt was so bombed out it was depressing to see. Living in these little villages where time had stood still, we had almost forgotten how the real world looked. My father lived in a tiny village at the foot of the same mountains where we lived. He had a really small apartment. He was in bed when we got there.

We met his secretary, a pretty blond who was probably fifteen years younger than my mother. She seemed to be taking care of him. Her name was Irma.

We sat down on chairs, and Mutti started talking to him. When my parents were in the middle of the conversation, Irma came into the room and told my father in no uncertain terms that we should not be with him. We would just upset him. It was very clear to us that she was living with him. My father had always been a kind of Romeo. My father sat up, grabbed a water glass, and raised it as if he was going to throw it at her, and yelled for her to get out. I have never seen anyone leave a room as quickly as she did.

Shortly after my parents got done talking, we left for home.

We all hugged and kissed my father, and told him we loved him.

From then on, we saw less and less of my father, but we saw more and more of Ernst. He was often invited for supper. When my brother and I went to bed at night, we could hear my mother and Ernst talking for a long time.

We started to have plays in school. It was a senior play, and most girls were between eighteen and nineteen. Everybody had missed so much time in school. Another friend of mine and I were asked to dance a minuet in this play. It was a play about the times of Mozart, and the minuet was written by him. Giesela and I were so much younger than the other girls, but we were a great match. We both were tall and slender. We had long hair and wore it in a very elegant bun. They made us long dresses, and I must say, we drifted elegantly across the stage to Mozart's music.

We wore makeup for the first time, and felt quite gorgeous. We were invited, after the play, which was a huge success, to a party at one of the girl's houses. It was in the town where I lived, but Giesela lived too far away, and couldn't go.

I was by far the youngest. I was nearly fifteen then. When I got to their house in my little village, we were served refreshments. The talk was very animated about the play. They also invited some of their male friends. There were probably about ten of us.

After a while, I could tell that the guys and girls moved a little closer to each other, and it wasn't long after that when the lights went off. I assume that some heavy making out was taking place. I sat there by myself, very bored, and hoping that they would turn the lights on again. After quite a long time, I said, "Excuse me, but I have to go home now."

Someone turned the lights on again, and our senior, who had

the most handsome and nicest guy there, said, "Meg, we will walk you home. You cannot walk up that hill in the dark by yourself." I thanked everyone for including me, and we were off. They were really very nice people. Eva was the senior's name, and the young man was Dieter. They were both very attractive people. Eva had long, real blond hair, and the guy was tall, dark, and handsome with black hair and blue eyes. Dieter was a "knock out."

It was quite a long walk. We had to climb the big hill, and go past the church and the cemetery. The cemetery looked quite spooky at night. Right by the gate and the high stone wall was some kind of monument with something on the top that looked like a big head, and it scared me half to death.

We started talking about the party. In my innocence, not yet been kissed, I said that I would never make out with someone I wasn't in love with. I thought it was gross. My new friends laughed, and told me that they would remind me of this sometime in the future.

I was home now, and they both wished me good night. My mother was home, and waiting up for me. I never mentioned any details about the party, just that it was fun.

My life was getting so much better. I learned so much in school. We had so many interesting subjects. First of all, German, then English, then they added Latin (I had five years of Latin), and last French. In addition to that, we had mathematics, geography, history, biology, music, sports, and art. We really had to study to have decent grades. We went to school from 8 a.m. until 1 p.m. then we went home and had tons of homework for most every subject.

I had all my chores too, so I could only socialize on the weekends. Marlis's mother invited me to their house in the next village quite often. Marlis had three brothers and the house was always full of happy noise. I loved going there. Somehow, the mother managed to feed me too, when I was there. My mother became very good friends with Marlis's mother also. Asta came from her little town and rode her bicycle to join us.

There was always a lot of talking, kidding, and laughing going on. My brother Manfred also had time on the weekends and sometimes the whole gang would go dancing together. Manfred fell in love with Asta's older sister Nani. She was really cute. She had blond hair and blue eyes, and she was a delicate looking girl. Each one of our little towns had little restaurants with great food and some of them had a ballroom and offered dancing to the public. It was more like a family affair. They had German bands, and we all danced like crazy.

When I was sixteen, my mother enrolled me in a ballroom dance school and all my girlfriends went too. It was an old custom that kids who came from nice families---boys and girls--would go to a ballroom dance school when they turned sixteen. They would learn how to dance and learn social etiquette. For instance: how to treat a lady, how to introduce people to each other, how to open a car door, and how to hold a door open to a restaurant. We actually had a lot of fun with that. We went once a week for two hours for ten weeks.

Now, my brother and I got serious about dancing. At least three times a week, we would roll the carpet back in the evening, and I would teach him what I had learned that week. The rumba was the first dance we learned, and you had to let your hips swing. We laughed ourselves sick when he tried to move his hips in a sexy way. But to be honest, we got quite good at it. I discovered another talent of mine - I was a good teacher! That would also be a valuable talent of mine in years to come.

In school, things went fine. We all suffered through math, Latin, French, and the rest went smoothly. We had a marvelous music teacher. He was very creative, and challenged us by singing classical music.

He had discovered my voice, and challenged me with difficult solos. I owed him a lot for how he taught me, and the joy he gave me. I enjoyed singing so much, and my fellow students and teachers encouraged me, so that my desire to sing grew each day. We had a great school, and because we all had been through so much, there was no jealousy or pettiness. There was no room for that in our lives.

Dieter started to call me every now and then to ask my mother if he could take me to a movie. He even told her what was playing.

We saw a lot of American movies in those years. My mother was extremely strict, and expected me home twenty minutes after the movie was out. After dating like that, Dieter and I would have a quick, hasty kiss. I felt like I was really living, and I started to like him a lot. He was six years older than I, and had a sweet personality. He even had my mother charmed.

The next thing that happened was that Dieter graduated from the University of Frankfurt as a full-fledged engineer. His father decided to send him to the United States for one year to learn about business.

Before Dieter left for the United States, he took me once more to the movies. When we walked home, it was dark. We were holding hands as we walked up the hill, past the church, and past the cemetery. We saw the lights of the village down below. It was a beautiful, clear and balmy night. We stopped walking, and turned toward each other. We reached out, he put his arms around my waist, and I put mine around his neck. We held each other tight, and I molded my body to his. This was the first time we were so close, and it felt so right.

We kissed for a long time, and we both got quite excited. He whispered, "I will miss you." I whispered back, "I will miss you, too." Then the tears started. "A year is not so long," he said. "It is a very long time," I sobbed now. We held each other a little bit longer, and then walked on in silence. We stopped every now and then, and kissed some more. We were getting quite passionate. By the time we got to my house, I was very upset. "I'll write," Dieter said. "I will write, too," I sobbed, and ran into the house. I turned one more time, and he stood there and waved to me. Then he walked off. When I got into our apartment, my mother just took one look at me, and opened her arms. She held me, and when she looked at my tear stained face, she said, "You are in love for the first time." I would really miss him.

Shortly after he left, his twin brother, Wolfgang, started to court me. They didn't look a bit alike. Dieter was the handsome one. Wolfgang wore glasses, and was also tall and slender. He had a bicycle with a motor, and in the morning, on the way to school, we could hear him from far away. It sounded like a very loud bee. If I was walking alone, he would invite me to sit on the back of his bike, and he got me to school in a hurry. He was a lot of fun.

We lived in this beautiful wine country, and every fall when the grapes were ripe and harvested, the farmers would make the wine. All the way up and down the mountain road, up and down the famous River Rhine, up the River Mosel, and many other places, there would be wine festivals.

They would erect huge tents with a bandstand, tables and chairs, or picnic tables. The wine fest would usually last for a week. There would be German food available; hot dogs, Bratwurst, smoked pork chops, potato salad, sauerkraut, French fries, and all kinds of German food. Everybody would go to the wine fest. You would see many people that you knew, and many people came from the surrounding cities to celebrate and taste the new wine. Beer was also very popular. The band played waltzes and polkas, among other popular music. Everybody sang and danced until midnight. Everyone said it would be a fun time.

Wolfgang called my mother and asked if he could come by and introduce himself. He wanted to invite me to the wine fest to eat and dance. My brother and some of the friends we had in common would be there also. He would come by with his father's truck on Saturday at 8 p.m. I was very excited. This was the first invitation I had gotten to something like this.

Saturday could not come soon enough. I was so excited. There would be about ten of us going, including my girlfriends with their dates. My brother invited Nani, Asta's sister.

We picked a place where we would meet, and Wolfgang picked everybody up with his father's truck. It was a covered truck with a long bench inside. Of course, I got to ride in the front. I was pretty happy about all that. From our town, we drove to the same town where we went to school. Wolfgang took a couple of curves pretty sharp, and we heard everybody screeching and laughing in the back. When we got there, we found us a couple of tables and seats. We were all quite excited. The music had just started to play, and we all rushed to the dance floor. Later on, we had a German hot dog and something to drink. There was a lot of laughing and dancing. It was great fun.

When it was time to leave, Wolfgang took everybody home. My brother wanted to spend a little more time with Nani, so he got off when she did. The last stretch to my house, Wolfgang and I were alone in the truck. We talked and were in good spirits. But I could not help thinking about Dieter and wondering what he was doing. Since he was so handsome, I was sure he would not be alone long. When we got to my house, Wolfgang got out of the truck and walked me to the door. We hugged and kissed each other on the cheek. I told him, "Thank you for a nice evening."

My mother was still up and asked me how it was. I brought her up to date on the evening. I also told her that I missed Dieter and that I did not think I would ever fall in love with Wolfgang, even though I liked his company.

My mother said, "Dolly, there is something I have been wanting to tell you. Don't ever have sex with someone you don't really love. Right now, you are too young anyway. Let it be special and wait until you are sure. On the other hand, don't marry any man you have not had sex with. It is an important part of marriage." I never forgot what she said to me.

The next day was Sunday and we woke up to the sound of the church bells ringing. It was such a beautiful sound. To this day I love the church bells, but we don't hear them often in the small towns in America anymore. What a sweet message they told. When we heard the church bells chiming, I asked my mother why we never go to church.

"It seems to be only the older villagers who go to church," my mother said. "During the war, Hitler sometimes persecuted people who went to church. Our whole lives were built on fear. After the war, we were refugees and with our lives having been so disrupted for such a long time, no one was in the habit of going to church anymore."

Another thing that bothered me was that there were hardly any young men in our community. Most everybody older than their mid-twenties and up had been called into the war and just now they were starting to come home. Some of them had lost an arm or a leg. It was tough for them.

A generation was lost or mutilated.

In the meantime, the young women were flirting with the American soldiers. I talked with my mother about that. Our soldiers coming back in the shape they were in, and the young women had American boyfriends. It was a messed up world full of tears. I remember it all. My mother said, "These have been tough times. People's lives have been turned upside down. They have been hurt; they have seen death; everyone is lonely; and they are scared. But we all, including my little girl, have to put things behind us and go on and live life." These words often come back to me.

My mother had done really well in her business venture. My uncle's letters of introduction opened a lot of doors for her, and she had gotten a lot of orders for the packaging of pharmaceuticals. She had made enough money and had gotten steady orders. She decided to buy a car so she didn't have to ride the train anymore. Riding the train at night was dangerous and time consuming.

We got to go with her; the excitement was almost unbearable. The three of us had nearly been one of the poorest families in the little town. No more charging bread and groceries. We were now buying a car. My mother knew the people of the Opel dealership and that is where we were headed. We all had dressed as nice as we could. From where we lived, it was a two mile walk.

My mother had already stopped by and talked to those people before, and they knew her. Some kind of financial arrangements had already been made. My mother showed us the car she wanted to buy. It was a white Opel with a black convertible roof.

My brother and I could hardly believe it. My mother got treated very courteously. I think people really respected her for saving our family. Thanks to her brother's help, we had recovered much quicker than some others.

My mother was a small person, maybe five feet three or four, so she wore high heels wherever she went. She was going to look her best, no matter what. I felt like a giant next to her, since I was five feet six, growing into five feet seven.

Anyway, the car was pulled up in the front, and we were ready for our test drive. They put the roof down for us so we could enjoy the convertible. It was a beautiful day with a gentle breeze. We drove back to the dealership and finished the paperwork. My mother said, "Let's go get Ernst." We drove to his house and picked him up. He was as excited as we were, and again we drove around along the mountain road, and the little main streets of the villages to admire ourselves driving by the shop windows where we could see our reflections.

That night, we celebrated with a wonderful home-cooked meal. The next day we were back to our old routine. My mother left for the road, only this time in her car. I walked to school, and my brother took the train to work.

That day as I was straightening the house, I knocked over a flower vase, which was sitting on top of Manfred's radio. It spilled the water straight into his radio.

I was devastated. The radio was still Manfred's most treasured possession. I tried to dry the radio out. I turned it upside down, and anything I could think of.

In between times, I would look out the window, hoping my mother would come home before my brother did, to help me out. She had gone on a short trip today, not one of her long ones to Switzerland or North Germany, where she would be staying overnight. I did my homework, and ran to the window again.

I started supper. Trying to be extra good, I cooked something nice; noodles and spaghetti sauce with lots of fresh tomatoes in the sauce.

Finally, my mother came. I told her what had happened, and she said, "Let's turn the radio on." We did, and oh no, only one station played. My mother went and got the hair dryer. We opened up the back with a knife - we didn't own a screwdriver, and proceeded to dry the radio with the hair dryer. When we thought it was dry, we plugged it in. You won't believe it. It didn't only play, it had one more station. I was overjoyed.

When my brother came home that night, the first thing he did, as always, was to turn his radio on and look for some music for supper. He was turning the dial with a frown on his face. Finally, I got the giggles really bad, and I asked him if something was wrong. He finally said, "I can't believe it. I have one more station than before." That's when my mother and I lost it, and with peels of laughter and doubling over, we told him what had happened. He looked at us very seriously and said, "NO more vases or anything on top of my radio." Then he joined us in our merriment.

One Friday night my mother said, "Manfred, Margret, I have a surprise for you tomorrow. Please don't make any plans for Saturday. We have plans together." We wanted her to tell us, but she wouldn't.

My brother and I slept in, but we heard her busying herself in the kitchen. I turned over in my bed, and went back to sleep. She woke us about ten o'clock. "Get up and get ready. Have a quick bite to eat. We are going hiking, with a picnic." We were ready in no time. My mother handed my brother a backpack and declared, "Let's go!"

We hopped into the car. I got to sit in the front with my mother. Manfred sat in the back. The top was down, and the wind was blowing. It all felt great.

"Okay, now tell us where we are going," we said.

"It's a surprise" was her answer. We just relaxed and looked at the scenery fly by. She drove us onto the interstate (autobahn), and we really got excited. We were going fast and the mountains flew by. The sky was blue with a few puffy clouds in it. This was living. Up to this point this was probably the most exciting day of my life.

I turned around and looked at my brother. We both beamed at each other. I turned to my mother and touched her hand. "Mutti," I said, "this is so wonderful. You have done so well. Thank you for all you have accomplished with all your hard work." She beamed back with a big smile as my brother touched and squeezed her shoulder. We were really happy knowing that we had all contributed.

"Okay," my mother said, "I will tell you now where we are going. We are going to Heidelberg."

"Oh fun," we said. We couldn't wait to get there. Heidelberg had a huge castle, even though it was only about an hour from us, we had never been there before.

Heidelberg also was a university city with a famous old university. The old part of the city had many old houses and cobblestone streets. The beautiful river, the Neckar, wound through the middle of the city with huge old bridges built across it with gigantic stones. We crossed a bridge, and there was the old city right in front of us and up above on the mountain was the gigantic castle. It was an inspiring view.

"Oh, it is so beautiful," were our shouts of admiration. We drove halfway up the mountain and parked our car in a parking area. Now we started walking, straight up toward the castle. It was quite a walk. I was the first one to start complaining, and here my brother was carrying the backpack. He never complained. He was such a good sport. It took us about an hour to get up to the castle, and another walk to get into the courtyard. The courtyard was beautiful with grass, and lots of blooming plants and trees. Since we were pretty tired, we decided to have our picnic first, and then explore the castle. Manfred put down the backpack, and my mother started unpacking it. Remember, we were not spoiled. This was a treat.

We had ham sandwiches, hardboiled eggs, and potato salad. For dessert, I will never forget, we had wonderfully ripe strawberries sugared with whipping cream on top. In a thermos bottle we had sweet tea. It was absolutely a feast. We sat on the grass on our jackets, and after we had eaten, we lay back on the grass and relaxed. I was watching the clouds drift across the blue sky. This was living.

The thought crossed my mind of what we had all been through, but it disappeared with the clouds drifting across the sky. We had come a long, treacherous way to get to this point. If there was a God in heaven, I wanted to thank him. I didn't know what my mother and brother were thinking. We were all very quiet. After a while, we stretched, and were ready to explore the castle. It was so huge. They had guided tours there.

To me, the most exciting thing was the tower. We started to climb up the circular stair. It was a long climb, and we had to stop a couple of times to catch our breath. We finally reached the top. There it was with its red roofs, the Neckar Valley. The river shimmering in the sunlight, winding through the city, around the bend as far as the eye could see. It went under the bridges, through the town, and through the lush Neckar Valley with its vineyards.

The river was speckled with pleasure boats on this beautiful day. I can still see it. After the tower, it was time for us to get back to the car and head for home. It had been an unforgettable day. We started to have many trips and excursions from then on, either on Saturday or Sunday. Those were the good times.

My brother and I went to visit our father. We took the train and the bus. It was really sad to see him. He was living with his secretary, and suffered a lot of anxiety. He thought often that he would have heart trouble, and started to drink wine to relax. He got into the habit of drinking too much, and then he didn't talk like the father we knew. It was upsetting to see him like that, and I was scared to visit him alone, even though he loved me. It was just tough to see him like that, and we saw him less and less.

My parents finally got a divorce, and even though we were all upset, it was better this way. My mother's relationship to Ernst got closer, and we saw a lot of him. The war and the after effects of the war had ruined so much in people's lives. There was nothing constant for us, or stable. Years after we had grown up they called us, "the lost generation" because we had no childhood.

We went on many more of those excursions on the weekends. Many times, we just went hiking close to where we lived. We would walk straight up the mountains. German forests have the most wonderful trails. Whole families go walking on Sundays all the time. Always, after you walked for a couple of hours, there was either a castle on the mountaintop with a restaurant in it, or a really nice cafe along the way. Germans love their coffee and cake on Sundays or their hot dogs and beer. We got very close to each other on these many walks.

My brother got quite close with Nani, and I went out weekly with Wolfgang. We started to fool around a lot, but I never fell in love with him, and don't think he fell in love with me. We were good friends and enjoyed each other's company.

It was almost time for Dieter to return, and I looked really forward to seeing him again. I had a lot of guy friends, and I was very popular, but I was always waiting for that person I would love. I broke quite a few hearts on the way. I was a very passionate girl and drove the boys quite crazy, but my heart was not involved, and I always remembered my mother's advice: "Don't ever have sex without love."

My mother's relationship with Ernst was very serious, and I believe they were in love. Ernst would stay late sometimes, and I could hear them whispering and laughing softly. A great longing came over me. I realized that I wanted to have someone who would really love me with his whole heart, mind, soul, and body. I had grown up, and I was ready for love. I could hardly go to sleep those nights. It took me a long time.

We had finished our ballroom classes, and I continued into the advanced ballroom class with my partner who was a handsome darling boy. He was one year younger than I was. We were good dance partners and saw each other on occasion outside the dance class. I felt about him like a younger brother. We did have a great victory in dance competition. We won the silver medal in the rumba, and the gold medal in the slow waltz. I loved ballroom dancing, and we were really thrilled to win. We had to compete with a lot of good dancers. I had taught my brother almost everything I had learned and made him a fake graduation certificate when I got my gold and silver certificate. He was really tickled. He laughed and gave me a big hug.

Wolfgang called to tell me that Dieter was coming back from the United States. He was supposed to arrive the next week on Friday. Wolfgang and I went to the movies that week, and he asked me, "How do you feel about Dieter? We have had a really good time with each other, and I enjoyed your company a lot, but would you like to date Dieter again?"

I replied, "I missed him, even though you have been a wonderful friend."

He looked at me and said, "Well, there is my answer. You sound as if you are still in love with him. You probably need to see him, and have a date or two to figure out if you have feelings for each other. I am not heartbroken, but I'll miss you."

I told him that was probably the best. I told him I would miss him, too.

When he dropped me off at home, after the movie, we hugged really tight and kissed. Then he left. I called after him, "I will call you." I hated to see him go. He was the ultimate reliable boyfriend. I didn't even know if Dieter had changed. He was too handsome to be all that reliable.

So often we choose the wrong men because of their looks and charm. Well, I was too excited to give that much thought. I couldn't wait to see Dieter, but I was sorry to see Wolfgang go. He was really a neat guy. He was studying to be an accountant. He did really well in his life.

The next day, on the way to school, I ran into some of my classmates. We were all pretty good friends. Among them was Olga. She was another year older than we were. She also came from Berlin, Their life had been filled with more danger than ours because her mother was half Jewish. She was a very dainty, dark haired woman. She was very nice. Her father was a charming man, and very likable. Olga was a tall, slender girl with dark hair and dark eyes, and definitely a leader. She was smart, and had a boyfriend with a big, black motorcycle. He was very macho and impressive. We definitely looked up to her.

Lately, we had been talking about sex among us girls, and what we would do if any of our boyfriends approached us. It was kind of scary. The information we had about it was very vague. We just knew we were not to do it; we shouldn't be found out; and we shouldn't get pregnant. There were about five of us walking together. Olga was entertaining us, and we listened spellbound. After we all promised we wouldn't tell, she told us, "I did it!"

We gasped, and our mouths hung open. "You mean it? You did it? Where? When? How was it? Did it hurt?'We were beside ourselves. We stopped walking, and stood in a huddle with disbelief in our eyes over such monumental news.

I said, "Tell us step by step."

She said, "We went for a ride on the motorcycle. It was a real pretty evening, and we stopped in the country." Evidently they had a blanket with them, and he spread the blanket on the grass. They must have been kissing and necking and gotten quite overheated. Her boyfriend looked very much like a man already.

It was getting dark and Olga said, "I need to go home or my mother will get really worried about me." So they folded their blanket. She said her boyfriend didn't want to leave but she convinced him that she had to go, even though he looked pretty unhappy about it. When they got home, it was dark. Olga and her parents lived in a big villa, three stories that had been divided up to make small apartments. They had a lot of trees and bushes around the house. It looked very pretty when you saw it during the day. It also had a pretty gazebo in the yard.

She said they got off the motorcycle, and he parked it by the side of the house. She said that they started kissing again, and then she said they did it.

We asked, "Where?"

She replied, "In the bushes." We gasped. She repeated to us that she did it in the bushes.

I said, "Weren't you afraid someone would see you?" She said it was dark, and there was no one around.

We asked, "Did it hurt?"

She said it did not hurt one bit, that it was kind of nice. She seemed quite proud of herself. She was the first one. After all this news Olga was definitely the leader of the gang. She was now surely way ahead of us in life's experiences.

Dieter's arrival was getting closer, and I was very excited. Wolfgang called me and said that he wanted to give Dieter a welcome home party. He wanted to know if I would help him get the gang together. That sounded great, and we shared the list of calls to be made.

Dieter was supposed to arrive on Friday. His parents were going to pick him up from the airport in Frankfurt. The welcome home party was supposed to be on Saturday. We chose the pub in the next little town which also had a band again that Saturday. We could eat first and then dance. We were all excited to hear what he had to tell. I especially could not wait to see him again.

My brother planned to come with Asta's sister, Nani. Marlis was going to bring her older brother. Asta had a boyfriend now. He was a very nice looking young man with a gentle demeanor who worked for his father's electric business. With two more couples, we were twelve people. We were looking forward to our party very much.

Dieter arrived on Friday, and he called me as soon as he got into town. He sounded the same, but I was sure that we both had changed quite a bit in looks. A year is a long time at that age. I know that I had changed a lot, I had quite a shapely figure. I was five foot-seven with all the right measurements---34-24-34. My hair was still chestnut brown. I still wore it straight, halfway down my back with bangs covering my forehead. My family always told me that I looked striking.

I hoped that Dieter would find me pretty. He asked if he could come over that evening. He wanted to take a little walk, and get to talk with me. It was all right with my mother. I could not wait to see him. He got to my house about 7 p.m. and rang the bell. I ran to the door as fast as I could, and opened the door. There he stood.

Just on impulse, I threw my arms around him, laughing and holding him tight. He moved me back a little laughingly and said, "Let me get a good look at you. You are beautiful and all grown up." I looked at him. He looked great. He had filled out and looked like a man. The boy was gone. We were both so excited and laughing. My mother came and greeted him. We talked a little about his trip. He said he loved the United States, but he was glad to be home again.

We said to my mother that we wanted to take a walk and to talk. We left the house and took the trail up the mountain through the vineyards. It was a beautiful evening, and the sun stood low over the horizon. We could look a long way across the plain where the River Rhine flowed in the distance. It was a moment to remember. Dieter looked at me, and then he gave me the most wonderful kiss, first tender, and then with passion. It was one of the moments that you never forget because it was so perfect. We hiked all the way to the top of the mountain and then sat down on a bench. As the sun was setting and dusk came, we sat there holding hands and talking and talking as it slowly got dark. We felt so close as we got up to walk back. As we said goodbye, I reminded him of his party the next day. He was happy about that. As he left, I had to look at him again, and saw his blue eyes and his black hair. He had an ever-present smile. He was truly tall, dark, and handsome.

The next day, he picked me up with his motorcycle. To own a car was still a real rarity in Germany. We were all still relatively poor. It took years to recover from the war.

We had a great get-together for Dieter, and he was so happy. I never left his side. It was such a wonderful feeling to have him back. That evening when he took me home we parked the motorcycle and just stood in each other's arms and kissed. We were halfway up the mountain and could see the village lights down below. It was so romantic. He told me that he was still in love with me and even more than when he left. I had to tell him that I felt the same way, and I realized how much in love I was with him. Dieter told me that he had dated quite a few girls, but that he had never really cared for someone as much as he cared for me. I guess it was my "first love." What a glorious feeling.

Dieter was to help his father in their machine factory. He was to learn the business. They also had a factory in Berlin, and his father was commuting. Dieter was supposed to do some of that too. As an engineer he was well qualified for both jobs.

I went to school and continued with my household chores, cooking, and shopping. We saw each other often and always on the weekends. This time was very special for both of us. I was almost 18 years old, and Dieter was going on 24. My desire to become a singer was still as strong as ever. I sat down with my mother and told her about my plans for the future. She explained to me that her music degree never helped her once times got so bad, and made it clear that she felt I needed to learn something that would support me during bad times. In other words, there could be no help from home. I was very disappointed and had a lot to think about.

One afternoon when I visited Asta at her father's parsonage, we started talking about our future. Asta wanted to be an elementary school teacher. I told her about my plans.

She helped me think about something that had not come to mind before. She said, "You know, you are so good in English. You could go to interpreter school. That will get you a very good job, or you could go to England like my sister did. She went to a branch of the Cambridge University in London.

She worked as an au pair girl, and she now has a really good job as an interpreter. You could do that, and pay for your own education with the job you get when you come back. Go to night school while you study voice." I was so excited when I left her house. It was definitely something to think about.

Things were really changing fast in our lives. We had to make decisions and shape our future. My brother got a promotion, and was transferred to another part of his company. It meant that he had to move away. I hated that, and he did too. He was supposed to get a much better salary, and he could always come home on the weekends if he took a train.

We performed a concert at school. I think it was a Schubert composition. It was very beautiful, and very long. It was between the choir and me, back and forth. It took a lot of practice. Our music teacher said that I could handle that easily, but the principal wanted to hire a professional singer. We had to sing it for our principal with me, and then she also auditioned it with the professional singer. We did so well that my music teacher was able to talk her into letting us sing it with me. We were very excited and nervous. When the concert came closer, I was very nervous.

The concert was a huge success. On the second night, we were not as nervous, but there were even more people there. It was sold out. Everything went fine. We were in the second half of the piece when I suddenly saw Dieter, fifth row center. For one moment, I lost my concentration, and missed my entrance. I was not singing, the choir was not singing, and the pianist stopped playing. Our teacher quietly raised his hands and whispered, "Page five from the top." The pianist came in, the choir came in, and thank God, I came in. We finished the concert without any more happenings. That is what happens when you have a lovesick soloist singing with her boyfriend present. We got a long applause probably because we recovered so quickly and finished with thundering applause.

The third night my mother and brother were there, but I didn't dare look into the audience. We were a great success again. Our principal had been a little upset about the second night, but she said that we recovered like pros. That was an exciting experience.

Our high school worked differently than in the U.S. We had

four years of elementary school, then the students who wanted to go to a university went into high school. High school had nine years altogether, but you could also graduate after seven years and go on to specialty schools like interpreter school, opera school, or school of dramatic arts. I was in my seventh year of high school. I spoke good English and pretty good French- I had five years of Latin, history, geography, algebra, and geometry. I was pretty well educated. I felt that I was getting older fast and needed to zero in on what I wanted to be. I planned to take the seven year graduation and go on to interpreter school. My mother took me to Darmstadt to check out an interpreter school they had there. I liked the school, and they were happy to take me. I decided with my mother's help to finish the year and then go there.

I was much happier since I had made a decision and saw a way to make my dreams come true. My brother agreed with me, and even Dieter thought it was a good idea, Of course, everybody thought that I could never make a living with my music, but the future would surprise them and me too.

Dieter had a very good friend by the name of Winfried, and Winfried and he had gone to the University in Frankfurt together. He was also an engineer. He had a very nice beautiful girlfriend with black hair and dark eyes and a voluptuous figure. Her name was Eve. I liked her very much, and she was always very nice to me. One day Dieter asked me if I wanted to go to the International Auto Fair in Frankfurt with him and his friends, Winfried and Eve.

Frankfurt was an hour and a half from where we lived, and I got quite excited. My mother said it was okay, and I counted the days. We were supposed to be gone all day. It was a huge exhibition. Dieter borrowed his father's truck, and we were to meet

Winfried at his apartment, park the truck, and go together in his car.

That day came, and after our trip to Frankfurt, which I spent sitting practically behind the wheel with Dieter, we met Winfried and Eve. We parked his car in the huge parking lot and started to walk. There was so much to see. It seemed we walked and looked for hours. Dieter held my hand the whole time. It was summertime and a hot day. After a couple of hours we stopped and had German hot dogs and beer. Refreshed, we went on until later afternoon. Eve and I talked quite a bit, and our two engineers had a great time analyzing the new cars.

When we were ready to go, we got Winfried's car and headed back to his apartment. He fixed us sandwiches, and we had a nice, light supper. The conversation was very animated, and we had a good time. All of a sudden, the mood seemed to change in the room and Winfried looked at Eve and then back at us. He said he and Eve wanted to be alone for a little while before he had to take her home. If we wanted to be alone, we could go into the guest room. Winfried and Eve were both a year older than we were, and I am sure that they had already had an intimate relationship for a while. I felt very awkward, but Winfried and Eve disappeared, and Dieter took my hand and led me to the guest room and closed the door behind us.

As time went by, Dieter and I got to know each other more intimately. Our relationship grew into a wonderful time of young love. We were happy and carefree.

Dieter and I went many places on his motorcycle. One time we wanted to go to a concert. We were dressed nicely. When we were on the interstate it started to rain, and we got soaking wet.

The people in their cars who passed us looked at us fuU of

pity. We got *so* soaked that we finally had to turn around. Dieter said that was it. He needed to buy a car. The next day he talked to his father and asked for help to finance his car. After all, he worked full time for him. A truck or a motorcycle was not always appropriate. His father helped him out as much as he could, and Dieter bought a little Isetta, one of those little after-war cars. When you opened the only door, the whole front of the car opened up and you got in and out that way. It was a crazy little car, but it got quite popular because it kept people out of the weather. It was really inexpensive. We had a lot of fun with that little car and felt like we had arrived. It sure beat getting soaked on a motorcycle.

Dieter started talking about getting engaged and how many children we wanted when we got married. I was happy that he was so in love with me, but I was only 18 years old and not quite ready for definite plans. I was just happy and still real serious about having a career with my voice.

My last high school year was coming to a close, and I enrolled at interpreter school. I was excited about that step in the right direction. I got a real good report card on which my principal wished me good luck in my musical endeavor and also wrote that I had a real talent in that direction and excelled vocally. I was very sad on that last day of school. I left many wonderful friends behind.

Now I started commuting by train to Darmstadt. I liked the school okay even though after a few weeks I feared this would also take a long time before I could take the interpreter exam. Dieter had to start commuting to Berlin every now and then, and I hated that. He had to drive right through communist territory. That was kind of dangerous.

My mother took me along a lot when she and Ernst went to gallery exhibitions of artists new and old. I learned so much about art that it was like a whole education on its own. I found it very interesting. She and Ernst also took me along when they went to see special American movies. I saw a lot of the old movies during that time and loved it.

My mother and Ernst started to fight and argue a lot. He was an artist, and he wanted to paint nudes. That was part of his training. My mother did not trust him to be faithful to her if he painted beautiful young women in the nude. The arguments sometimes went on into the night. I felt really bad for them, but it bothered me a lot that they argued so much. My mother asked me what she should do. I suggested she move to a bigger city and try to find a nice man closer to her own age. Two years later she took my advice.

When Dieter came back we had a lot to catch up on. We saw each other many evenings and cruised around with his little Isetta. The more Dieter was gone, the more I thought about doing what Nani had done and going to England. She gave me the address of the agency she went through, and I wrote them a letter. They wrote back and said that they always needed girls from good families who spoke English to be "a mother's helper."

They said they screened the homes carefully and would always stay in touch with their girls. The girls received a certain amount of money and two full days off a week. Most of them came to learn the language fluently and used their free time to take courses at Cambridge University in London. The ladies of the house were supposed to have a cleaning lady once a week so the au pair girls did not have to do heavy housework. This all sounded pretty good to me. I discussed all this with my family and with Dieter when he came back.

Dieter and I had gotten very close, and when he had to go for several weeks at a time, it became harder and harder to say goodbye.

The next time he came home I told him about all of this. He was going to be gone for eight weeks this time. I told him I was going to go away for a year. I had to sign a contract and commit myself for that period. My mother told me she could give me the money for the trip to England and a little bit of spending money to tide me over. I was then on my own.

When it was time for me to go, Dieter and I made passionate love one more time. It was bittersweet. Then we had a tearful goodbye, and he held me like he would never let me go. A year is a long time. Would we still love each other after mother's separation? If I wanted to be a singer, I had to do this. I was scared but determined.

The next letter I received from the agency told me about the family who wished to hire me. It was a young couple in their mid-thirties with two children: a six year old boy and an 18-month old baby girl. The family was Jewish, and their parents had escaped from Berlin, Germany before the war.

I was a little concerned about that, but if they wanted to have me in their home it was fine with me too. I was supposed to start as soon as possible. I wrote to them and told them that I came to learn the language and wanted to spend my free time taking courses at Cambridge. I also told them that I had no experience with children, but I looked forward to helping take care of them very much.

They wrote me a nice, long letter back, and a date was chosen for my arrival. It was close to Christmas by now, so I wanted to leave in January. I was supposed to take the train from Darmstadt to Ostend, and the ferry to Dover, then another connecting train to London, England.

It was getting more and more scary. I didn't see Dieter any more before Christmas, and I started to get ready for a year away from home. I mostly wore straight skirts with white blouses or turtleneck sweaters.

I wore flat ballet-type shoes. I wore a suede leather jacket. I had a couple of nice dresses and a brown corduroy suit, straight skirt and jacket with a tight yellow sleeveless turtleneck sweater. It was quite sexy. I actually looked sexy in anything I wore. I also took a warm winter coat. All of this went in one big suitcase which turned out to be very hard for me to handle.

The day of my departure came closer and closer. My mother and I started to get very sad. My mother had been my only constant companion through many difficult years. As the time grew closer I realized how difficult this separation would be for me. I was 18 years old, and I went to a foreign country all by myself. If I thought it was hard to leave Dieter behind, it was almost unbearable to leave my mother. If my brother had been there, I would not have been able to do it.

Chapter Three

Leaving for England

The day of my departure, Ernst came early to our house to help us get through this. My train was supposed to leave at 8 a.m. from Darmstadt, and I was supposed to be at the train station in London around 10:30 p.m.

When we were standing on the platform, waiting for the train, I started to cry, and could not stop. I started to sob when the train came in. My mother was crying also. We hugged each other fiercely. Ernst took my suitcase, and put it on the train. He hugged me tight. The conductor whistled, and the train took off. I was so upset that it was like physical pain. But, my great adventure had just begun.

The train was speeding down the track. It was very fast. This was an intercity train. It only stopped in the larger cities. Before I knew it, we were in Frankfurt.

The cities and countryside took turns rushing by the windows while I sat and thought about my family, and what a big step I had taken. I was quite scared. Soon my thoughts turned to my destination.

Was my English good enough? Were they nice people? Would they be good to me? I had so many questions.

After so many hours we got to Ostende. It is right at the shores of the North Sea, a rough ocean with many resorts. I remember it was pretty windy. Ostende had beautiful beaches and was one of the popular vacation sites. We now had to leave the train and board the ferry for England. The ferry was not there yet, and I had plenty of time to lug my big suitcase to the place where we were to board the ferry. I stood there with other passengers looking across the water waiting on the ferry. It was a beautiful day, and the sun was shining on the water and the waves.

Everything was glistening in the sunlight. Cars started to line up ready to get on the ferry. All of a sudden a shout went up, "There it is."

We could see a dot in the distance. The dot got bigger and bigger until we could make out the shape of a big ship. It wasn't much longer until we could see the details. The ferry had several decks. There were a lot of people on the ferry and plenty of cars on the car deck. I was getting really excited.

We had to wait until everybody had disembarked, and then it was our turn. I can't remember who got on first, the cars or the passengers. It was time to lug my suitcase again. A nice looking middle-aged man offered me his help, and I got a seat on the passenger deck by the window. The gentleman who had helped me wanted to know where I was going. I pretty much told him the whole story. He was English and had the prettiest accent. I was able to understand him very well, which gave me a lot of confidence. I needed it at that time.

I started watching how we were doing, slowly leaving the coast behind. It disappeared into the mist. About an hour and a half later we saw the English coastline appear faintly in the distance. I think in those days it took us between two and three hours to cross the channel. The water got kind of rough at that point, and rocked us a little.

The English gentleman told me that this was actually a smooth crossing. In another hour, we could see the white cliffs of Dover. Now I was really getting excited. It was a beautiful sight. The famous white cliffs of Dover reached out of the ocean towards the sky.

Soon, it was time to disembark. I was getting very tired. It had already been a long day, and the sun was setting slowly. My new friend and I introduced ourselves as we were talking. He said his name was James. He took my suitcase and hauled it toward the exit.

Soon we disembarked. When we had reached the station, we had to wait for the train. It was going to be a little bit late. I just collapsed on a bench, wrapped my coat around me, and tried to relax. It was almost an hour before the train pulled in. Once again, I got help from James with my suitcase. We found a compartment to sit in, and shortly after that, the train departed. We were supposed to arrive in London around 10:30 p.m. We would be a little late.

I was so tired, I fell asleep for a little while. When I awoke and tried to look out the window, I could not see anything. It was so dark. Once in a while, the lights of a little village would fly by the window. They had a dining car on the train, and after a while, someone came through and sold drinks and sandwiches. I was starved, and got something to eat and drink.

About another hour went by, and the conductor came through and told us we had 20 minutes before we got to London. Now, I was really getting nervous. I got my hairbrush out, and brushed my hair and repaired my lipstick. I wore very little lipstick, but even a little bit helps. After a while the train slowed down. There were many lights outside. We came through a suburb with nothing but townhouses. Then we saw taller buildings and some cars on the road. The train slowed down some more, and we pulled into Victoria Station. My friend got up and had the suitcase by the door in no time at all.

When the train stopped, we were the first ones out. He put the suitcase in the middle of the platform, and wished me good luck. We shook hands. I hated to see him go. I said, "Thank you for everything." He replied, "Good luck to you." I immediately looked around for the couple I was to meet. The train had been 20 minutes late. I couldn't see anyone who seemed to be looking for me, and I got nervous. I pulled my suitcase toward the exit, and then I stopped and waited. I looked at everyone coming in and going out, but didn't see anyone who seemed to be looking for me. I got very scared.

I saw the conductor, and asked him for help. He asked me where the family lived. I told him they lived in Hendon. He said that was northwest. He told me to go down the stairs, and pointed them out to me. He said I could also take the escalator. He told me to go downstairs to buy the ticket to Hendon. He said it comes right after Golders Green, and then I would have to catch the bus. He said everything would close down pretty soon.

Somehow I got downstairs, purchased a ticket, and got directions. I saw a conductor coming from the platform. He took one look at me, and saw that I was close to tears. He asked me where I had to go, and he took my suitcase to the platform. He stayed with me to make sure I got on the right train. He reminded me when to get off. I could have kissed him. The English were so sweet. I never met such sweet people in all my life. It was about a

15 minute ride, and I was in Hendon. The subway is unbelievably fast. I had to get to the outside of the small train station and look for the conductor. He asked me where I had to go. He said the bus didn't stop there.

He turned around to his five passengers, and told them that I had traveled all the way from Germany today, and missed my people at Victoria Station. He asked if they minded if he stopped at my street. It was one block away. Sounds of compassion and absolute agreement came from the few passengers.

I was so relieved. All I could say was, "Thank you. Thank you so much." By then, I was crying. True to his word, it was only a 10 minute ride. The bus driver dropped me off at my new address. Everybody waved goodbye to me, and wished me good luck. I waved back with tears in my eyes. The house was a pretty big townhouse with a fence around it. Right by the gate was a bell. With shaking hands, I rang the bell. The house was dark. A minute went by. I rang the bell again. Someone opened the window upstairs, and stuck their head out.

They shouted, "Hello?" I called, "Mrs. Igra, this is Margret.

She said, "Oh my God. It is Margret. I will be right down." Soon after, the front door light came on, and a lady and gentleman opened the door. They came to the gate, and clucked over me like two mother hens. They said, "We didn't see you. We looked and waited, but couldn't find you. Come in. How in the world did you find your way with that huge suitcase?"

I told them the whole story, and once in a while, a tear rolled down my face. It had been a rough start. I still didn't understand how they did not see me. I was about the last person standing there. I figured they must have been at the wrong platform.

Mr. Igra took my suitcase upstairs. Mrs. Igra took me into

the breakfast room, and fixed me a nice, hot cup of tea, and two pieces of toast with butter and orange marmalade. I started to feel much better. She took me upstairs to my room, which was freezing cold, but had a big comforter on the bed. The bathroom was right next door. I brushed my teeth and washed my hands, and went to bed. I was asleep in an instant. My last thought was of my mother, and a tear rolled down my cheek.

Mrs. Igra woke me up at 9 o'clock by knocking at my door. I got up, cleaned up, and dressed. I was downstairs in about 20 minutes. Mrs. Igra had a cup of hot tea for me with plenty of milk and sugar.

I learned to love to drink my tea that way. For breakfast, I had two pieces of toast with butter and marmalade. I was still a bit tired from my trip and all the excitement of the night before.

The first thing I noticed was a huge pile of laundry on the kitchen floor. Mrs Igra said, "Margret, I would like you to sort out the laundry and work the washing machine." It was a wringer washing machine. She told me that her little six year old boy was in school until three o'clock, and her baby, Brenda, had awakened real early in the morning. She had put her down for a little catnap after breakfast. She assisted me through the laundry process until Brenda woke up and called for her mama. She went upstairs to get the baby while I continued with the laundry. It was a pretty day, so we could hang the laundry outside, and let the sun dry it a little.

She then asked me to wash the kitchen floor and the breakfast room floor. She also wanted me to take everything out of the refrigerator and wash it out. She had boiled a chicken, and she brought that out for lunch. We ate a piece of boiled chicken with a piece of toast, and some green beans. I saw right away that she was a terrible cook, but I politely ate what I could get down. After lunch, we cleared it away. She told me I could freshen up a little, and walk with her and the baby to school to pick up Irving. Brenda rode in her big, navy blue English pram, loving every minute of it. We got to the school, and looked around for Irving. Soon, he came skipping out the door. He was a skinny little boy, but he was very lively. Mrs. Igra introduced me to Irving. I bent down to his level, smiled at him, and said, "Hello Irving. How are you?"

He was a friendly littly guy, but pretty spoiled, as I found out later. Brenda was just a beautiful little girl. She looked at me and smiled all the time. I couldn't wait until her mother let me hold her. When we got home, we had tea again. The children had milk and cookies. I got to hold the baby then, and sat on the floor in the big foyer, and played with the children. I enjoyed that time so much.

The children took to me instantly. That made me happy. Then, it was time to bring the laundry in.

It was getting cold. Since it was wintertime, we had to hang the laundry over a contraption in the breakfast room, right by the pot belly stove. The houses, even though they were nice, did not have central heat. There was the wood burning stove in the breakfast room, which pretty much heated the downstairs. There was an open gas fireplace, which heated the living and dining room.

Upstairs, the master bedroom had a gas fireplace like Irving's room. The baby's room had electric heat, and so did mine. I remembered that we already had steam heat all over the house in Berlin, but now, of course, we had only wood burning stoves in our apartment for warmth and to heat bath water.

The whole house was furnished really pretty, and I thought it was very comfortable. There was also a little fenced in back yard. Hendon was a nice suburb, with pleasant one-family homes.

Mrs. Igra was not really a pretty woman. She was tall and slender with dark hair, and dark eyes. She was always very polite to me. We now seated the children at the table. They each got a little white meat, cut into pieces, some potatoes mashed in butter, green beans, and a glass of milk. Mr. Igra got the white chicken. Mrs. Igra took a drumstick, and put the neck on my plate. When we sat down, I had to tell her, very politely, that I would not be able to eat the neck. She just swapped our plates, and hungrily ate the neck. I could tell she was very frugal with their spending.

After dinner, I cleaned up the kitchen while Mr. and Mrs. Igra played with the children a little. Then we took the children up-stairs, bathed one after the other, and then put them to bed. Mrs. Igra read a book to Irving in his room while I got to read a little baby book to Brenda.

I got to hold her on my lap in her rocking chair while I read to her. I was used to hard work, but I must say, I was really tired. There had not been a moment's break.

I really liked the children, especially the baby. We both liked each other.

I told the Igras good night, and took a bath, and went to bed. I did not fall asleep. I passed out.

Tuesday was no different than Monday. I cleaned all day. In addition, Mrs. Igra showed me how to get the pot belly stove ready for the night, and how to light it in the morning. I was supposed to get up before Mr. Igra, and have a nice fire burning before he came downstairs.

I had to get up at 7 a.m. Mrs. Igra fixed Mr. Igra breakfast in the mornings. They were very strict Jews. For instance, they did not mix their dishes that were used for meat with the dishes used for dairy. They had two sets of each. On Saturday, she wore a little lace head cover for supper. He had a little black cap, and they said some prayers.

Wednesday was my day off. I could not wait. I had to stay until everybody had their lunch. I then cleaned it up. It was just a half-day off. I got the directions to Cambridge University, and headed for the subway. It was pretty easy to find. This was just a branch of Cambridge University, but it was quite large. I went to the main office and looked for someone to help me enroll in two courses: certificate of proficiency in English literature and the London Chamber of Commerce Certificate.

I could attend both classes on Wednesday afternoons. That left me the evenings at home for homework, and Sundays I could sightsee. I was very excited with that solution. I paid for the course, and headed back to the subway for Piccadilly. Picadilly was kind of in the middle of everything.

Everybody goes to Picadilly Square, including hundreds of piegons. There was the famous bird lady. "Feed the birds, two pence a bag," she would say. Like the bird lady from Mary Poppins. There were so many people, and so many birds.

There were several art galleries there. I inquired, and found out that they were free. I walked a lot and found Westminster Abbey. After quite a walk, I also found Buckingham Palace. It was surrounded with a huge wrought iron fence. There were also the gate houses and huge gates, and two guards with red uniforms and big, tall fur hats. They either stood in front of their guard houses or walked up and down with their rifles shouldered. I was fascinated along with several tourists, who stood there and stared as I did. You could talk to the guards, and look at them, and speak to them. They were not allowed to blink their eyes or talk to anyone. I was fascinated.

I was getting a little hungry. It was going on five o'clock. I had heard so much about English tea time, that I decided it was my next stop. I saw a bobby standing at the corner. I knew how friendly they were. I went up to him. "Excuse me, officer. Can you tell me where I can find a nice tea shop for high tea?" I asked. He replied, "Of course, young lady. I will show you." He walked with me for about three blocks. There was a department store with a cafe. He told me the tea shop was on the first floor. It was called Lyon's Tea Shop. He said I would have a fine high tea there. I thanked him so much, and went inside Lyon's. I picked out some little cakes, and a couple of little finger sandwiches with a small pot of high tea. I sat down at a little table. I put some cream and sugar in my tea. It was so delicious!

It was slowly getting dark outside now, and I didn't want to get into a scary situation. I headed for the subway. I found from the map where the train to Hendon would leave. I did not have to wait long on the platform. There were plenty of people around, and I got reassured that I was on the right platform. The train came, and the doors flew open. Everybody ran in. The doors shut, and we were on our way. It didn't take long until we were in Hendon. I decided not to take the bus, but to walk.

When I got to the house, Mrs. Igra couldn't wait to have a report. She and Mr. Igra were amazed at all I had done, and I was very satisfied with my adventures. The children were still up, and I helped Mrs. Igra put them to bed. I liked that, and so did the children. Mr. and Mrs. Igra watched a little TV. I was already looking forward to Sunday. Asta and Nani had an aunt in London;

Aunt Gretchen. She was supposed to be really nice, and she had already told them she would look after me.

The next morning, I got Aunt Gretchen's telephone number out and called her. She answered the phone, and when she heard my name she said, "Margret, I have waited to hear from you. How are you doing?" I told her I was doing fine, and was looking forward to meeting her. She asked me when my day off was, and I told her on Sunday. She said she'd like me to come and have afternoon tea, and meet her. I told her I'd be delighted to. She gave me directions to where she lived, right in the richest historic district. She told me to be there around five o'clock, and to call if I got lost. I was really looking forward to Sunday. I told Mrs. Igra about my plans. She was quite impressed.

Thursday came, and Mrs. Igra had a lot of work for me to do. I had to vacuum the whole house, and clean the bathroom. In the early afternoon, we walked to the school again to pick up Irving.

When he saw us, he came running, and threw himself into my arms. I was happy to see that he liked me. When we got home, I helped Mrs. Igra with food preparations; tea and cookies, and something for supper. I had been busy again, and by the time we were done, I sat down in the kitchen and wrote a long letter to my mother. I told her how much I missed her, but I thought the time for her and Ernst alone was good for them. I reminded her of my advice if things didn't get better.

Friday was another busy day, except that Mrs. Igra's mother came to visit. She was a very nice lady, maybe a little simpler than the Igras. She brought a big casserole for the whole family. I loved that because it was very good. She was definitely the cook in the family. I thought to myself, it wouldn't hurt if she had taught her daughter to cook a little. My mother was a fabulous cook, and had taught me all the good German dishes.

Saturday was a quieter day. Mr. Igra stayed home, and we did not do any housework. That day, I asked Mrs. Igra when her cleaning lady was coming. I told her that the agency had told me that she had a cleaning lady to help us. She said that the cleaning lady had just quit, but she was going to get another one.

Saturday afternoon, I took the children for a little walk around the neighborhood. Brenda was in the buggy, and Irving was helping me push it. I thanked him very much for his help, and it made him very proud. This week I had learned something very important about myself; I loved children.

That evening, I watched a variety show on TV with the Igras, and then I went to bed, looking forward to Sunday. When the next morning came, I didn't have to get up until 8 o'clock. We all had breakfast. We even had scrambled eggs and smoked herring, an English specialty. After breakfast, we did some straightening up, had a sandwich later, then I was free.

I headed straight for the subway and Picadilly to take a look in the art galleries. I remember they were free. First, I had to feed the piegons, who landed on my head, my arms and shoulders, and ran around my feet. They did scare me a little, but I just loved feeding them, like so many other people.

Then I headed into the Tate Gallery. I didn't remember the name of the others. There were several there as I remember. I saw wonderful exhibitions of the French painter, Gauguin, who had gone to the South Sea Islands, and stayed most of his life. He painted nearly naked, and some totally naked women there. The women looked very beautiful. The colors of the paintings were striking. Most of the women had big, dark eyes and long, black hair.

I noticed a nice-looking young man there. He had blond hair, blue eyes. He wore gray pants with a white shirt, and a navy blue blazer. He must have been in his late twenties. He looked at me quite often, and then we smiled at each other. I left after that.

I headed for the River Thames. I had walked a lot in Germany, so walking in England didn't bother me at all. I found the river with all its houseboats that were anchored there. People lived on those houseboats. I learned to love walking there, and observing how the people lived there. After a while, I walked on, and came to a huge bridge built of stones. I walked out on the bridge, and when I stopped and looked back, I saw the Houses of Parliament with the tower, and the famous Big Ben on it. As I stopped, Big Ben chimed four o'clock. Where did the time go when I was having so much fun? I walked back off the bridge.

This time, I was looking for a bus stop. There were some people queuing up at the bus stop, so I showed a lady the address I was looking for. After consulting the person next to her, they told me what bus to take, and where to get off. It was not far from there.

I was quite excited to meet Aunt Gretchen. My German friends had told me how nice she was. I found the house at a square of beautiful, stately homes. I do not remember the address. This was so many years ago. The house was very impressive. It surely had a lot of history, and was 3 stories high. It had a wrought iron fence, and a wrought iron gate, which was closed. There was a bell, which I rang, and after a while, someone opened the front door and looked out.

It was a nice-looking lady past middle age. She smiled at me and said, "Are you Margret?" I smiled back and said, "Are you Aunt Gretchen?" She pushed the button, which opened the gate, and I walked in.

When I got up the steps, Aunt Gretchen opened her arms and gve me a big hug. She said, "Welcome." She had already made me feel so comfortable. I almost cried, and realized what a rough week it had been. At the same time, I was so grateful to meet Aunt Gretchen.

She ushered me into the house, the likes of which I had never seen before. It was so elegant, full of antiques, and yet not over-done or cluttered. Some things were a little faded, which gave it a certain modesty. Nothing was showy, just elegant. The floors were parquet, with true Persian rugs. In some places, there were marble floors. There were beautiful chandeliers. The way the light broke in them, I knew they were crystal. The wood on the furniture and the banister of the stairway were polished to a sheen. I just loved it. She took me to the kitchen and breakfast room. It had a cheer-ful fire burning in the open fireplace with cozy armchairs sitting in front of the fire. There was a little tea cart, set with china, and some lovely pastries, and little finger sandwiches. It was all so exciting. Aunt Gretchen asked me to sit down and make myself comfortable. She asked me about my first week as she was pour-ing steaming, strong tea for me with cream and sugar.

I told her all about my first week pretty much day by day. Of course, I also told her about my arrival. She listened attentively. Then she looked at me and said, "I cannot believe what you have been through. How could they leave you at the station? You're not supposed to work like you have done this week. Where was the cleaning lady?'She felt like we should call the agency and tell them what went on. She said that she had an au pair from Germany and a cleaning lady, and that she did the cooking herself. She was very angry with the Igras, but I insisted that I wanted to try to make it a little longer. She told me I was a gorgeous girl, and she hated to see people taking advantage of me.

At that moment, a nice-looking girl, maybe a little bit older than me, came in. She was the German au pair girl. Aunt Gretchen introduced us. She was a nice-looking girl. We shook hands and smiled. We didn't really take to each other at that time, but later on we became pretty good friends. She said she was on the way to the movies, and she left. Aunt Gretchen and I started drinking our tea and eating the most delicious of snacks. You could tell they were all homemade. Aunt Gretchen told me that she was working for a lord, a very nice and courteous man. She said she loved working for him. I asked how old he was. She said in his late 50s.

Aunt Gretchen was a nice-looking lady with bright blue, intelligent eyes. She had a beautiful smile. She was not exactly elegant, but she was very wholesome looking. Someone would immediately take a liking to her. She was also from Berlin, and so was her au pair, Helga. Aunt Gretchen asked me why I had come to England. I told her all about my dreams and ambitions.

She thought that was wonderful, and wished that my dreams would come true. I asked her what life would be like if we could not follow our dreams. Her reply was, "More power to you."

We talked for another hour or so, and then I felt it was time for me to go. I thanked Aunt Gretchen so much for the invitation and the lovely teatime.

When I got outside, it was already dark. I went straight to the subway and took the train to Hendon. Again, I walked home because it wasn't all that far.

Monday was the repetition of the week before. My only fun was my walk to school with the baby, and picking up Irving.

Tuesday was the same except I wrote a long letter to Dieter and sent him my address. I could not wait for Wednesday to come, and have my first day and evening at the university. I was excited about Cambridge University, and had told Dieter all about it. I really missed Dieter. It would have been such a comfort to feel his arms around me sometimes. I was leading a lonely life, and I was very much taken advantage of.

I always looked forward to putting the baby to bed, sitting in her chair, holding her close, rocking her, and reading to her. I read to her almost until she fell asleep. When her little head started to get heavy, I carried her to bed, and she was ready to go to sleep. She got to the point where she wanted me to put her to bed. I loved that child. She had blond, curly hair and big blue eyes. Irving was blond headed too, but he had green eyes. Mrs. Igra was the only dark-headed person in the family.

I went to bed early Tuesday night because I knew that the next day would be tiring. By noon on Wednesday, I was free to go. Mrs. Igra wished me good luck. I kissed the baby goodbye, and was off to my new adventure.

I went directly to Cambridge University to find my way around. I went to the office and got the classroom numbers. I found the classes and decided to take a walk. I was back by 2:30 p.m. It was not long before the other students started to straggle in. A really cute girl came in. She had black hair and blue eyes.

She looked around, lost. She said, "Bon jour." I knew she had problems, and she seemed very insecure. I also said, "Bon jour." I had 3 years of French in high school.

We struck up a conversation. That was my first friendship. In the future, we were to spend time with each other. Since my English was better than hers, I was able to help her. My French was mediocre. Her name was Danielle, and we really liked each other. Our teacher then came in. He was a man in his late 40s; Mr. Blackburn. He seemed businesslike, but pleasant. We discussed business letters and letterheads. We read and typed some, all pertaining to business. The hour went quickly. Danielle and I decided to find us a tea shop since we had to wait an hour for our next class in English literature. She was taking the same classes as I. We found the tea shop, and had our tea and refreshments, and talked nonstop. We really hit it off.

We hurried back to our next class to meet our next teacher. She was different from the first teacher. She was an older lady who exuded wealth and elegance. The jewelry she wore looked like antiques. She wore large diamond rings. She looked very intelligent. She told us about her course. We could stay with her for one year. By the end of that year, we would be able to read Shakespeare and translate it. We would translate modern writers and write essays. We were overwhelmed and excited. The classes would be taught in English. This was the tempo I was looking for.

We dove headfirst into literature, and the next three hours flew by. We had to buy three books that day. Since I had proudly accepted my first two paychecks, it was no problem for me. On the way out, one of the students told us that our teacher and her husband were Lord and Lady Davenport. We were very impressed. She was supposed to be a fabulous teacher.

Danielle and I decided to go to a pub, which had bountiful food, buffet style. We walked a little and found one. The food buffet looked great. We sat down at the bar and each got a glass of wine and the buffet.

We were starved by then, and it tasted great. By nine o'clock, we were ready to go home. She took the subway with me, but she didn't live quite as far out as I did.

When I got home, I was very excited. Mrs. Igra couldn't wait to hear my report. She was a great listener. I was disappointed that the children were already asleep. Mrs. Igra assured me that she and the children had missed me greatly.

I spent most evenings now with homework and reading. My days were full. I received a letter from my mother, and one from Dieter. They both told me in different ways that they missed me very much. I took my letters to my room so I could read them again and again, and cry some tears in private over them. Dieter said he was spending much time in Berlin, and hardly ever got to go home anymore. He said it wouldn't be the same anyway without me there.

My mother said it was really lonely for her without me and my brother. That night I wrote to all three of them; my mother, my brother, and Dieter.

The next Sunday I planned to go back to Piccadilly, and go to the gallery next door to the Tate, where I had been before. I got to Picadilly and fed my friends, the piegons, first of all. They were just as pushy, landing on me and looking for food. Of course, I had to buy some bird food from the old lady first.

When I was done feeding the pigeons, it was quite a job getting them off me. I finally had to walk away, and they flew off.

I headed straight to the gallery, and went inside. The pictures in there were more of the old masters. There was the original Rembrandt, "The man with the golden helmet." I was thrilled. I wanted to walk around and look at various things, and also planned to take the bus out to the Tower of London. All of a sudden, I saw the nice-looking young man whom I had seen at the Tate gallery before.

He came straight toward me with a smile and said, "What a coincidence to see you again. You must love art as much as I do."

I smiled and said, "It's good to see you. Yes, I grew up with art." We talked for a while. He told me his name was James Gardener. We shook hands. I said, "I am Margret Messer."

I told him that he was the second James I had met. The first one had carried my tremendously huge suitcase on my journey to London. We laughed about that. He asked me what my plans were for the rest of the afternoon. I kind of liked him, so I said I didn't really have any. Then, he asked me if I liked music. Of course I did. He told me that the choir at Westminster Abbey had a rehearsal that afternoon, and asked if I was interested in listening to part of it. I was delighted. He led the way to Westminster Abbey. When we stepped into that enormous, awe-inspiring church, we saw a lot of people sitting there waiting for the rehearsal to begin. It was very quiet. People only whispered. All of a sudden, the choir came in and sat down behind the altar. It was a huge choir. Everybody sat up, and it became totally quiet. The organ started to play, and then they started to sing. They started out softly, and then the music swelled. It would build, and then get soft again. When that choir sang quietly, they had a flute-like quality. It sounded like one voice. It was unbelievable. I could have cried. It was so beautiful.

We stayed for a long time. After an hour, they were still rehearsing. I signaled to James that I wanted to leave. He went with me. When we got outside, he asked me if I wanted to have tea. I thought about it for a minute, and then said I would love to. He said about two blocks from there was a really nice hotel with a pretty tea room. That sounded all right to me. We walked a couple blocks, and there was the Russell Hotel. It was very pretty. We walked in, and went into the tearoom. A pianist was playing softly. The tables were set with beautiful china. I liked it very much.

We had tea and different little things to eat, and got acquainted. James told me that he was an architect, and was with a firm, which was buiding a lot in London and the surrounding area. He gave me his card with his office number on it. I felt quite safe with him, and started telling a little bit of my life. He asked a lot of questions. He wanted to know where we were during the war, about my parents, and my dreams. We talked a lot. In the end, he asked me if I had a boyfriend. I told him that I did, but I probably would not see him for a year.

He told me that he was not attached to anyone right now. He asked me if he could see me again. I was pretty happy about that. We had become friends. I gave him my phone number, and we made plans to meet the next Sunday. He offered to take me home to Hendon, but I preferred to go by "the tube." That's the British name for the subway.

He walked me to the subway and stood waving when I went into the subway station. I did not feel so lonely that evening. I realized that I was not used to being alone. I left my family behind; my girlfriends, my boyfriend, and I was only 18 years old. I was practically alone. I had met Aunt Gretchen, but did not know her very well. I had met baby Brenda, but she was just a baby. She was someone to hold and love. Now, I had a new friend, James Gardener, but I still felt very alone in this big, foggy city. There were no vineyards, no mountains, and no walking trails. In bad weather, when it was raining, the city was so foggy that you could barely see the gas streetlights or your own hand in front of your eyes. It could be very spooky.

Even though I had met all these people, I felt lonely most of the time. My salvation was that I stayed so busy. Besides all the housework and helping with the children, I had a lot of homework now. I would study at night, after the children had gone to bed, sitting at the table in the breakfast room until 12 or 1:00 in the morning. One night, the Igras went out, and I was babysitting, studying as usual in the breakfast room.

I fell asleep at the table, and didn't wake up until the Igras walked in. That's when I decided to take up smoking. In the evenings, when I got tired, I would light a cigarette, and it helped me stay awake.

In school I did very well. My teacher often praised me. We had to write an essay, and mine turned out so well that my teacher circulated it through all the classes to read to the students.

James called me and said that he had tickets for Sunday evening to the Royal Festival Hall. He wanted me to go with him to the symphony concert. I told him I would be delighted. We decided where and when we would meet. He said he would drive me home afterwards so I didn't have to take the subway. I really looked forward to Sunday.

Between my work, homework, children, and school, the week flew by. I talked to Aunt Gretchen once that week on the phone. I also got a letter from my mother, and a letter from Dieter. I cried over both letters. I got so homesick. Three days later, I got a letter from my brother, Manfred. He was lonely too, and I cried even more. Before I knew, it was Saturday, and I started getting excited over the concert on Sunday.

Now, I had to think about what I would wear. I decided to

wear my pretty dark brown corduroy suit. It had a narrow skirt with a slit up the back, and a pretty straight jacket. I would wear it with a tight, yellow sleeveless sweater. It looked very good on me. For the occasion, I would wear a pair of dark brown high heel shoes.

Sunday was here, and I was terribly excited. Even Mrs. Igra got excited for me. James and I were going to meet at Picadilly at two o'clock. I was there early, I thought, when I saw him standing by the statue. We walked toward each other smiling. When we got to each other, I gave him a big hug. I was so excited. We decided to take a walk, then we would have tea and go to the Royal Festival Hall.

We took a nice walk around and talked a lot. There was so much to learn about each other. We had our tea, and after that we took his car, a little Austin-Healey, over to the Royal Festival Hall and parked it there.

The Royal Festival Hall was a huge, modem building, right by the River Thames. It had a domelike roof. It was very imposing, sitting there above the river. Wide, beautiful steps went down to the river, and there was a nice promenade to walk on.

The concert was supposed to start at 5 o'clock. After a short look around, we went back up and entered the concert hall. It was huge, and very plush inside. The domelike roof looked like a night sky from the inside, dark blue with thousands of little lights twinkling like stars. I was breathless. I had never seen anything like it. We had good seats. I couldn't wait for it to start. There was a huge stage on which the orchestra was tuning up. It got quiet, and the tuning stopped. It was so quiet. In walked a good-looking man with silvery hair from behind the curtain. He was very handsome, and had a great profile. He wore a black tuxedo, and walked to the conductor's stand. He turned around and bowed, and was greeted by a thundering applause.

He motioned for the orchestra to rise. They got a big round of applause, and he motioned for them to sit down. Now it was totally quiet while the conductor raised his baton. As he brought it down, the music started with all the violins playing. I was immediately transported into another world, and was so emotionally overwhelmed that tears welled up in my eyes. James looked at me and reached for my hand. He held my hand through the whole concert.

I forgot about the world around me until the intermission. The conductor left the stage during a roaring applause, and a standing ovation.

To me, all this was new. I had never been to a concert before. There were no concert halls left in Germany, and the Frankfurt Opera House was badly damaged by air raids. London had also been bombed by German planes, but not as badly as Germany.

James still held my hand and suggested we get a drink during intermission. A lot of people got up to stretch their legs and get refreshments. James got us two glasses of champagne.

We stood in the big lobby and sipped our champagne, and looked around at all the different people. They were all dressed up. James wore a blazer, white shirt and tie, charcoal gray pants, and black, shiny shoes. He was a good looking man, medium height, and slender with blond hair and blue eyes. I liked him a lot, but he didn't have that vibrant smile that Dieter had, which went from his lips all the way into his eyes. Dieter was a happy-go-lucky man. James was a bit more serious.

We had a lovely time during intermission. Then, we heard a gong, which meant intermission was over. We returned to our seats, and anxiously awaited the conductor to return. The lights went down as he returned to his podium, with everyone cheering him and the orchestra. As the lights went down and the first strains of the music started to play, I looked up at the dome and the dark blue with the many shimmering lights. It reminded me again of the night sky. I experienced a moment of great happiness. I was the one this time to take James's hand. As he turned to me, I whispered, "Thank you." He smiled at me.

We had another forty-five minutes or so of being transported into another world, and then it was over. After three curtain calls for the conductor, and the orchestra rising and sitting down again, the conductor left during a standing ovation.

We left the Royal Festival Hall with everyone, and came out into the cool but beautiful night. Everything was lit up, so we chose to take the stairs down by the River Thames, and take a short stroll on the promenade.

We walked a little ways, and then stopped under the bridge and looked at the reflection of the lights on the water. All of a sudden, we turned toward each other and started kissing wildly. When we stopped, James took me by the shoulders and smiled at me and said, "What was all that about?"

"I am just so happy tonight," I said. I asked James if he would take me home now. He was happy to do it. It had been a great date. All the way to Hendon and at every red light we kissed.

We said goodbye. He asked if he could pick me up at the school on Wednesday, and take me to a little supper at eight. I said that was fine, and I would look forward to it.

I fixed my lipstick and went into the house. Mrs. Igra came out of the living room, anxious to get the report about my date and the Royal Festival Hall. I told her all about the concert, and how great it was. She said, "Your eyes are sparkling." Then she got nosy, and asked if I liked James. I said that I liked him a lot.

That week went by quickly. I worked hard, and studied at the kitchen table at night, reading, translating from English to German, and from German to English, essays, etc. After school, Lady Davenport called my name, and said that she would like to talk to me for a minute. She gave me her address and phone number, and told me that she would like to invite me to her home Sunday afternoon for tea. She wanted to make a suggestion to me. I thanked her and said I would be there. I was pretty puzzled and excited. Lady Davenport had invited me to her home for Sunday afternoon tea.

James was waiting in front of the building for me. He asked if I wanted to go to a nice restaurant or to his favorite pub, where they had really good food and nice atmosphere. I voted for the pub. We hopped into his car, and after a few blocks, he parked his car and escorted me into a really cozy looking pub. In an English pub in those days, you could sit down and read a newspaper, or sit at a table with other people and find a conversation. There was always food around, and I always loved the relaxed way of the English people.

We were lucky, and did find a little table just for the two of us. We told each other all the news since Sunday, ate a nice little supper with a glass of wine, and had a nice, relaxing time. By 10:00 I was so tired. The late hours of the week were catching up with me. I could hardly keep my eyes open. James insisted on taking me home, even though it was a long trip by car. I was too tired to fight it. I told him that I would call him to see if we could get together after my tea with Lady Davenport.

He stopped at the corner of my street and just put his arms

around me and held me. I put my head on his shoulder and almost fell asleep. After a while, I said I had to go inside, and we kissed. I went inside. I went straight up to my room and fell into bed. When I fell asleep, I was thinking about James and then about Dieter. I knew that I still loved Dieter, and I also knew that I should tell James, or should I just wait to see what the future brought?

I finished the week with my usual workload and lots of studying. Time flew. The cleaning lady never showed up, and I stayed really busy. I called Aunt Gretchen and told her what I had been up to, and also about my invitation to my teacher's house. I also told Mrs. Igra because it was on my mind. My happy moments at the Igras were spent with the children, and especially with Brenda, the baby. We loved each other.

Sunday came, and I dressed as nice as I could for my visit. I had the address and instructions to Lord and Lady Davenport's house. The house was just as grand as the house where Aunt Gretchen lived.

I rang the bell, and a maidservant answered the door. I said, "I am Margret Messer, and Lady Davenport is expecting me."

She said, "Come on in." She led me to a study. Lady Davenport was sitting at a big desk, smoking her cigarettes, and evidently correcting papers. She got up and stretched out both hands.

She said, "Margret, it is so good to see you." She asked me to sit down in an armchair, and she sat down across from me. She told me how glad she was that I was in her class, and that I was an outstanding student. She said she enjoyed my essays. I was really happy to hear all that. Then she asked me questions about where I lived and worked. She wanted to know if these were nice people, and did they have children. She asked me about my duties there. In between, she pulled the bell pull. The maid came in, and she asked for the tea tray. We had tea and everything that went with it. Then she said, "Margret, I have a proposition for you. It seems to me you are working a awfully hard, and you're actually being taken advantage of. I wanted to ask you if you would like to live with us in this house. I would pay you twice what you make now, and all I want you to do is to help me with correcting papers, maybe two hours a day. You could continue to study at Cambridge, and make a good profession of it. I think you would do a really good job, and I would love to have you here. Your life would be a whole lot better, and more fun, and give you more opportunity. What do you think?"

I was stunned, and just looked at her for a second or two. I then told her how stunned I was about this great offer, but if she would please give me the opportunity to think this over.

I would let her know in school on Wednesday. We had about finished our tea, and I told her that the only thing I would have a hard time with was saying goodbye to the baby. I told her I'd never been around children before, and that I had gotten very attached to Brenda. I thanked her from the bottom of my heart, and promised an answer on Wednesday.

It had gotten quite late in the afternoon, and I had not made a date with James. I called him from a pay phone. He answered, and I told him that I would go walking on the River Thames, and wait on him. He said he would look for me. I walked along the river, and it always amazed me how many people had children and dogs on those boats. What a job, to watch your children and keep them safe on a houseboat.

As I was walking along, I kept thinking about this great opportunity Lady Davenport offered me. What in the world would

I do? I thought of the baby. I thought of wanting to go back home. I was very homesick for my mother and my brother. I thought of Dieter. I thought of James. He was so in love with me, and I just knew he wanted to marry me if I just gave him the smallest sign. A whole new future was mapped out here for me, a whole new road. My future at home was just a plan, but nothing concrete. I didn't know yet how often in life we get to choose one road or another. I didn't know yet either that I often chose the rockier one.

I heard a voice calling my name. It called me back to reality. It was James. He just parked his car, and came to join me. We walked along the river together while I told him everything. He got really excited and asked, "Well, are you going to do it?" I told him all my thoughts about little Brenda, and that it would mean that I stayed in England longer than planned. I told him that I would give her an answer on Wednesday. He put his arms around me and said, "It would be so great! Just think of the opportunity. We can be together too if you wanted to."

I told him I was ready to be alone, and think about things. This time I would take the subway. When I got to Mrs. Igra's house, I just watched a little TV with them. Mrs. Igra wanted to talk about my invitation from Lady Davenport, but I just told her that it was very nice, and that she just wanted to tell me how well I was doing. Monday and Tuesday flew by, and it was Wednesday. I had come to a decision. It had been difficult, but Brenda, and my being homesick had won. I know my life would probably have been easier had I decided to stay in England.

We never know, do we? There were two people who were really disappointed; my teacher and James. Afterwards, I told Mrs. Igra what had been going on. She was much nicer to me from then on, and even helped me a little. I got more time with Brenda. Aunt Gretchen thought I made the wrong decision. Had I known the heartbreak in my future, I would have decided differently.

One morning after I had lit the pot belly stove in the breakfast room, Mr. Igra came down and said that Mrs. Igra was sick. Could I take care of the children and feed them? He would take Irving to school, and call the family doctor.

I had just fed and dressed the children when the family doctor showed up. Mr. Igra took him upstairs, and they stayed in the master bedroom for a long time. Finally, Mr. Igra called me upstairs. They called me into the bedroom, and told me that Mrs. Igra was very sick, and the doctor suggested that she go to the hospital. She was crying really hard. I cannot remember what she had but it was her throat, and it was supposed to be very contagious.

Mr. Igra asked me if I could take care of the children if her mother did all the cooking. I told them that I could, but I wanted to know why she had to go to the hospital. The doctor said, "What she has is contagious. She can't get near the children. Anyone who takes care of her would have to wear a sterile coat and mask, and wash their hands when leaving this room."

I don't know what possessed me, but I volunteered to take care of her if Mrs. Igra's mother would supply the food. That is what we did. The grandmother came every day and cooked, and sometimes played with the children. She was a really nice grandmother.

I took care of Mrs. Igra, wore the sterile coats and masks, and somehow managed. In the beginning, she had a really high fever, The fever broke, but she had to remain in bed Mr. Igra came home earlier at night, and brought her supper, and did the evening shift. The grandmother and I did very light cleaning, and things went relatively well. They took over on Wednesday and Sunday afternoons to give me a break. By the time 10 days had passed, we had it down pat. She now could get up for a couple of hours in the afternoon. I would wrap her up in an easy chair, and bring her a foot stool. I've never seen anyone so grateful. When she was well, Mr. Igra said we all needed a vacation. We would be going to the seaside. It was summer.

Little Brenda now thought I was her mama, and only wanted me to take care of her. Irving was a big helper. He enjoyed that. With all the hard work, it had been a very good experience for me. The Igra's were very thankful.

I had a lot of school work now in both courses. James was still my faithful friend. We planned to go to the Tower of London the next weekend. Then, we would be going on vacation. The Tower of London was terrific and spooky. First of all, the black ravens of the Tower of London greeted us in the courtyard. Then we took the tour. We saw the crown jewels. We saw little prisons in the tower where the English kings had locked up all kinds of people who threatened the succession to the throne, even 2 little children. The tower told cruel stories.

We had taken a double-decker bus out to the tower, and I really looked forward to the trip back.

We saw London Bridge, and traveled along the River Thames. Afterwards, James took me to a really nice restaurant. James started to mean a lot to me. I don't know what I would have done without him. I felt very close to him, but I was not in love.

Now, it was time to get ready for our vacation. We were going to Brighton for 10 days. The Igras had rented an apartment. James could hardly stand the thought. I would miss him too. The excitement was at an all time high the day we packed up the car and got ready to leave.

The children were very excited, and so was I.

It was not a terribly long trip. When we got there, we looked for our apartment, which was on the first floor, two blocks from the beach. This was the North Sea, so it was a pretty rough ocean.

The sun was shining, and we got to take a walk that first day on the beach. From then on, we went mornings and afternoons. We played in the sand and walked on the beach. I was the only one who swam in the waves. They said, "Margret has no nerves."

On my afternoons off, I took long walks and felt lonely for James. I guess I was really getting very attached to him after all. I had no idea that he had come to Brighton, and was searching up and down the beach for me until I came back to London, and he told me.

The whole time, I remember, we lived practically on smoked herring. I got pretty sick of it because they were full of little bitty bones. By the time we had to return to London, we all were brown as berries, the picture of health. I could not wait to see James.

That Wednesday in school the teacher who taught The London Chamber of Commerce told us that we could take the test for that particular paper in two weeks. He thought we were all ready for it. I was pretty excited. It was supposed to be a written test with an oral portion.

Lady Davenport said some of us could take the test for her course in October. I would be home for Christmas! I would see my little family again; my mother and my brother, Manfred. James was waiting for me in front of the school. I told him all bout it.

I felt so sorry for James. He tried to be happy for me, but he was very quiet the rest of the evening. We went to a pub and ate something, and had a couple beers. We walked to the subway. We stood there and talked a little, and then we hugged. He held me tight, and after a long kiss, I went into the subway.

Mrs. Igra was waiting for me, and I told her the news about my exams. I also told her that I would want to go home for Christmas. She acted absolutely disgusted with me.

I said, "You know, that is almost three months away. That gives you time to find another girl, and I will help you train her."

She was not pleased. I went to bed upset that night, thinking about how I took care of her and the children. Evidently, she had already forgotten that. The next day, I heard her call the agency and heard her complaining about me. Anyway, she couldn't do anything about it. If she had been nasty to me, I could have spent those three months at my teacher's, and helped her correct papers. I think she remembered that because she did not mention it again.

Several days later, I asked her if the agency was looking for a new girl for her. She said yes, they were, and she wanted another German girl. They were trying to get her there in time for me to train her.

I told Aunt Gretchen about it, and she said, "Mrs. Igra is going to be surprised. She took such advantage of you. She's not going to find someone like you again." She invited me for tea the following Sunday. I looked forward to seeing her very much. She wanted to know all about James and Lady Davenport. She also pointed out the opportunity I was turning down. I knew all that, but I still wanted to study voice, and I wanted to be closer to my mother.

I saw the other girl, Helga. She had no plans to go home yet. She had a good life with Aunt Gretchen.

Wednesday, when I came out of school, James's little Austin-Healey was parked about a block away. I ran to it. I was really glad to see him. I jumped in the car and threw my arms around him, and here we went kissing again. Then we looked at each other real serious and I said, "I don't know what I will do without you. You are the best boyfriend."

He replied, "I don't know what I'll do without you either. I can't even imagine London without you here. Couldn't you just stay? We will make a future together."

I looked at him sadly and said, "I just can't leave my mother alone, and you know I want to study voice."

"Well, you could study here too." He was right about that, but my poor mother.

I told him maybe I would come back. We both had to be happy with that for now.

The next few weeks just flew by. I was very busy with school, but I always saved time for James. I needed the break too.

At night, I would rock Brenda for a really long time. She still preferred me to her mama. I loved that child. Irving was sweet too, but he was just a wild little boy, and not cuddly like the baby.

The exam for the London Chamber of Commerce came rapidly closer. I stayed up late, and smoked quite a few cigarettes in that kitchen at night. The day of the test was almost here. First, we had a written test, and the oral was separate.

We had the written test, and I felt very comfortable with that. Then came the oral test, and we were all very nervous about that.

The person who gave us the oral test was unknown to us,

and he did not know us either. When I walked into the room for my oral test, I met a very courteous, white-haired gentleman. He looked very dignified in a black suit. He asked me my name and introduced himself. He asked me some questions about myself, and then some pertaining to business questions and letters. We had a really good conversation, and I was not scared at all anymore. He finally said that I had done a very good job, and he would give me a really good grade. I would receive the certificate within ten days. I thanked him very much and walked out with a bright smile. A few days later I received the certificate with "Distinction in the oral portion." I was ecstatic.

James told me that he wanted to celebrate my success by taking me to Covent Garden to the ballet. That was something else I had never done before. I could hardly wait.

On Sunday, he picked me up at the Igra's house. They were very impressed by him. He wore a dark suit and looked smashing. I wore the only cocktail dress I had brought. It was my mother's, but it fit me perfectly. It was a sexy dress, and I looked fabulous in it. He looked stunned when he saw me in it. Even the Igras barely recognized their au pair. We went to the car, and he held the door open as I sat down, as dignified as I could. First, he took me to a very nice restaurant, and we had a lovely dinner. I almost inhaled the dinner, after all the bad food I had eaten at the Igras. We strolled along the little roads in Soho to the theater.

Pretty soon we got to the theater. The place was old fashioned, and that was its personal charm. It was so exciting. People were very dressed up, and the hum of many voices filled the air. We found our seats, which were excellent. He took such good care of me. I was just beaming at him.

He smiled back at me the whole time. Finally, the lights went down, and the curtain slowly opened. The music started. The dancers, who were standing in frozen positions, started to move, and I was frozen in time. I could hardly breathe, and for the first time I was totally immersed in dreamlike music and movement. The ballet dancers were so beautiful in their ethereal costumes. It was like a totally different world. The men leaped and lifted the girls. The spins and turns, and the beautiful soft arms on all the female dancers were like a dream. I was so spellbound that when intermission came, I just whispered in his ear, "I love you." He looked at me, stunned. I had to love him. He had been so good to me. It was a magical moment.

James suggested a little refreshment. He got us two glasses of champagne. I smiled at him and said, "I could get used to the good life, no problem."

He laughed and then he said, "By the way, have you noticed that people stare at you? You look stunningly beautiful." I was surprised and pleased. I told him I'd not noticed. James said,

"That is part of your special charm." He gave me a little kiss on the cheek. A bell rang, and everybody headed back to their seats. The magic of the music and dance gripped me one more time.

It was late when it was over. We held hands and took a little stroll around, and then he took me to Hendon. We sat in the car, holding each other, and I said, "I don't even know how to thank you for all the wonderful experiences you have given me. You are everything good and beautiful that happened to me in London."

We held each other, and we touched each other, but he never pressured me, even though I could tell he felt passionate about me. We knew this couldn't last.

Three weeks later, just before my Cambridge exam, I went to

see Aunt Gretchen, and brought her up to date. She said again that Mrs. Igra was in for a lesson. She would not find such a goodhearted girl again. Aunt Gretchen was a wonderful person, and I would miss her.

Now, our exams were just around the corner. One day for translations, German into English, and English into German. The next day was essays. Since my essays had always been so good I was not worried. We had an oral part. We were so relieved when it was over. We were told that we passed, but we were to get our certificate in the mail. I had done it! What a feeling of accomplishment, and all in only nine months.

The new German girl had arrived. She was a pretty little blond from Munich, but I don't think she had ever done any work at home. She was sweet, but she complained all the time. I hoped that this would work out, but I kind of doubted it. I worked very hard all the way to the last day. At night, I would just cuddle little Brenda. Leaving her just about broke my heart.

The worst was yet to come. Mr and Mrs. Igra took me to the station where we met Aunt Gretchen and James. The train was already there, so James lifted my huge suitcase onto the train. I gave a quick hug to Mr. and Mrs. Igra and Aunt Gretchen, and thanked them. I gave a long and desperate hug to James. We kissed each other, and the tears started to flow. I whispered, "I will see you again." But, I never did.

"Be safe. I love you," he whispered.

It was almost as hard to leave there as it had been to leave home. I waved and shouted, "Thank you for everything, James," as the train pulled out of the station. I had seen so many beautiful and good things with James. I would never forget him, and I never did.

Chapter Four

Home Again

A great sadness came over me as the train carried me away from London. I thought of all the good times I had had there. I thought of the hard work I had to do. I thought of the children I learned to love. I thought of the baby that I adored. I thought of what I had accomplished in a short time. I thought of James and his kindness, and how he worshipped me. There was not anything he would not have done for me. He showed me the beauty of concerts, ballets, and the wonderful sights of London. He had taken me to fine dinners. All in all, he was the perfect boyfriend. He gave me the things that made my stay unforgettable. I also thought of the opportunities I had turned down.

As we neared Dover and the channel, my thoughts turned slowly to my mother, my brother, and going home. The channel did not look so friendly today. It looked all gray and wavy. The wind was blowing. It looked pretty rough.

The ferry was already there, and it was rocking quite a bit in the waves. This time, there was no knight in shining armor, and I had to drag my suitcase onto the ferry. I headed for the middle deck.

Someone had told me once that when you're in a storm on a

ship, to go to the center of the ship. You don't feel the rocking quite as badly. It was pretty rough, though, and all the way across I had to fight nausea. When we got closer to the German coast, the wind stilled a little. When I saw the German coast, I got really excited. I am going home, my heart sang.

As we disembarked the ferry, and I was dragging my suitcase, a nice young man offered to help. "Where are you going?" he asked.

I said, "I'm going to Darmstadt." Well, he was going there too.

I had another travel companion, but I had so much on my mind that I did not talk to him very much. It was Saturday, and I wondered if my brother would be there, too. I looked out the window after we had passed Frankfurt, and I saw things I recognized. I was getting hungry. I had been too excited to eat or drink anything.

The conductor came through. "Five minutes to Darmstadt," he said. My heart started to race. Here we were pulling into the station. I saw my mother and my brother as the train slowed down. Even Ernst was there. The nice, young man lifted my suitcase to the platform, and I thanked him. My family came running. I just opened my arms and ran toward them. My brother picked me up first and swung me around. Then, my mother opened her arms and we held each other. Then, Ernst, who had stayed in the background, gave me a huge hug. I know I was beaming from ear to ear. I was finally home. I had to hug everybody one more time to make sure it was real.

We went to the car, loaded my luggage, and off we went toward town. I'd been away for almost a year, and everything looked a little different to me. We got home to our apartment, and everything was small and shabby. The big, beautiful homes I had seen, and the nice houses in Hendon, in comparison, you could see how Germany had suffered. We still had a long way to go.

I was happy, though to be with my family. We couldn't talk enough about what had happened while I was gone. My brother, Manfred had gotten a promotion, and had a little apartment of his own. He was very proud of that fact. He looked all grown up. He was working hard and making progress. My mother's business had grown, and she thought she would soon be able to buy a condominium, maybe in Mannheim.

Ernst was busily painting, and he had sold quite a few pictures. I told them about my "London Chamber of Commerce" certificate with distinction, and the "Certificate of Proficiency in English Literature." We had all achieved something. I told my mother that I needed to take a typewriting class, and then look for a job in Heidelberg because that's where the school of dramatic arts was located.

My mother was so glad that I was back home, and had done so well. "Even if you go to Heidelberg, at least you are not in London, England." she said. Then I knew that I had done the right thing for my family. Whether I had done the right thing for myself, I still didn't know. Time would tell.

I arrived on Saturday, and we still had all of Sunday to talk. We started with our traditional breakfast; soft boiled eggs, crisp German rolls, German ham, Swiss cheese, butter and jellies, and several pots of hot, strong tea just like I had in England, with milk and sugar. My mother drank her tea English style, because when my parents were first married, they lived in London, England for three years. My father had a really good job there as a doctor of chemistry.

We sat and talked and drank one cup of tea after the other. Sunday morning was always our time to talk.

My brother, Manfred was willing to take the train early in the morning to get to work. Later on, we took a walk straight up the mountain to the castle. On the way back, we went through the vineyards. We looked down from the mountain and saw way in the distance, the River Rhine glistening in the sunlight. Now, I was really home.

I was sad the next morning when my brother, Manfred had to leave for the train station. We hugged each other and he said, "I'm so glad you are home."

I said, "I really missed you."

The next morning during our breakfast, my mother and I made a plan. I told her the first thing I had to do was take a typewriting class. Then, I needed to find a job in Heidelberg, find a place to live, and then enroll in the school of dramatic arts as soon as possible. My mother was so glad that I was home that she didn't object to anything. I told her that I had a little bit of money, but not much, and I would like to do some work for her until my first paycheck. That was no problem. She wanted me to type some of her business mail. I said I was glad to. The first thing was getting enrolled in a little business school in a typewriting class. They started classes just about weekly, so I was going to start the following week on Monday.

The gentleman who ran the school had also given some classes in high school. He was a very good-looking man, but he had broken many a young girl's heart. His reputation was not too great. I was not surprised that my second day in class, he asked me to stay to talk to him after class. He asked me for a date. He was going to take me to Heidelberg, take his paddle boat along, and we would spend the day on the river. I told him I would think about it, and then I declined.

I practiced typing so hard that I ended up having to bandage my wrists. In the meantime, I had found out how fast one was required to type to be able to get a good job. I also found out that the American headquarters and European Exchange System were always looking for good bilingual secretaries or interpreters.

My typing class was only four weeks. By then, I was going stir crazy. It was time for me to move on. I took a day trip to Heidelberg. First, I went to a German agency and applied for a suitable job. Then, I went to the American personnel office, and also applied there. They had me take the test right away, and made a copy of my certificates. Within three days, I had a phone call from both places to come and see them. There was also an offer to work for a goldsmith, a designer, the son of the own-er in a famous jewelry store. I had an offer from the European Exchange System. They had two other girls working in the office. Both were experienced, and I thought that for the beginning, it was the easier job.

Now, it was time for me to find a place to live. I looked in the newspaper, and found a nice large bedroom and private bath in the apartment of an officer's widow. She seemed very nice. She said that I could move in anytime. I told her it would take me a week. Within a week, I was ready to go to work. I was really excited.

One more thing, I went to the School of Dramatic Arts and enrolled. After that, I had to audition and read for the head teach-er. She seemed to like me very much. She was an older lady with timeless beauty. I couldn't wait to get started. It was three nights a week, from 7 - 10 p.m. Finally!

My mother helped me bring my clothes and some books to my new room. She also met Mrs. Mueller. She was sorry to see me go so quickly, but she understood. I went home every other weekend on the train to visit my mother.

Each time I stopped at the flower shop and brought my mother a bouquet of flowers.

I started working for EES, and it was quite a trip to where they were located. First, I took the streetcar to the main railroad station. That's where a bus was waiting for the employees to take us out of town to where they were located. All in all, it took about 45 minutes from my door to their offices.

There were two other ladies working there, a young woman who was single in her late twenties, and a young newlywed Hungarian woman. She spoke German with an accent, but she was fluent. What my job was, I found out from the older girl. She was the main secretary there and also had to write a lot of letters. The Hungarian girl and I had to type most of the contracts. That's where the American army received all their goods in the grocery stores, beauty shops, and dry cleaners. All these people had a contract with EES to supply Americans with all their needs.

I had worked there a few days when someone knocked at the office door, stuck his head in with a huge mile smile and called, "Good morning, ladies." He popped in like a breath of fresh air. "How is everybody today?" Then he noticed me and asked, "And who is this young lady?" I couldn't help but laugh. Then the secretary introduced me. His name was Oscar Kunze. He had the friendliest face, sparkling blue eyes, red hair in a crew cut and was about six feet tall with a very athletic build. He was well-dressed and very "easy on the eyes." We shook hands, and then he wanted to know all kinds of things about me. We had a good conversation.

Then we had some business to conduct, and he said goodbye with as much spirit as his hello. I liked him right away. Before he left he wished me good luck with my new job.

We had two bosses. The younger one had a really bad reputation as a womanizer. The older one was quite unfriendly and terribly moody. When he came in during the morning and slammed the door, our secretary would get a pained exppression on her face and wait for his summons. We just rolled our eyes and waited for the first explosion, which would practically make the windows rattle. I soon learned if I just typed my contracts, and stayed out of his way, I had nothing to fear.

The next Sunday, I went to see my mother. While I was there, Dieter called from Berlin. I was so happy to hear his voice. He told me that he was coming home for three days over Christmas. We were both very excited, knowing that we would see each other soon.

Christmas was only one month away. I scraped my money together to be able to buy Christmas gifts. I bought a beautiful, warm scarf for my mother, and a small bottle of her favorite perfume. For my brother, I bought a beautiful, warm sweater. For Emst, I bought some cologne, and for Dieter, a warm, red scarf to go with his camel hair coat. I was very proud of my gifts, and very broke.

I started acting school. We learned how to breathe properly when speaking or singing. We had to act out parts without speaking, just with facial expressions and body language. It was very interesting. We had expressive dance instruction, and a little bit of ballet. I felt I was finally living. There were some really good, young actors in that school who were about ready to take their state exams. I was the newest member, but I was the prettiest. I was not vain, but that was just how it was, and I was grateful for that. It can only help in the future.

It was tough on me right now. I didn't have much money. I could only grab a hot dog after I got out of the office, before I went to school. I had reading for school, but only half as much as I did for Cambridge.

I did not eat very well. I did not want to get into the widow's hair by cooking in her kitchen. She had to take another student in, a young man who went to medical school. Heidelberg had a world-famous University Clinic. Now, there was even more traffic in the kitchen than before. On free evenings, I took walks through Heidelberg, and I would eat something small at a little sidewalk cafe.

Oscar stopped in at the office quite often to bring us new contracts to write for people who wanted to open a business with European Exchange System. He stayed a little while, sometimes, and he would ask me where I had been, and where my family lived. I told him about my year in England, and that I went to see my mother every other Sunday. I told him about acting school, and what I had learned. Be asked me if he could give me a ride from the office to my school, where he happened to be going right by. I said I would appreciate that. Sometimes those evenings were pretty tough. Everybody loved Oscar, so the first time he came to give me a ride, I got some really dark looks from the Hungarian girl, but she got over it.

Christmas came closer, and Dieter would be home. We were getting three days off work. I was really excited. My brother, Manfred would be home too. Life was really good. I wished everyone in the office a Merry Christmas, and they did the same to me. Oscar came in to give me a ride. For each one of us he had a little package wrapped in red paper with a big golden bow. It turned out that for each of us he had a little bottle of very expensive perfume.

When we wished each other a Merry Christmas, we hugged and he said, "I am looking forward to seeing you again in three days." I smiled at him as I walked into my apartment. The next morning, I was up early, and went to the station to catch my train home. I stopped at the flower shop and bought my mother a Christmas candle decorated with branches and pine cones.

She was so surprised, and loved it. We expected Manfred within a couple of hours. The excitement was great. We went to the station at the time he was supposed to arrive, and waited for him on the platform. Soon, the train came, stopped with a lot of noise, and there was my brother, the first one off. There was a lot of hugging and Merry Christmas shouts, and then the three of us held hands, and walked to the car together. We were happy. How times had changed.

We decorated the tree together. It was just a small one, but oh, it looked so cheerful. We sang Christmas songs as we decorated, and drank lots of local wine from the vineyards.

The next day was Christmas Eve, and our pile of gifts was very small. But, they were given with hearts so full of love.

I had written to the Igras for Christmas, and my heart was still full of affection for those sweet children, especially "my baby." I got a letter from them, and they said they missed me. The new German girl had not worked out, and Mrs. Igra was searching for a new one. I had written to Gretchen and thanked her for everything. She wrote, "I always told you, Mrs. Igra was taking advantage of you. This serves her right." I had written to James. He wrote to me a very loving letter, and said that he would probably take a contract to build schools in Bermuda. He said right now, he could not stand London without me.

I sent my teacher a Christmas card, and thanked her for everything. I was grateful for the good people I had met, and who helped me during a time that was not easy. I was in the Christmas spirit, and was very, very happy. Tomorrow, I would see Dieter! I was very nervous about that.

Would we still be close?

It was now Christmas Eve. Dieter called in the morning, and wanted to come over to see me. I was all excited. He was there shortly after we had talked. The doorbell rang, and then he was there, more handsome than ever.

He said hello to everyone, and wished us a Mery Christmas. Then, I got my coat on. We bundled up and went for a walk. It was a cold, snowy day, just like it was supposed to be. We walked into the woods, which were very silent, just like snow always makes everything so still.

We held hands, and we were kind of shy. I didn't know what all had happened in his life. He asked me a lot of questions about England, and I told him about all the people I had met, and the opportunities I had found. I told him about my friend, James, but that we had only been friends, and that I often thought about him. I also told him about the wonderful things that James had shown me. Dieter told me mostly about work in Berlin, and how hard it was to get in and out of Berlin since one had to go through the Russian sector. I felt there was a lot that he didn't tell me, but I was happy to be with him. We hugged and kissed, and went back to the house. It was simply too cold.

Since it was almost Christmas, we had to be with our families. We made plans to see each other again the next day.

When he left, I walked him to the door. He gave me a little package. I opened it, and it was a beautiful gold bracelet. He also gave me a framed picture of himself on a gorgeous horse, and he told me he had joined an equestrian club, and rode; hunter jumper. He looked like a movie star. He had a big happy go lucky smile on his face. Several girls stood around him, and looked up to him on the horse, adoringly. I could tell that his life was a lot different from mine. I gave him his gift, and he seemed to like it. I had wondered if he would ask me to join him in Berlin, but he didn't bring that up. I had really dreamed of having him make love to me again, but I felt our wonderful relationship was going to end soon. We hugged and kissed, and I went inside, kind of sad.

He had been my first love, and I had adored him.

Christmas was wonderful, and even though I already missed Dieter, I was very happy with my family. Everybody loved their gifts. My mother had given me a beautiful, black skirt and a red silk blouse. I loved it. My brother had a wonderful camel hair jacket for me. Those were both great gifts, and when I put them on, I looked smashing.

I wore Dieter's bracelet with it. Ernst came over later on Christmas Eve, and also had gifts for us. He gave me a black silk scarf, which I could wear around my neck with all the things I had gotten for Christmas. Also, I could use it to tie my hair back in a ponytail. We had a lovely supper of cold meats, cheeses, hard boiled eggs, cold turkey, homemade potato salad, and wine and beer. My mother played the piano, and we sang German Christmas carols. One song was about the softly falling snow, and the stillness of the lake and nature around it. When we looked out the window, that's exactly what it was doing. The snow was falling softly, and then the church bells started to chime. We opened the window to hear the bells and smell the clear, cold air. At that moment, the telephone rang. It was Dieter. He missed me. We were going to see each other the next day. He was going to pick me up after breakfast. Dieter came about 11:00 the next day, Christmas day. In Germany, the big holiday was always Christmas Eve.

We got in his car and looked at each other. "Where to?" Dieter asked. He said his family was visiting family. Wolfgang was skiing, and the house was empty. Did I want to spend some time with him at his house? I thought hard. I really wanted to be with him one more time, even though I was pretty sure that our time together was probably over. We had met the first time when I was 16, and now I was 19. He had been my first love, and he told me that I was his first serious relationship. It was hard to let go. As I thought about it, I knew that I could not just let him go like this.

We had to have closure to this, our first love. So, I agreed to go with him to his house.

When we entered his house, it was really festive with the Christmas tree. We went into the living room. Dieter got a bottle of very fine wine and poured it for us. We toasted and clicked glasses to a Merry Christmas and a happy future. I knew he had to go back to Berlin the next day, and I had to go back to work in Heidelberg early the next morning. I looked at him sadly. He came to where I sat and picked me up, and put me on his lap. He held me and started stroking my hair. I put my head on his shoulder, and closed my eyes. It was all very bittersweet. We started kissing, and things got heated. It had been a long time. He finally took my hand, and we went to his bedroom. We sat down on his bed, and took each other's clothes off, between kisses. Then, we started to make love to each other, very gently and very intensely.

I think we both knew a new era had started, and it would be the last time, and it was.

The next morning, my brother and I were at the station early. Mutti had taken us. We took trains in different directions. As we stood waiting for the train, my mother said she had looked at a condominium in Mannheim, right at the River Rhine, and was considering buying it. There was a long promenade alone the river where one could walk. It was beautiful with the big ships coming in. We both encouraged her very much to get out of our little town, and move somewhere pretty and classy. She said she was seriously thinking about it. Then the train came. My brother's train came first. We hugged and kissed and waved, and he was off again. I encouraged my mother some more, that if she could afford it, she should move. That condo sounded just right for her.

It did not take me long to get back into my routine. I would go to work early in the morning, and go to the School of Dramatic Arts three nights a week, and study some of the other nights. After three days, Oscar showed up in the office. It was a Wednesday night. He asked me if he could drop me off at school, and I gladly accepted.

On the way into the city we talked. He asked if I wanted to go with him to his friend's pub after school, and have supper. He said his friend's food was first class. That sounded really good to me.

When I got out at 10 p.m., Oscar was in front of my school. I was so glad to see him. I was still sad about Dieter. This was a good diversion for me. We drove to the north end of Heidelberg and stopped in front of an old historic looking building on a cobblestone street. When we went inside, it was a real cozy restaurant with stained glass windows, big wooden tables and chairs, and pretty colored glass lights. It was a really cozy atmosphere. We sat down in the restaurant. The waitress came, and I ordered a glass of wine, and Oscar ordered a beer. She then brought the menu. My favorite meal of all times had been "Wiener Schnitzel." Oscar said his friend, Bill made a fabulous Wiener Schnitzel. I should order it. He was going to have one too.

Shortly after that, Bill came out, and Oscar introduced us. Bill was very friendly, tall, and skinny with a crew cut, and a very friendly face. I think we liked each other right away.

When our drinks came, we started talking. Oscar asked me about my ambitions and plans for the future. So, I told him all about my decision making, my year in England, and my plan to become a singer. He was pretty impressed about my long range plans. Then, I asked him if he had any special plans. He said, for now, EES was fine, but his long range plan was that he wanted to immigrate to Canada. He had a sponsor there. It could take a year, but that was what he planned to do. Oh God, I thought, don't let me fall in love with him. I laughed and said, "We better not get used to each other, had we?" He said, "Well, I wouldn't mind at all if you fell in love with me," and we laughed.

Our food came, and it smelled so good. We were so hungry that eating was our main interest for a while.

Bill came in from the kitchen, again, to see if we liked everything. I smiled and said, "The best Schnitzel ever." Bill had a happy grin on his face, and went back to the kitchen. Then I asked Oscar if he had any special hobbies. He said he was a semi-pro soccer player, and really loved his sport. He practiced several times a week, and had many Sunday games. No wonder he looked so athletic and tough. I liked that.

After a while, Bill came and invited us to the back. He had a nice, big room to hang out in behind the kitchen, and he was through with cooking. We sat in the back room and visited. He also had a big billiard table. It was getting late, and we said good night, and Oscar took me back to my apartment building. We hugged, and I thanked him. We waved at each other as I walked toward the door.

Friday came fast since I was so busy. Oscar called me and said he was tied up that afternoon, but he would like to pick me up after school, and take me out to eat a little something. I said I would really look forward to that.

In school that night, I had to do a love scene with another student, without words. It was kind of weird, but very interesting. The third time we did it to our teacher's satisfaction. That was not so easy. I told Oscar all about it when I saw him afterwards. He was so different from James. I just didn't have any chemistry with James, but there was plenty with Oscar.

Well, I thought a year was a long time. Things can change. We had a great winter with lots of snow. We would take long walks in the hills around Heidelberg. It was great. Heidelberg looked like something out of a fairy tale with its old down town and the castle up above. This weekend, I was not going home. I decided I didn't like my room any more; no privacy. I was going to try to find something else. Oscar told me he lived with his parents. He said they had a decent place.

The next weekend we went to the movies and saw, "Love is a Many Splendored Thing." It was an American movie about lovers who were separated through the war. She kept waiting for him until she found out that he had been killed. She stood by a tree, overlooking the ocean, and the tears rolled down her face as the music played, "Love is a Many Splendored Thing." To me, being so in love, it was the saddest thing, and I cried all the way out of the movie theater, and then some. Oscar had his arm around me and tried to console me. He even dried my tears. It was awful. I think the actors were Jennifer Jones and William Holden. I can't be sure because it was 50 years ago. It was so powerful that it moved me. I just about had Oscar crying too.

I heard about an old hotel on Main Street in Heidelberg, which was renting their rooms by the month. I went to look at it, and it was old, but very clean, and close to everything. I rented a room and bath, starting the next month, and gave my landlady a notice. It had a little two-burner stove in there, and I could fix hot drinks and soup. I was happy about that. I couldn't wait to show Oscar.

In school, I got my first small speaking part. I was thrilled. I also found out that I had a lot to learn. Projecting a voice, and still trying to sound natural was not an easy thing to do. I enjoyed my dancing class. My life was very full. I went to see my mother that weekend, and Manfred came too, so we had another short weekend together. All the hard times we had been through really had brought us close.

My mother went on vacation. The doctor had told her she needed a rest. Her relationship with Ernst hadn't gotten easier either. She decided to go to the Black Forest, where we had been as a family during the war, for vacation. We had stayed in a hotel in the middle of the woods with the huge clearing behind the hotel, flanked by the forest. At night, when we sat in the dining room, the deer came out of the forest and grazed.

It was such a beautiful place. The air was so good, and smelled like pine needles. That's where my mother decided to take her two-week vacation. When I told Oscar that was where my mother went, he asked if I wanted to visit her. He said he would take me there. I was so excited, and we planned to go to see her the next weekend. That evening we sat for a long time in his car with our arms around each other.

I had noticed that some of his friends called him, "Okker." I liked that better than Oscar, so I asked him if I could call him Okker, too. That was fine with him, so from then on he was "Okker." I was still living with the widow, so I could not ask him up. All of a sudden, he said,

"Let's go visit my sister." It was about 9:00, but he insisted they didn't go to bed early.

We drove to where they lived and rang the bell. His brother-in-law opened the door and asked us in. His sister showed up, and they were really excited to see us. We had a nice visit. Lewis said goodbye, and his sister said, "You have to take Meg over to our parents too. I know they would love to meet her." He promised he would.

We planned to drive to the Black Forest the next Saturday morning, and come back Sunday evening. Okker had a little Renault. It was a nice little French car. We packed up early on Saturday morning. We were very excited. I called my mother, and told her that we were coming. She was excited. She was getting lonely. By then, she had been there for a week. When we were ready, we hopped into the car. I had to throw my arms around Okker's neck and give him a big kiss. "Thank you, thank you, thank you," I said. I gave him another big kiss. He grinned, and off we went.

We headed straight for the interstate (autobahn) and headed south. We had fun. We were talking and laughing, and even singing. The interstate had some really great restaurants on it for travelers.

Around lunchtime, Okker said, "Let's stop and have lunch." We parked the car and went inside. It was a big, nice place. I had a Black Forest ham and Swiss cheese plate with potato salad, crisp German rolls, tomatoes, and pickles. We were not far from the Black Forest now, and I was getting a little nervous. My mother could be just a little stuck-up. That's just how she was. She had never met Okker, and I hoped she would like him. He was just a great loveable bear, a down-home guy, good natured, and lots of fun.

He was also a hard worker. He not only brought all the contracts in, but he also supervised how all those dealers ran their business, and complied with the rules. You could tell, I thought he was a super guy.

We passed through Baden-Baden, a beautiful city mostly for vacationers. Baden-Baden had beautiful hotels and parks, and no industry. It was just a healthy place to spend a vacation for most retirees. After that, we headed straight into the Black Forest. After a while, we parked the car, and took a short walk among the huge spruce trees. The ground was soft with pine needles, and the air smelled so good, like a whole forest full of Christmas trees. We stopped and just listened to the quiet, and then we hugged and kissed, and got back in the car to continue our trip.

The little town we went through next was called Freudenstadt, and it was known for its beauty and beneficial air. It's only about one hour from Baden-Baden. We came to the marketplace with a huge fountain in the center. It had geraniums all around it, and a statue in the center. Cobblestones were all around it. There were lots of little shops, with overhanging roofs so the visitors could always stay dry, even if it was raining. All the roofs had red tiles. The sides of the buildings were stucco. Everything was really colorful and pretty. Now, we had to take a little road straight into the woods. The little road wound around for about two miles, and then in the middle of a forest in the large clearing, was the hotel.

It had a low roof and lots of long wooden balconies all round, The view from the rooms was beautiful.

Then a childhood memory came rushing back to me. My father had sent my mother and my brother and me to this place during the war for a vacation. We loved it. One day my brother and I and other children were outside picking blackberries along the edge of the woods when suddenly out of a clear blue sky planes dived down opening machine gun fire on us. We all screamed and ran into the woods where they could not see us. It all came back to me. I screamed and threw myself at Okker's chest and clung to him. I was shaking. After a few seconds it was over, and I told him what I had just remembered. He told me he had no such memories because he had lived in Heidelberg all his life, and Heidelberg was never attacked.

We parked the car, went into the hotel, and asked for my mother at the reception. They called up to her room. After about five minutes, she came down the steps. She was smiling, and I rushed to her and put my arms around her. Okker had followed me, and I introduced him.

Luckily, she seemed to like him and thanked him for bringing me there. She asked us to join her in the dining room and have hot tea or coffee and cake.

The view from the dining room was gorgeous. I did remember how we used to watch the deer come out of the woods at night to graze and how beautiful that was. After our refreshment, we took a little walk through the woods, and then it was time to head back because we planned to go all the way back to Heidelberg.

Before we left my mother reminded me of one evening when we spent time in this hotel. It was dinner time and everyone was seated in the dining room when she received a phone call and had to leave the table. When she came back, she had tears in her eyes, and told us that she just found out that our home in Berlin had been bombed, and had burned to the ground.

I started to cry really hard. I had said, "My pear tree, my pear tree," My little room had a small balcony and the pear tree grew right up to it. The pears were wonderfully juicy, and I loved them. I mourned the pear tree more than anything. Even in a beautiful place like the Black Forest, the war memories followed us. The only thing left of our home was the steel triangle of the grand piano, which was lying in the back yard. My mother mourned her grand piano.

Well, it was time to say goodbye to my mother. We wished her a good vacation, and lovingly hugged her. We waved and left for our trip back home.

I was sitting really close to Okker, and looked at him adoringly and said, "Thank you so much for bringing me on this trip."

"You are so welcome," he said, and smiled at me. He was such a neat guy.

I put my head on Okker's shoulder and nodded off a little bit. I woke up when we got into Baden-Baden. "Let's just have a cup of coffee and head on to Heidelberg," he said. That was fine with me. In no time, we were on the interstate (autobahn). By eight o'clock, we were close to

Heidelberg. We decided to drive on, and have dinner at Bill's. There was no better food around.

The time flew, and soon we were in Heidelberg. Bill's restaurant was quiet, so he cooked our supper and closed up. We went to the back of the restaurant. A few of their friends showed up, and we started to talk and party a little. We danced and played pool, and told stories. We drank wine and had a wonderful time. It was getting very late. When finally everybody started to leave, Okker and I were dead tired.

Bill could tell we were tired. He said, "You guys have traveled so far today, why don't you stay in the hotel part tonight? My mom is out of town."

Okker and I looked at each other, and we both wanted to stay. Okker said, "That would be great if you don't think you would get into trouble with that."

Bill said, "'It is my business too, and I invite you to spend the night, and not to drive anymore."

Okker and I both said, "Thank you so much. We appreciate it."

We visited with Bill a little bit longer, and then he showed us which room we could have, and he gave us a key. We went with Bill, and helped him lock up the place. He had no hotel guests that night. After he was done, we said good night and went to our room. I was very nervous. Okker and I had never really been alone together. Okker looked at me after we had gone into the room. He put his arms around me, and asked me, "Are you all right?"

I just smiled at him and said, "I am fine." Then he started to kiss me. We kissed so passionately that I forgot about being nervous. He held my hand, and we walked over to the bed. We sat down next to each other, and **as** we kissed, we feverishly took off each other's clothes. We tossed the big feather quilt to the floor and lay down on the bed. We held each other, and we touched each other all over, and we kissed. Those kisses were sweeter than wine!

As Okker looked down on me he said, "You are so beautiful. I've dreamed about you like this." All I could do was hold him tight, and press myself as closely to him as I could.

We made passionate love. It was the greatest experience I ever had. We were perfect for each other, and we couldn't get enough. When we finally rested, and he lay next to me, I raised up on my elbow, and looked at him.

He lay there totally relaxed, with his arms flung wide. He had the perfect body. He was a little over six feet with perfect muscle tone.

I loved him so much that I prayed, "Dear God, please don't ever take him away from me," but, the cards were stacked against me. I lay down and laid my head on his shoulder. I closed my eyes, and a lonely tear rolled down my face.

I woke up in the middle of the night, as my face was being kissed all over. Our arms and legs were wrapped around each other, and our passion was aroused again. We made passionate love again, and then drifted off in each other's arms, with the big feather quilt all around us.

When we awoke again, it was almost 9:00 a.m. We showered and got dressed, and went into the kitchen to greet Bill. He was bustling around the kitchen. It smelled deliciously like fresh brewed coffee and fresh rolls heating in the oven. "Oh Bill, it smells so good in your kitchen," I said. "Can I move in?"

He laughed and looked at me. "Anytime, darling, anytime." We thanked him for putting us up. It was great.

Okker said, "We want to take you to dinner one night when you are free, and you can bring a date."

Bill was delighted. "Wednesday would be great," he said.

"So, Wednesday it will be," said Okker.

We asked Bill if he would like to get his girlfriend, and take a walk with us. He declined, but said he was looking forward to Wednesday. We thanked him so much for his hospitality. I hugged him and gave him a little peck of a kiss, and he blushed.

We got into Okker's car and took off. We drove to the Neckar Valley and found a place to park, then headed out for a nice walk. A lot of people were walking; couples, whole families with their children, and their dogs too. Everyone was in a festive mood.

Winter had blossomed into spring, and everything looked so beautiful with many bright blossoms, the sunshine, and the silver ribbon of the Neckar. Summer was right around the corner, and all of a sudden I shivered. How long would I have this wonderful man who was so perfect for me? I hoped so much that he would change his mind. We were both so in love with each other. Well, it was up to him, and I did not want to ruin our time together.

A few weeks later, he got some paperwork to fill out, and he also had an interview at the Canadian embassy. I did not ask him any questions. To me, it was a painful subject. I guess he was just as determined with his plans as I was with mine. We wanted a better life, and a country with more opportunity than we had at that time.

My mother was in the process of buying her condo at the Rhine River, and was very excited. We were very happy for her. It was a big decision for her because she would finally break up with Ernst. Life was full of constant changes. It was tough. I already asked myself if I should have stayed in England. I was headed for heartbreak. Okker started talking about sending for me as soon as he was established enough to sponsor me. I clung to that hope, even though I knew we were talking about a long time to wait, and all that could happen before he could sponsor me.

I got ready to move into that old hotel on Main Street. I hated to say goodbye to my nice landlady, but I needed a little more privacy. Okker helped me move my stuff, which was not much. He saw my room with the kitchen and bath. I introduced him to the doorman. I didn't think it would hurt if I did that. We finally had a place where we could be alone together, at least once in a while, I thought.

We were both really excited about that. After he helped me move, he said, "Meggie, let me invite you to dinner somewhere, and we will celebrate." I was all for it.

When we were done moving, we cleaned up, and one thing led to another. We ended up chasing each other around in that small space, with lots of suppressed giggles. He had to try out the bed, and as he tossed me, I almost suffocated from giggles. We had a very nice christening of this little bitty apartment. Then we went out to eat, and had a most enjoyable evening with more than one glass of wine. Then he brought me back to the hotel, and suggested to see me to my room. I looked at him sternly, like a prim and proper schoolteacher, shook my finger at him and said, "No sir, once is enough." He laughed very happily, slapped me on the derriere, kissed me, and finally let me go. I was very happy the doorman was not on his post.

Spring turned into a lovely summer. Heidelberg had a couple of great civic swimming pools in the park-like setting with little restaurants, ice cream stands, and hot dog stands. One could spend a great Sunday there, all day.

We started going there on the weekends with Okker and Bill's group of friends. It was a fun thing to do, and the weekends just flew by. I wore my little bikini, and thought I looked so sexy. So did the other girls. The men wore those little European swimming trunks that really didn't hide anything, a little embarrassing.

The summer seemed to go by quickly, and Okker mentioned that his papers for Canada could come quite soon. I felt like a needle was piercing my heart. He told me for the first time that his sponsor in Canada was a young woman. He said, "You know, first, one doesn't meet anyone who you might be interested in. Then I met this nice girl, who was ready to immigrate, and offered to sponsor me. She is barely gone, and here you come, and I love you so much."

I said, "I wish you weren't going because I love you so much too."

He said, "I will send for you." He looked me deep in the eyes, and our eyes were full of sorrow.

The next weekend, I went to see my mother. She was in the middle of packing for her move. I helped her pack things for two days. She was excited about her new condo but sad about leaving our little town and leaving Ernst behind. I kept telling her starting over was the right thing to do, She had hired movers to help her, and I promised to come to Mannheim the next weekend to help her.

Okker drove me from Heidelberg to Mannheim which was a very short trip. He stayed around too, and we both helped unpack boxes. Mutti was very grateful. Okker went home at bedtime. He had a soccer game on Sunday and promised to come and get me late Sunday afternoon. I had a nice evening with my mother on her first night there. When I left with Okker on Sunday afternoon, I promised to come back soon.

On our way back, I practically sat on Okker's lap. We ate a bite in a sidewalk cafe when we got back to Heidelberg. It was a beautiful summer's evening, and we watched the world go by holding hands and sipping wine. When we got back to my hotel, I asked him to come up, and he did. We went to bed, made love, and slept in each other's arms. Okker got up before the doorman was on duty. This was the summer of our love. I will never forget!

My father had had so much trouble with his heart that he had to give up and ask his brother to take him in. He wanted to bring his secretary/girlfriend, but my Uncle Fritz said, "You can only bring her along if you marry her." So my father married his secretary, and they moved in with my Aunt Pia and Uncle Fritz.

I went to visit him, and of course, really looked forward to seeing my uncle and aunt. My visit with my father was not successful. He still drank excessively, and I simply could not tolerate it. People are so different when they are under the influence. You can hardly recognize that same person you loved. After that visit, years went by before I would see my father again, whom I had admired and loved so much. My mother turned out to be the stronger person when things were bad for the two of them. I was very sad when I left after my visit. The war had taken its toll.

When I came back to Heidelberg, I could not wait to see Okker. I had called him that I was coming home, and he was at the train station. When I stepped off the platform, I saw him immediately. I put my suitcase down and flew toward him, straight into his arms. He held me real tight. When I looked at him, his face was real serious, and I got this horrible gut feeling that something was not good. Even right now, I don't want to write about it. I said, "Is something wrong?"

"Not really," he said, "except that I got news from the Canadian consulate. They said that I would have my papers, and would be able to immigrate within the next three months." I just stood like I had been hit by lightning. I know my eyes were as big as saucers. I was unable to say anything.

All of a sudden, the tears started to come. First, one rolled down my face, and then another and another. It was a river that did not want to end. I just stared at him. Then the pain started. It hurt so bad that I thought nothing could ever hurt so much again. But, I didn't know much about life yet. I never talked to him about any of this again. I just ignored it, tried not to think about it, and tried to live in the moment, the moment where each one brought me closer to his departure.

We spent as much time together as we could. We held each other so tight as if we could change things that way. We made love like there was no tomorrow. One day Okker said, "Please don't cry anymore. I will write to you, and I will send for you"

I just looked at him with sad eyes, and whispered, "I will write to you too."

We spent many evenings with Bill and their friends trying to be happy. All of a sudden the time was there, the time to say goodbye. He was supposed to fly out the next morning. That evening he took me to my mother's. We got out of the car and kissed like we never wanted to let go. "I love you so much," he said.

"I love you so much too," I whispered. Then he got into his car, blew me a kiss, and off he went. It was pitch dark by then and I sank to the ground. I hugged my knees and rocked myself and sobbed. I don't know for how long. It was a long time. I wanted to die.

After what seemed forever, I dragged myself to the door and rang the bell. My mother answered the intercom. "Who is there," she asked?

"It's me," I said in an almost unrecognizable voice. My mother pushed the buzzer, and I went in. She was waiting at her apartment door. She took one look at me and opened her arms.

"Is he gone?" I just nodded.

She sat me down on the couch and just held my hand, and we didn't say anything. I thought, "Goodbye my love, goodbye."

The next day I called in sick at work, and the next, and the next. Then I went back to work and gave two weeks notice. I just couldn't work there anymore. Everything reminded me of Okker. I worked my notice. Nobody ever mentioned him. I think they knew that I thought that I was dying inside.

After my notice, I went back to the lady who had given me my first job and asked if she could transfer me to the United States Headquarters in Europe which was also in Heidelberg. I told her that I had heard that they paid much better, and I needed the money for school.

She said, "As a matter of fact, I have an opening in the Judge Advocate Division. Come with me. I will introduce you." She liked me. We went straight over to Headquarters USAREUR, and on the third floor I met my new bosses. I was to fill in for a lady on maternity leave. They thought that possibly she would not come back. I met the Captain, the Major, and two high ranking civilians. They all spoke to me and asked me questions. They were all very nice to me. They were about middle aged. The pay was much better than what I got before. They asked me when I wanted to start.

I said, "Next week."

They said, "Great!" I was thrilled.

Chapter Five

Love and Marriage Go Together Like a Horse and Carriage

I had almost a whole week off. I went to school three nights, and studied some of the roles I had for homework. I went to see Bill, and ate his Wiener schnitzel. He would only let me pay once. I took many walks to places where Okker and I used to walk. I mourned him.

I went by train to see my mother. By Monday, I was ready to go to work.

I loved the pomp and circumstance of Headquarters USAREUR. I loved it when at 5 p.m., the flag was lowered. The trumpet played retreat, everybody stopped, and people in uniform saluted. I liked my building. I liked my bosses; Captain Eppley, Mr. Davis, Mr. Frazier, and Major Dunn. The civilians were in their thirties, and Captain Eppley was in his forties, and Major Dunn was in his fifties. They were really polite, and nice bosses. The office was responsible for all the mail that went from this huge headquarters to Washington, D.C. In those days, there were no computers, only typewriters. I was a pretty good typist, but not really prepared for this job. Every letter that I typed had to be typed flawlessly. I could not correct anything or use white out. These letters could have no corrections. The result was that the first four weeks of my new job, I filled my waste paper basket with countless sheets of typewriting papa.

Every time I made a mistake, I had to pull the sheet out and stuff it in my waste basket.

My bosses walked by and grinned when they saw all the paper in my basket, but slowly things got better, and I learned not to make mistakes. I didn't know how I did it, but I did.

I had a colleague, a middle aged German guy, who seemed very nice and efficient at his job. He was very encouraging to me. We got along well. He talked a lot about a friend of his, a guy, but I never got suspicious until one day the military police showed up and took him away. He looked at me while he was being taken away like a deer caught in the headlights of a car. The poor guy was gay, and in those days, it was against the law. I felt really sorry for him. I asked my bosses if he would get to come back again, and they said they didn't think so. I had gotten really good by then with my typing and after a few days my bosses asked me if I thought I could handle the office by myself. I said I thought so. So I got a pay raise and took on all the work. I continued with my studies and did real well in school too. From that time on my bosses always brought me lunch from the cafeteria and coffee in between. I got spoiled.

In school we were learning how to interact with each other. We got many lines to read and show anger, sadness, laughter, mistrust, any emotion you can think of. It was really challenging, and I got better and better at it and really enjoyed it. Two or three of our classmates were ready to graduate and passed with flying colors. They were now official members of the actor's guild. I moved up in ranks, and I was not the least experienced anymore.

I had to memorize parts of plays and perform them with class-mates. After that we had times of discussion and a critique from our classmates. That's how we all learned I still loved my dance classes and learned a lot.

On the weekends, I often visited my mother in Mannheim. My brother and I coordinated our visits so we could see each other. My mother's condo was beautiful, and she had furnished it very tastefully.

It was not gaudy but elegantly simple. I loved it. She had start-ed to date and was pretty happy. She did very well in her job and so did my brother.

At work this young sergeant showed up every morning with the mail. I found out later that he was the boss of top secret mail. He always took the mail directly to my bosses, and then he would stop at my desk, wish me good morning, and inquire how I was doing. I was polite to him, but I gave him no encour-agement. He was of medium height, had brown eyes with dark blond hair. He had a nice physique, but I was not one bit inter-ested. I walked around with my nose up in the air and remained unapproachable.

I didn't think I ever wanted to date again. I just was not over Okker. Okker and I had written each other regularly. They were really nice love letters. But one day I got an airmail letter with a Canadian stamp, but it wasn't Okker's handwriting. I opened the letter, and started to read it.

She introduced herself as Helga Braun, Okker's sponsor. She told me that she and Okker met in Heidelberg while she was on vacation and fell in love with each other. She said she came back to Heidelberg and told him she was glad to sponsor him if he wanted to immigrate to Canada.

She said Okker fell for the idea, and they pursued the process. She said, "Now he is here, and your letters started arriving. I want you to know that I had been very serious in my intentions for Okker and also wanted you to know that if you are not serious about Okker to please stop writing to him." I about went into shock.

I did not answer this letter, but soon after I received a letter from Okker. He wrote, "Please write to me. I still want us to be together as soon as I can sponsor you. I love you."

I cried, and I believed Okker, but I could not stand the thought of him living with another girl who proclaimed to love him. I just really had to get over him. I wrote him a sad goodbye letter and cried myself to sleep.

Now I had been hurt twice. I was learning about the pain of love. I knew I would never forget Okker. He was the great love of my youth.

I tried to do a good job in the office. I tried to excel in school. I was even more driven than before. I didn't have Dieter. I didn't have James, and I didn't have Okker, Sometimes I went to visit Bill who was always so happy to see me. We were good friends. He knew what had happened and how much I missed Okker.

He kept telling me, "He is going to come back. He is not happy there. Don't give up on him." But I couldn't live like that, and who wanted to be without a partner? I thought men were pretty wonderful.

We were preparing for a theater production in my school, and I got a pretty good part. That was exciting. We practiced a lot, and the performance date came closer and closer. It was Shakespeare's Midsummer Night's Dream. It was great fun. When the evening of the performance came, I was nervous as a cat. I missed Okker so much. I wanted him to see me in my stage play. Well, we were very successful, and our teacher was very proud of all of us. She had us working hard, and the results were great.

The young sergeant at work started writing poems to me. Every morning he dropped a new poem in my mailbox written to Meg by Allen Revier. They were pretty good, and they were always about love. I guess he was falling in love with me, but I wasn't ready. I always told him that his poems were very good, and he should keep writing.

It was late summer now, but we still had beautiful days. One Sunday I did not know what to do with myself so I put on my black one piece swimming suit, wrapped a skirt around my waist, put some necessities in my bag, and headed for the swimming pool. There were a lot of people enjoying this late summer's day.

I found myself a nice spot, spread a blanket out, and started putting lotion on myself, and lay down in the sun.

All of a sudden someone said, "Hi, how are you?" I looked up, and there was the young mail sergeant standing over me, smiling.

I smiled at him and said, "I am fine. How are you?"

He said, "You know my name, right? Allen Revier. And you are?"

"Meg Messer," I said.

"Do you mind if I sit here next to you for a minute?"

I really did not want company, but I didn't want to be rude, so I said, "Go ahead for a minute."

He sat there for about a half hour and told me about himself and where he was from, South Dakota. He said he wanted to be a journalist. When he was out of the army he wanted to go back to college. He seemed really nice. After that I told him I was going for a swim, and I guess he didn't want to be pushy so he let me go without following me.

After my swim, I towel dried, combed my hair, and got ready to leave. I saw Allen watching me, and I waved to him as I left. I took the streetcar back to the center of town to my hotel. I dried my hair, put a pretty summer dress on, and decided to have a nice supper with Bill. He was busy cooking in the kitchen, but it never got late on a Sunday, so I ordered my meal and it wasn't long before he came out of the kitchen and brought me my dinner, Wiener schnitzel. It was the best food on earth.

He brought himself something to eat too. The waitress brought us two glasses of wine, and we had a good time eating and talking. I was glad I had this friend. Bill told me again that Okker was not happy, and he thought he would come back.

I felt as long as Okker did not write this to me, I could not rely on it.

The next morning, Allen Revier came to my office with the top secret mail for my bosses, and then with my mail for the in-box. He asked me if he could invite me for coffee and cake some-time after work. I said I didn't have much time after work, but I could spare about forty-five minutes, and then I went to school.

So, a couple of days later, he asked me again, and I said I could have a cup of coffee with him after work that day. We had a really nice conversation, and then he walked me to school. I was a little embarrassed when he wore his uniform. I really didn't want to date an American soldier. It was not the thing to do.

Working there at Headquarters USAREUR, I had gotten used to the Americans, and I especially liked my bosses. They were fine gentlemen, and they spoiled me very much. I did a really good job for them, doing two people's jobs. They often praised me. In return, I never had to get them coffee. They took turns doing that, and always asked me what I would like to have.

One day I got scared to death. All four of my bosses gathered at my desk, and said that Colonel Williams had called, and asked for them to send me to his office. I had never talked to Col. Williams before, and I was convinced it was something bad. So did my bosses.

"Don't worry," they said. "Just go down and smile at him, and we will be here waiting for you."

I quickly brushed through my hair, and went downstairs, shaking in my shoes. Colonel Williams was the big man at Judge Advocate Division. I found his office, and told the secretary that I was there to see Col. Williams.

She announced me, and I heard him call, "Come in here, young lady."

I went into his office, smiled and said, "Hello sir."

"Miss Messer, right?"

I said, "Yes sir."

He said, "I am so glad to meet such a lovely young lady. I have talked to you on the telephone, and I have seen you in the hall. I heard from your bosses that you are doing a great job doing two people's jobs, and I wanted to congratulate you on your job performance and your lovely manners. We are lucky to have you here."

I couldn't believe my ears, and I felt all flushed and hot from nerves. I thanked the colonel for taking the time to tell me this. He shook my hand, and I had a big smile for him. Then I left and flew up the stairs, and couldn't wait to tell my bosses. I went to their office and they all said,

"What did he want?" I told them everything. I got congratulated, and I was really happy. That was a good day.

Allen Revier and I started meeting once in a while for coffee and cake after work and before I went to school. He told me a lot about his life. He had been the youngest child in an orphanage in Nebraska called, "Boys Town." The way that had happened was that his father went into the army. I think they had the draft in those days. So his father left his wife, his children, and his very old mother behind. Allen and his two older brothers had their mother and grandmother to take care of them. The young mother got restless and took on a singing job and left the boys with the grandmother. The old grandmother ran out of money and got sick, and the boys were put into Boys Town. Allen was very young, but some kind soul made sure that he didn't get separated from his brothers and let him stay in Boys Town. He was there for two or three years when his Uncle Simpson found out, and his wife insisted to at least rescue little Allen.

So, they went and got him and brought him home to Mitchell, South Dakota.

Allen considered his Uncle Simpson and Aunt Hazel his parents. When Allen was in his first year in college, his Aunt Hazel died of cancer. Uncle Simpson and Allen were grief stricken. The two of them lived together, and managed somehow. Then Uncle Simpson decided to get married again, and married Hazel's sister, who had a hard time living up to everyone's expectations.

Allen had loved Hazel, but he hated her sister, Leone. He was as mean to her as he could be, and invented many nasty little tricks to play on her. After he made her life miserable, he joined the army.

That's where I met him. Now, he had fallen desperately in love with me. After I knew him a little better, he constantly told me that he wanted to marry me, and he hoped that some day he could convince me. He was a nice looking and very charismatic young man with a great sense of humor. But, I was in no mood to marry anyone. I still carried a torch for Okker. The thing we had in common the most, was that we both felt like lost children; me because of Okker, and him because of his childhood, and the death of his Aunt Hazel.

That's how we finally found each other. We were two young people, lonely at heart.

We started doing things together. We would go to dinner in the evenings when I didn't go to school. We went to movies. We took evening walks, and finished the nights with a glass of wine in an outdoor cafe. We talked a lot. We both liked to read, so we started reading a lot. I had to memorize a lot of parts in plays. He started writing a lot, and he let me read his material. We both felt that we had a companion for our lonely heart. We were the same age, only three months apart.

Sometimes we went to the enlisted club and "boogied." We both loved to dance, and got really good at it. Allen was a good kisser, and we did that a lot, too. My relationship developed very differently than it had with Okker. I did not fall head-over-heels in love, but our relationship grew. Allen's enthusiasm carried me along, and I looked forward to seeing him each time. I didn't think much about the future at all, or I would not have had this relationship. After all, he was from a different country than I was. I was kind of drifting, not giving it much thought. But, some day it would really hit me and my family hard. When we are young, how can we just let ourselves get carried away, like a leaf in the wind?

One weekend when I went up to see my mother, I received

a telegram. I couldn't imagine what it was. I opened it up, and there were the words, "Love and marriage, love and marriage, go together like a horse and carriage, as was told by my mother, you can't have one without the other, signed, love, Allen."

My mother was nosy, and wanted to see my telegram, so I showed it to her and said, "This is just a friend of mine." "Ja, ja," she said. "Sounds like more than a friend to me."

One day as I came to work, one of the secretaries on the second floor asked me if she could talk to me for a minute. She was a very voluptuous girl with olive colored skin. I said, "Of course, do you want to talk in my office?"

That would be great," she said.

We reached my office, and I turned to her expectantly. She said, "I need to talk to you about Allen Revier. He is not a good man. He got a friend of ours, a Dutch girl, pregnant, and now he does not want to take the responsibility." I was shocked, and did not know what to say.

I said, "I have no idea what happened, but I will ask him. Thank you for speaking to me," and I turned away. I thought to myself, what is next?

When I saw Allen later, I asked him if we could talk for a few minutes after work, and he said, "Of course." We decided to meet in front of the Kasern and walk a little ways.

After work, we met and took a little stroll away from the headquarters. I was kind of quiet, and he looked at me expectantly. I told him about the girl, "Lola," who had talked to me and came with me to my office, I told him what she said. "Is that true?" I asked him.

He told me that there was some truth to that. He had dated her a few times, and they had sex, but that they had nothing in common and stopped dating. Shortly after that she dated another American sergeant with whom she went a little bit longer than with him. He said he was not the only romance she had had. "She has a pretty bad time trying to pin this on anybody because she was not exactly monogamous during that time." He thought that it might go to court, but he didn't know for sure.

I was pretty upset and just asked him to keep me up to date. After that I went to school. I did not talk to him for a couple of weeks. Then he came to the office and told me that he was off the hook because she had had more than one person who could be the father. I never heard any more about it until thirty years later. Allen and I resumed our relationship.

At the end of the summer Heidelberg had a huge festival. People came from everywhere to taste the new wine. There was lots of music and festivities. One of the high points of the festival was the fireworks over the Neckar River. We took the train up to the castle and found us a place where we could look down on the river. There were thousands of people up by the castle, thousands down in the city along the river, and even on the bridges. You could hear music from everywhere.

People were dancing in the streets. All of a sudden, the first fireworks went up and as it went high into the sky, it opened into a huge display of stars in many different colors. It was followed by many more in grand displays of lights and colors. People cheered and clapped. It was a magic night.

I had gotten another raise, and at the same time, I found out about a little apartment in Ziegelhausen, a couple of villages down the river. It was for rent at a very reasonable price. Of course, it would take me longer to get to and from work, but I was sick and tired of being so confined.

I asked Allen if he wanted to come along when I looked at it, and he was very excited. We took the streetcar along the river, and it took no time at all to get there, maybe 15 minutes. The lady had a little apartment in the bottom of her house with an entrance to the yard, and in that same yard, a little bitty house built right over a little creek. It had a gas heater and an open fireplace. That's the one I took. I was so excited. I liked my landlady, and she said I could move in the next week. It was not as practical as my room in the middle of the city, but I was ready for some nature again. I also looked forward to having more space. There was a kitchen with a stove, a fridge, a full bathroom, a large living room, and a bedroom. It was reasonable because it was a ways from the city.

It had a nice porch into the yard, and when you sat outside, you could hear the creek rushing by under the house.

Allen was so excited he couldn't contain himself. He said if I took that house, he was going to buy a car. I couldn't wait until the moving date.

The week went fast, and it was time to pack up my few belongings. Allen had bought a used Chevy, and we packed it full, and drove out to Ziegelhausen. It was a beautiful day, and the sun shown on the river and the vineyards by the little village. The little colorful villages looked cheerful in the setting sun.

The landlady took me to the little house, and we made the rounds to make sure everything was all right. Then she gave me a key, and I gave her a deposit check and the first month's rent. Then she reached out her hand and welcomed me.

My landlady's sister also worked at Headquarters USAREUR, and I had often seen her. She was unmarried, and the landlady was widowed.

The landlady had a boyfriend, and the three of them spent

almost every weekend, when it was pretty weather, basking in the sun on their back porch in colorful array of "none clothing."

They had a beautiful black German shepherd, and he was supposed to bite almost everyone, but I had always been, and still am, crazy about dogs, and we made fast friends.

Allen and I spread my few belongings around my house; sheets and blankets, towels, soap, my few dishes, etc. Now, we needed to go to the grocery store. There was a little grocery store not too far, and we got the most necessary items; bread, eggs, butter, milk, jam, coffee, and fruit.

We took our treasures home and decided to go eat out. This was on Allen. We found a nice little pub, and ate Bratwurst, pan fried potatoes, and a salad. I drank a glass of wine, and Allen had a beer.

Later on, we sat on the back porch and listened to the creek and talked softly. It had gotten dark swiftly, and we were tired from all our activities. The next day was Sunday, and we didn't need to go to work. I asked Allen if he wanted to spend the night, and he very much wanted to.

We closed all the drapes, and locked all the doors. We showered together, and fell into bed. We made long, slow, sweet love, and fell asleep from exhaustion. Allen was a sweet lover, and he made me feel good. We fell asleep in each other's arms.

When we awoke in the morning, Allen looked at me and said, "Please marry me." We looked at each other, and I put my arms around him, and he did the same.

I said "Yes, I will," He was so happy, and so was I. It just felt right!

When I told my mother, she was very surprised, but also very excited. She bought imported lace from Brussels Belgium for my veil, which was an off-white material with gold threads in it to be sewn by our seamstress. There was no big fashion for weddings and brides in Germany at that time, and I wanted to have something special. The dress was sewed with a princess waist-- very form-fitting in the waistline. The veil framed my face and my shoulders halfway down my back. I thought I looked like a princess. Our rings were heavy, wide, gold bands that we wore on or right finger until we got married, then we would move them to our left ring finger.

We planned to get married in a civil marriage first, and then in church. My best girlfriend's father was a minister in the next little village, in the Protestant Church there. It was a beautiful old church. The cemetery was next to the church. There were huge, old oak trees there. The monuments were so old that you could not read anything on some of them. Of course, there were new stones too. The church was built out of huge stones, and had a bell tower with real bells.

The little church sat on a hill, with a stone wall around it. It was a very beautiful setting. The parsonage was within the protective walls of the church. Our pastor had to baptize me first, in order to be married in the church. The next day was the wedding.

When we awoke the next morning, God had colored everything overnight with a blanket of pure, white snow. Everything looked so beautiful.

We arrived at the church in a Mercedes taxi. We pulled up in front of the church steps. Family and friends were awaiting us there in a procession. The pastor greeted us, and told us to follow him. Allen and I were right behin him, then my mother and brother, then my two close girlfriends as maids of honor, and then other family and friends. The bells were ringing.

The pastor led us to the front of the altar where we stood. Everyone else sat down. The organ started to play, and a fabulous violinist started to play. He was from the Opera House in Frankfurt, and was a gift from our pastor and his family. It was so beautiful, and it was very touching. It almost made me cry.

After the ceremony, when I turned, my mother was the first one I faced. It hit me that I would be leaving her, and I started to cry hard. She and I just clung to each other.

When we came out, the snow had started to fall softly again. Everybody hugged us and congratulated us. Then we all went to our cars. The black Mercedes was there waiting for us, and we went to our favorite restaurant and had a wedding feast.

We sang, we danced, we ate, and we drank wine and champagne. It was a lovely wedding.

The next day we went back to our little house. We had one more day off, and then we had to go back to work.

At work, everybody congratulated us. We were very excited, and then we settled into a lovely comfortable life.

It was strange, but we were very much in tune with each other. Allen would have done anything for me. It was a happy time, and then I got pregnant. It was not planned, but we were happy about it except for one thing.

I was sick morning, noon, and night with an upset stomach. I missed a lot of work, and my bosses did not know what to do. 1 finally had to send my resignation. I worked a two week notice as well as I could. My bosses and I were very sad.

We had a lot less money now, but we actually managed. We cooked most of our meals, and for entertainment we would take walks or have coffee in a sidewalk cafe. We went people watching or saw an occasional movie.

We took our landlady's pitch black German shepherd with us when we walked along the Neckar River. His name was "Arco," and he had a reputation. When we walked on the sidewalk with him, people would step off the sidewalk and let us pass. He loved us and we loved him. But, he didn't love many other people. When people walked by our property, he made a big show of wanting to tear them apart. We had no unknown visitors, ever. Arco spent as much or more time with us as with his family. We really loved that dog.

Pregnancy was not the most favorite time of my life. It slowly turned into a real burden. Most of you know what I mean.

We went to see the movie, "The Bridge on the River Kwai," a war movie I cannot stand to watch anyway. This bridge was built during the war in the Burma area to re-supply Japanese troops. It seemed that all the solders were such young men. They were boys. The day they were going to cross the bridge for the first time, it blew up and killed so many men. (That's how I remember it.) And it was so awful I had to leave the movie theater crying and sobbing. When I got outside, I said to Allen, "How can I have a baby when we know there will be other wars, and our baby could be one of those young men that gets blown up, and what for?" I was inconsolable, and that's just how it is, history repeats itself.

Today it is no different. Wars are fought, and often the reason is not clear. Young soldiers get blown up and civilians get killed just as it was in my time.

Thank God there are lots of good days and good things that happen.

The months went by with me getting bigger and getting excited about our baby. We started buying baby furniture and things that we needed. My mother gave us a beautiful baby pram that could be converted into a stroller. Allen's uncle and aunt sent money for a crib, and pretty soon we had everything we needed. Winter turned into spring, and in the summer our little boy was born in the American Army Hospital in Heidelberg. I don't like to talk about the birth much. All I want to say is that it was 23 hours of labor and natural child birth, and my husband was not allowed near me. I was not only in intense pain, but also I was alone and scared.

Stephan James Revier was our pride and joy, and things went very smooth except for three days when I had to go back to the hospital with a high fever. Allen had to take care of the baby. One evening when he came to see me, he looked as white as a sheet. He was afraid he had killed our baby when he bathed him, and the umbilical cord fell off. He wrapped Stephan up and rushed him to the Army Hospital only to be reassured that everything was fine.

Well, we made it through those rough spots, and things went pretty smooth then. Now when we went walking, we had a baby buggy and a dog. Arco did not look too friendly when people wanted to see the beautiful baby, but he had mellowed some, and I think he was proud of Stephan too. We did have a beautiful baby. He had lots of dark hair and brown eyes with the longest eyelashes you have ever seen.

My mother came to visit, and admire her first grandchild, but she was not too excited about it. My mother was clearly not too crazy about children, and never offered to babysit. Let's say it was not her strongest suit.

Now, Allen's uncle and aunt announced their arrival. They wanted to visit and meet me, and see our baby, whom they considered a grandchild.

We were very excited, and found them a quaint hotel in walking distance from our little house. They came all the way from Mitchell, South Dakota. They flew from Mitchell to Minneapolis, to New York, to Frankfurt, and then to Heidelberg. What a tip for people who were not exactly young any more, especially since many planes were propeller driven, and were not always jets. We picked them up at the airport in Heidelberg.

When they came through the gate, I thought Allen would have a seizure, he was so excited. I saw a nice looking, well-dressed middle-aged couple with very expectant smiles. I liked them right away. They were not elegant, but solid looking pleasant people. That was such a long way for them to come. There were introductions, and hugs and lots of excitement. We had left Stephan with the landladies, who were babysitting him. They were so nice.

We took Leone and Jim Simpson to the taxi, and took them home as directly as we could because they were very tired. They did enjoy the trip through Heidelberg though, and along the Neckar Valley with the vineyards growing up the mountains. The sun was shining, and it was a beautiful day just for them.

We took them to the hotel, and got them settled in. It was very clean, with a beautiful view across the Neckar, and the vineyards on the other side. We made a date to meet for supper there. We didn't want to wear them out, and they needed to catch up a little on their rest.

Today was Friday, and on Sunday our little Stephan was supposed to get baptized. That was also one of the reasons the Simpsons had come to visit. It was an important event for all of us.

I had talked to the minister of the Protestant church there, and he invited us to come on Sunday afternoon to baptize little Stephan at 3:00 p.m. I had bought him a little white satin suit with a little cap, short pants, and little satin booties. I couldn't wait to put it on him. I had a pretty three-quarter length flowery summer dress on, and Allen was to wear a suit and tie. Mutti, (my mother) was supposed to come too.

We were very excited. Sunday came very quickly, and before we knew it, we were headed for the church with my mother and the Simpsons. We were about ten minutes early, but the pastor was already there waiting for us. He had a little sermon; the organist played a couple of sweet songs on the organ; and then our little Stephan was baptized.

I was holding him, so I handed him to the pastor. Stephan looked at the pastor with big eyes in his black robe and never cried. Allen was standing next to me, and we were holding hands. My eyes teared up when the pastor said that even though little Stephan might go to a far away country someday, God would always be with him. I looked at my mother, and she was crying, but it was a happy day anyway, and our beautiful boy never shed a tear.

The next day we turned into tourists for the Simpsons. We took the car, put the buggy in the trunk, and headed for downtown Heidelberg. I had a bag of bottles and diapers with me.

We drove up to the castle courtyard and started walking all over the castle area with Stephan in his buggy. He loved it and slept the whole time. Later on, we went back down to Heidelberg and ate something in a sidewalk cafe. Stephan had his diaper changed and got a bottle. He loved outings and was never a problem. We walked some more in Heidelberg out to the middle of the big old bridge, and got the view of the city when we turned back.

The Simpsons were overwhelmed by the beauty of the city.

It had been a beautiful day, and the Simpsons were so happy to have seen such a lovely place. It was their first trip to another country.

The next day, Mutti invited us for lunch at her condo in Mannheim, at the River Rhine. We packed our car up again; bottles, diaper bag, and the buggy in the trunk.

It was not a long trip, and we made it okay. The building in which my mother's condo was located was real pretty. Every condo had a balcony looking at the River Rhine. The balconies were full of flowers hanging out of window boxes. All of Germany had an abundance of flowers blooming everywhere. The Simpsons were really having a good time, and admired all the beauty.

We parked the car, and went to the door and rang the bell. My mother's voice answered, "Who is calling, please?"

I said, "It is us." The buzzer rang, and we could go into the hallway.

By then my mother, who had a downstairs condo, was at the door. She looked real pretty and excited. Jim Simpson was a handsome man, and Leone was a neat looking woman. She was not pretty like my mother, but she was a pleasant looking lady. Mutti asked us in. I was proud of my mother's place. It was beautifully furnished, with lots of windows, and had a great view of the river. Nobody knew how hard it had been to get to where she was now.

She asked us to have a seat in the seating area by the window. There was a very wide path going along the river for people to walk or ride a bicycle on the path. No cars were allowed.

My mother and I excused ourselves, and went to the kitchen. Allen gave Stephan his bottle and changed his diaper, and everything was peaceful from that area.

My mother had already set the dining room table. In the kitchen we prepared the plates. She had baked little Cornish hens, mashed potatoes, and fresh asparagus. On the table she had a carafe of water, one of red wine, and one of white wine. She also had some crisp, hot, white bread fresh from the oven with fresh butter and Edam cheese.

She invited us all to sit down. I took Stephan over; he was about ready to drift off in his little baby chair; then I went around the table offering red or white wine or water. Everybody was very relaxed and the conversation was lively. The Simpsons were very lively and told my mother how much they enjoyed the surroundings and her hospitality. It was a fun luncheon. Then they started to tell me about the state of South Dakota and how different it was from what I was used to.

They told Allen and me that they hoped we would come to see them first when Allen got out of the army and would consider settling there. I said, "If Allen wants to do that, we will certainly consider it."

I had absolutely no idea what South Dakota was like. It was like nothing I had ever seen in Europe with its huge wheat and corn fields, its grandness, and its loneliness.

The lunch went by quickly with so much to talk about. For dessert, my mother had gone to one of the many fabulous cafes and gotten an assortment of pastries. She had fixed coffee, and we had that with our pastries. It was quite a feast.

After lunch we moved back to the sitting area by the windows and started to watch the traffic on the river. There was always something to see. The big barges lay low in the water because they were loaded full with goods which traveled from Amsterdam,

Holland to Switzerland, and vice versa. The big pleasure boats, which were like hotels, stopped in little and big towns along the river. I loved the barges. People lived on those. They had little children with swimming vests on and haltars.

In confined areas, they had dogs. The women hung their laundry out to dry. You could tell where the living quarters were. I have always loved to watch boats.

It was a beautiful day, and I asked if anyone would like to take a little walk. We decided that would be a nice thing to do. So, we took the buggy out of the back of the car, and took a nice stroll along the river. Stephan was busily watching us and the blue sky above him. When we came back, he got cleaned up, got some baby food and a bottle, and it was time to go back to Heidelberg.

When we said goodbye, I whispered in my mother's ear, "Mutti, that was fabulous."

"Thank you." She smiled at me.

The Simpsons had been gracious guests, and complimented my mother on her hospitality, her great food, and her home. In the car, they told me how much they liked my mother. They told Allen that he had done really well, without their help, picking a wife, a son, and a mother-in-law. Everybody laughed and was happy.

We stayed really busy, and before we knew it, it was time for the Simpsons to return to the United States. They said that they had had a wonderful time, and that they hated to go, but it was time to check on their business at home. We all hugged at the airport, and watched them board the plane. I had liked them very much, but I secretly wondered if I would like South Dakota. Europe was so beautiful, and I hated to even think about leaving.

Allen and I really got along well, and we were very much in love by now, but I secretly asked myself why I had married someone who would take me so far from home.

I also started to miss my singing and studying, but I thought, if I let myself forget about it for a while, the opportunity would come back, and it did.

Sometimes you have to put your dreams on hold but don't ever give them up. With the decisions I had made in my life so far, I started to realize that I had taken the long way around.

I had had the opportunity to take some short cuts, but I didn't. For now, my path was laid out for me. I dedicated my time to my little boy and my young husband. We were both just barely grown up, but we lived up to our responsibilities in an optimistic way and were really building our relationship and our little family.

Thanksgiving came and my mother, who now had a nice boyfriend near her own age, went on vacation with him. She invited my brother and his fiancee Asta, my best girlfriend, to her condo in Manheim, so that we could celebrate Thanksgiving there since our little house was too tiny. I cooked my first turkey. My mother-in-law had sent me an American cookbook, and I cooked that turkey right out of that cookbook. It turned out great.

Manfred, Asta, Allen, and I had the most wonderful time that Thanksgiving. We ate and drank and joked. Our little Stephan was just such an uncomplicated baby. We had great fun.

We spent the night there. The next day we cleaned everything up spotless. We had had some serious conversations especially about Allen's and my plans, which were very sketchy. Allen wanted to go back to college in evening classes in Mitchell, and I still had my plans to better myself. We saw things easier than they would turn out to be. We had quite a few mountains to climb which at times seemed impossible, but in the long run, we managed it. At this point in my life, I am so afraid of decisions because only afterwards do you see if they were the right decisions or the wrong ones. I can truly say, though with each decision we grew and matured.

It was really hard to say goodbye to my brother and my girlfriend because we did not know exactly when Allen would get his discharge out of the army. It was a scary thought. We even talked about reenlisting, but that didn't seem to solve our problems in the long run unless Allen wanted to make the army his career.

We didn't think so.

The months flew by. Christmas came and went. We all met at Mutti's and had a wonderful family Christmas. Everybody had something under the tree. Stephan was crawling by then, and we had to watch him closely. We got some snow, and we all had serious winter coats. We walked a lot in the snow with Stephan and really enjoyed the change of season. Everything looked so beautiful.

Winter turned into spring and all the tender green came out, along with all the blossoms on the many fruit trees. Spring is so magical. Everything is reborn, and it will make a believer out of almost everybody. The rebirth of nature, I love it.

Allen wrote some beautiful poems about that.

He had very deep feelings about life, and he was very observant.

As summer neared, we got the news that Allen's discharge papers would be there on July 1st.

My heart had the most sinking, scared feeling. Here it was the news that I dreaded so much.

Allen said, "Don't be scared. If you don't like South Dakota,

I will reenlist for Germany, and I will get a promotion and a really good bonus. Let's just go see how it would work out. It is not going to cost us anything. So this is what I told myself and my mother too. "If I don't like it in South Dakota, Allen will reenlist, and we will come back and make a lot more money."

The mover came and put all our belongings in a container except for our buggy. The container was supposed to reach us in South Dakota in about three months. Our furniture traveled by boat first, and then by train or truck. Our buggy traveled with us by plane.

CHAPTER SIX

COMING TO AMERICA-SOUTH DAKOTA

We were to fly with TWA out of Frankfurt into New York. I was scared, curious, and excited. I remember being on the plane, buckling myself in, and buckling my baby in. When that machine took off down the runway, I thought I was going to die of heart failure. It was so scary. I had never flown before.

I think it was a ten or twelve hour flight. When we approached New York and were supposed to buckle up, Allen and I had our first fight. He buckled himself in. I tried to buckle my baby and myself and was so nervous. I had everything all tangled up. "Just take care of yourself and don't care about us." I was almost in tears. That he started to laugh did not help at all. But he came right away to our rescue, and by the time we saw the runaway, Stephan and I were safely buckled up and ready to land.

Now it was something like four o'clock in the morning. We were transported to, I think, Fort Hamilton, where they had accommodations. The next morning our papers could be taken care of. We found our room and cleaned Stephan up and fed him some baby food and a bottle. Then we found something to eat for us in an overnight snack bar. There were very few travelers walking around. Everybody else was asleep. Allen just had to call his uncle and aunt and tell them that we were in New York. It was the middle of the night, but they didn't seem to mind. They were excited too. Well, we finally settled down and went to sleep. Everything else seemed kind of blurry until we flew out west.

We had to stay one more day and flew out the following morning to Minneapolis. This was a jet plane, and it was not a bad flight. From Minneapolis we had to board a little bitty plane. It had room for about fourteen passengers. We landed, I think, two times in small towns before we got to Mitchell. Since the plane was small, takeoffs and landings were pretty rough. I didn't know the air had bumps. Stephan, who had been a really good traveler, didn't like that so much either and cried some.

From the air, South Dakota was totally flat, and all you saw was the farmland down below marked and divided by small roads running in squares. It all looked like a huge checkerboard, interrupted by huge farm buildings, silos, barns, and a main farmhouse. It showed how big these South Dakota farms were sitting right in the middle of their land. Wheat and corn were growing in abundance. The farmers also raised chickens and cows, etc. These farms were huge investments not counting all their machinery.

Allen was getting more and more excited, and I was getting very nervous. We approached Mitchell next. We saw a runway, a rather small building, and a group of people looking up to the sky. Not far in the distance we saw a medium sized town. It all looked quite lonely and very flat. There were hardly any trees, and Allen explained to me that almost every tree had been planted by human hand. This used to be the prairie.

We had one more landing to endure, and then the plane stopped close to that small building which was the airport and a few hangars.

The small group of people was the Simpsons, Allen's cousin, Bill, a good looking man, and his cute little wife, Alice Mae. And last, but not least, ten year old Jeanny, eight year old Billy, and a blond baby about Stephan's age. Everybody acted very excited, and I was so glad that I knew the Simpsons who hugged me warmly. It was a pretty, sunny day, and the warm wind was blowing around us. The prairie.

Everyone was very friendly and hugged and welcomed me. Allen looked very excited and happy. He came over to me and gave me a big hug and said, "And this is my Meggie."

The Simpsons took us to their house where we were supposed to stay temporarily. It was a pretty three bedroom house on a pretty street with lots of old trees lining the sidewalks.

Mitchell was a small town of about twenty-five thousand people. It was the center for everything for the people living in the country. People came from all around for their doctors, lawyers, shopping, schools, and whatever else they needed.

There were some one-room schoolhouses in the country, but I think a lot of kids were bussed to the middle schools and high schools if possible.

There were no big stores only some specialty shops and one or two boutiques. Almost all of us did our Christmas shopping through the Sears Roebuck catalogue. It was so big and fat. There was hardly anything you couldn't get through the Sears catalogue.

We stayed at Leone and Jim's house for several weeks. Then we could tell that it was getting too much for Leone who got up some mornings at four o'clock to take little chickens out of the incubators. They bred and hatched a certain kind of chicken. This was the business they were in.

Their product was so superb that it was marketed all over the world. They had specially trained Japanese people to check which baby chickens were male and which were female. The females got delivered to huge farms, and the males were disposed of which I couldn't stand at all.

Anyway, Leone was overworked and worrying abut meals became too much for her. I was not that confident about my cooking, but I did start surprising her with suppers when they came home after an especially long day. Allen had expected more money than he received. When he came home after the first week with forty dollars, we couldn't believe it.

We did not know how to live on that, but we started looking for houses. We really needed some yard. We had a baby. We found an old farmhouse with a little back yard and a big old front porch. It was pretty old-fashioned, but it gave us lots of room. It cost us $40 dollars a month, and it was going to be a tight money situation. Allen was very disappointed. He had expected so much more.

Mitchell had a small university called Dakota Wesley University. I met the lady who taught dance at the university and asked her if she would teach me so I could teach the children of the community. She was a teacher from New York and was quite knowledgeable. She agreed to teach me.

After about three months I started advertising for beginner ballet. Of course, I kept taking my lessons. With what I had learned in Heidelberg, I was only about one year ahead of my students. I had absolutely no competition, and the children flocked to me. Mitchell had a nice bowling alley, and they let me use a large all-purpose room for free since many of the parents bowled while I taught their children. I have always loved children, and they loved me too. My teacher helped me buy ballet records for beginners.

Within three months I was making almost $100 a week. This shows how great the need was for things like that in this isolated little prairie town.

We started going to church with the Simpsons on Sundays. The whole family went. So we got all dressed up and went too. It was a Methodist church, and I got very used to going to church. I didn't understand why there were so many different churches. I was used to the Catholic Church and the Protestant church in Germany. But it was just the way it was, and I accepted it. Allen and I were soon asked to join the church choir.

We soon met some wonderful people through the choir. We became very popular and were included in many things. Our organist was a wonderful lady and the soul of our choir. I also met Barbara Farmer and Liz Reynolds. We were all close in age. They both had beautiful voices and were accomplished soloists. They both had a degree in music. We got so close to those two I wish today I could still locate them just to talk to them. We lost touch through our travels.

When we moved into our old farmhouse, the Simpsons gave Allen his bed and dresser from his room. They also bought us a dining room set, and Alice Mae gave us an old playpen with a nice thick pad and that was Stephan's bed and playpen for now. We bought two pots, a frying pan, plastic dishes, and cheap silverware. We were set. Now came the question of transportation, so we bought two bicycles. Mine had a basket in the front, and Allen fixed it so Stephan could ride seeing everything that was going on. We took our bikes way out into the country. It was easy biking because everything was so flat. While teaching ballet and biking for fun, I was as little as I had ever been.

It was still hard to live on what we had so Allen started to bring home some of the rejected chickens from the hatchery. Our garage was a separate building from the house in the alley.

Allen fixed it up like a barn. We raised the chickens and twice a week Allen would kill one and clean it, and we fixed chicken soup or roast chicken. That helped a lot.

The summer was hot and even though I taught and studied ballet, we took the bikes out on the weekends into the country. Groceries were a problem. I could get some butter or a quart of milk with the bicycle, but when we needed more we had to take Allen's company van and get our groceries that way.

We bought a used washing machine, a wringer washer. It was a whole lot easier than what I had to do in Germany when I had to boil all the diapers, and then wring them out by hand.

Allen was a very loving husband. He helped me a lot at night. We both worked so hard we would just fall into bed at night. We managed somehow, but we could have never made it on Allen's income alone. I don't know how the Simpsons thought we could. Most of the time when I taught, I would take my baby with me. Often I would take a babysitter to entertain him. I did not like to leave Stephan when I had to teach so he grew up with a lot of music and a lot of children around him who all talked to him when they came into the studio.

We lived on a tight budget. It was a simple life, but it was okay. We made a lot of friends who always included us when they did something fun. We naturally did not belong to the country club, but our friends who were quite wealthy always took us along on any events. I think that disturbed the Simpsons a little, especially Bill and Alice Mae who were not as socially accepted as we were.

Our church organist, Mary Kaye, took me under her wing. Her husband was a lawyer, and they had a lovely tasteful home she always invited us to. She was my American mother. I loved and appreciated her. My two girlfriends, Liz and Barbara, were in that same group. I did not feel lonely because we had such wonderful friends.

My ballet teacher at the college helped me buy some wonderful children's ballet records. She taught me some children's dances. I got so good that I started writing lots of children's dances myself. My students started performing after just a few months into their lessons. People asked me to bring my little dancers to parties and city events. We became very popular, and I now had a waiting list for my classes. I continued to learn from my teacher who was very pleased with me.

I had discovered another talent of mine. My first talent was my voice, and then I discovered my love for children. Now I had discovered the imagination to write stories and dances for my little dancers. I had been given so much. I sometimes asked myself where it all came from because I had a minimum of training. From somewhere inside me came all these ideas and talents. I was not overly religious, but I believed in God and Jesus, and more and more often I thought that God had blessed me richly with all these talents, and I used every one of them to my limit.

Sitting here thinking about my life and how it all played out, I could cry over the sad things, and I could cry in gratitude over all the gifts that had been given to me to help us and fill my life with joy to this day.

One morning toward the end of October, I woke up and the wind was whistling around the house and inside the house, it was kind of chilly. I went to the window, and to my horror, I saw the snow flying by our bedroom window, sideways. It was astounding. We had a blizzard in October, and you couldn't see anything but snow. Allen got up and stood beside me. He put his arm around me and said, "Welcome to South Dakota."

The phone rang, and for the time being, work was postponed until later.

These storms would come up really suddenly, and were quite treacherous. People had been known to perish in these "whiteouts" because they could not find their way home. I now had an idea how dangerous this part of the country could be.

November came, and with it my first Thanksgiving in America. We all went to Alice Mae's house. They traded Thanksgiving off in the family. Christmas Eve was at the Simpson's house every year. This year I met the Simpson's daughter, Betty, and her husband, Kelly, and their two children. I really liked them. They were really nice people, and a lot of fun. Alice Mae did a really nice Thanksgiving with a huge turkey, and lots of goodies. Everyone else brought one dish too. It was quite a celebration. Stephan just loved all the other children. It was fun to be a part of a big family.

In church, my girlfriends and Mary Kay finally talked me into singing a solo. I was so scared that I didn't want to do it. My girlfriends said they would sit right next to me, and nothing could go wrong. Well, my hands shook so badly that they had to hold my music. Otherwise, it was okay. Well, they had made up their minds to get me used to singing solo, and all three persisted until I got so used to it that I could control my fear.

Christmas came, and it was even more fun than I could imagine. Everybody brought all their gifts to Grandma and Grandpa's, and the pile of gifts in all colors under the tree was almost obscene. I had never seen anything like it. Mr. Simpson called each name out, and handed them one gift at a time, and we all watched. It took a long time, but it made it real special.

The time just flew by. The busier you are, the faster time flies. We had friends who raised German shepherds, and Allen and I fell in love with these noble dogs. Allen had to have a German shepherd and our friends gave Allen a really good deal. He was a beautiful and perfect dog. We got him as a puppy, and as soon as he was old enough, Allen took him every Sunday afternoon to dog training. We called him Arco like the dog we walked all the time in Heidelberg.

Arm was tan and black. Before we knew it, Arco was one year old, and Stephan was two.

I thought about my brother a lot, and what we meant to each other. I very much wanted a brother or sister for Stephan by the time he was three. Allen and I discussed it and agreed the time was now. We were not well-to-do, but we thought it was pretty much now or never. It took me a while to get pregnant, but three months before Stephan turned three, our little Renee was born. Allen passed out in front of the delivery room and had to be put in a wheelchair. Most of us know that childbirth is not child's play.

I had been in labor with Stephan for 23 hours, but Renee came quickly. I was so exhausted with my first baby but I was very alert with my second one. I really enjoyed holding her the first time and looking into her eyes which seemed to watch me. We were so happy we could hardly bear it.

Renee was born in March, and by May we would walk her in her buggy, all bundled up with blankets over her. Stephan got to help me push the buggy, and it made him so proud. He was a wonderful big brother. We had a great sidewalk on our long street, and it gave us lots of opportunity to push the buggy and later for Stephan to ride his tricycle.

My mother came to the United States when Renee was eight weeks old. You should have seen her get off that little plane in Mitchell-grand as can be, high heeled shoes on, elegant suit, and mink jacket.

I was so happy to see her; I didn't know what to do. I just hugged her and held her, and didn't want to let her go. Her first words were, "What a trip, oh my God." The same welcoming committee that had been there for me was also there for her. She was very excited over her two grandchildren and had to kiss them both.

We were all invited for lunch at the Simpsons and Mutti liked their house and seemed to have a good time. She was tired, though, and after lunch we took her home and everybody had a nap.

We planned to take my mother on a trip so she could see something of South Dakota. Alice Mae had promised to take care of Stephan. He loved coming to her house because he got to play with little Jimmy, who was the same age as Stephan.

Since I was nursing Renee, she got to come with us on the trip. I was very excited. We had quite a trip mapped out. First, we planned to go through the badlands, Rapid City, and then into the Black Hills, and then Mount Rushmore. Allen was allowed to use a really nice station wagon from the hatchery so I got to sit in the back with my baby. My mother sat in the front which she loved. I could also nurse my baby easily in the back of the station wagon.

First, we headed toward Sioux Falls, South Dakota, and then toward the Black Hills, but first, we had to cross the "Bad Lands."

The "Bad Lands" were like a desert with lots of rock formations. The wind had whistled through that desert and shaped the rocks into strange shapes. Tall, skinny rocks would jut up toward the skies, and other rocks had holes blown through them by the ever-present wind. We got out of the car several times, and all we could hear was the wind whining, crying, and whistling through all the different shapes the wind had produced for many hundreds of years.

Nothing survived in the Bad Lands. Nothing wanted to live in the Bad Lands, and if anything got lost there by accident, it would stay there for a long time in the form of a skeleton. It was a very spooky place, and I was happy when we left it behind and saw the city of Rapid City and the skyline of the Black Hills in the distance. We found us a nice hotel or motel in Rapid City and spent the night. I liked Rapid City. It was a brand new town and very clean, and it was built along a river.

The next day we headed for the hills. When we got closer to the mountains, we would see buffalo lying on the road sunning themselves. Traffic had to wait until they decided to get up and find a quieter place to sun themselves.

The Black Hills reminded me a lot of the Black Forest in Germany. The trees from the distance had the same color with dark needles. As we got into the mountains, the air smelled so deliciously clean.

We headed straight for Mount Rushmore. I had heard a lot about it and was very excited. All of a sudden, we saw the presidents' faces looming high above us. It was breathtaking. The faces were huge, and you could see every little line in each face. We looked at it for a long time. Then we parked our car and went inside the large restaurant built almost totally out of glass so one could see the presidents well from the inside. The windows on the inside were at least two stories tall, and part of the ceiling was glass too. It was beautiful.

The waiters and waitresses looked like college students and were very courteous. They paid a lot of attention to us and our tiny baby, Renee. We had a nice lunch, and then all the wait staff came to our table and sang to us, "Ain't she sweet?" We were very excited. We toured a little more and then headed back to Rapid City. We stayed in the same hotel where we had spent the night before and headed home the next day.

Stephan was so happy to see us, and we were glad to be home again. My mother stayed for three weeks. She said she had to go home because her boyfriend, who had fought under Rommel in Africa and had been the youngest Colonel in the German Army, wanted her to come home after three weeks because he wanted to marry her. They were really in love, and I was so happy for her. She deserved someone to love her so much.

The day she left, I was so upset that my milk dried up. Now my baby and I were both crying. We had to get formula and bottles and fix that for her while she was crying the whole time. I was also crying the whole time. When we had fixed the bottle, I offered it to her, and she refused it screaming. We spent three very upsetting days until she finally drank some formula, and then accepted it, and started guzzling her milk again. I was very sad, but my milk was gone.

Well, our life went back to normal again, and I went back to teaching ballet. I now had a babysitter and both my little ones had to stay at home when I went to teach. They didn't like it, and I didn't like it, but that's how it had to be.

I was asked by my choir director to sing for a funeral. Even though I had been through so much, I had never seen a dead person. I was not familiar with the funeral customs in the United States with an open coffin. After much begging I agreed to do it. The pay was $25 which was enormous for us.

Mary was going to play the organ. She assured me that there was nothing to it. I was just helping the family by singing something comforting for them. The song was, "Abide with Me."

The day came, and I dressed appropriately and came to the church. I went up to the choir loft.

My friend was there, and the coffin was wide open. I honestly thought I would pass out. To this day I remember what the old gentleman looked like. It absolutely shocked me. Everyone in my family wants to be cremated with a memorial service at the funeral. I sang the song, and I tried to look at everyone else, and I never sang at a funeral again where there was an open coffin.

A friend of mine told me a really funny story. He was also a professional musician like I was later on. He tried to partially retire from being on the road so much, so he started singing for weddings and funerals for some extra money.

He was hired to sing for this funeral for a gentleman he knew. He said he sat there close to the altar three steps up and waited and waited. The church was getting quite warm and when he finally got up to sing he was a little dizzy. Well, he put his music on the music stand and started to sing. The words of the music started to blur in front of his eyes. He got really dizzy and the next thing he knew he was on the floor with people bending over him. He had passed out and rolled down the three steps from the altar right in front of the coffin with music stand and all.

When he came home to his wife, she had already heard the news. Small town! He immediately accepted several contracts for him and his band and never ever sang for a funeral again. He never did pass out again even when he sang in front of several thousand people like he did in the Pavilion in Myrtle Beach.

My three friends, Mary the organist, Liz, and Barbara belonged to this Monday Musical Club. We had great programs, and everyone was in charge of a program at least once a year.

Barbara, Liz, and I always did something together, and we were a great team. We were in our twenties and very much appreciated by the older members. There was a lot of talent in that group, and we never missed a meeting. Everybody was so supportive of each other. I learned so much from the friends I made in Mitchell, South Dakota. My life would not have been so rewarding without them.

Mitchell was not a particularly pretty town except it had that famous "Corn Palace," a huge building in the center of town that was decorated with corn of all different colors. It depicted scenes of Indian motifs, and tourists always came to see it. The Corn Palace was redecorated every fall with new pictures, and people came from everywhere to see the new pictures on the Corn Palace. Also a week of festivities followed.

One year, Lawrence Welk came, and I got to audition for him. He was very nice to me. I sang, "The Autumn Leaves Drift by my Window." I was not a bit nervous. He said that he liked my voice very much, but my singing style was a lot like the style of his "champagne lady." He could use only one of those. But, he said if he ever was in the same town as I was, I should make sure to look him up again. I thanked him. It was a good experience.

Looking back, I really did not have my own style yet, and I had a way to go.

Sadly, my little Renee started getting sick a lot. When everybody around us got a cold, she got a serious respiratory infection. When she had her first seizure, I almost died of fear. She had to be rushed to the hospital while I was holding her tongue down in the back of a taxi. After many tests, the doctors determined that she was born with bad tonsils, and that made everything so much worse than it did for other children. It made life very stressful for her and for me. I was forever bathing her in the middle of the night to get her fever down, or rushing to the hospital.

She often had to stay in the hospital for a few days, and I had to learn to sleep in a chair. It was so rough, but she was too young to have her tonsils out. I am grateful they had antibiotics in those days, or my little girl would not have survived.

We constantly had hospital bills that the insurance would not pay, and we got deeper and deeper into debt. When the weather got warm again, Renee did better, and Allen and I could join our friends again for some fun.

Our puppy Arco grew up fast, and he would watch the children when they played outside. It was amazing; by instinct he knew to watch the children. He was a really good dog and gave all of us a lot of pleasure. Renee had a little baby chair in which she could lay back, and I could strap her in so she couldn't fall out. She liked to sit in that little chair on the front porch. She would look around and finally fall asleep. Arco would sit right next to her with his ears pricked up ever watchful until she woke up, and I brought her in.

Allen had met two influential people from the company his uncle had his franchise with, and he told them both when he was able to talk to them alone, that he needed a job. He was not making enough to support his family.

Spring came, and everything started to look better. Shortly after that he got an invitation from the president of the Babcock Company to come to Ithaca, New York for an interview. We were so excited. We bought Allen a brand new suit, shirts, shoes, and anything else he needed.

They sent him an airplane round trip ticket to Ithaca. When he left from the Mitchell airport, I hugged and kissed him and told him, "My prayers are going with you." He almost cried. He had hit rock bottom. But we had hope.

When he called me the next day and said he had a job, and we were supposed to move to the state of New York, I started to squeal, and then 1 started to sob uncontrollably. His pay was going to be $200 a week, all moving expenses paid, and a company car all paid for.

When he came home, we thought we had won the lottery. I was supposed to go with Allen to the Albany area, and find a location we liked and a house we would like to move into. They were going to help us financially with settling in.

Allen had to give his uncle notice, and everybody was quite upset but us. When I look back, I know how good this move was for us. We had so many financial problems; we could have never dug our way out.

At our last Monday Musical Club meeting, Liz, Barbara, Mary, and I cried for two hours. I hated to leave all my wonderful friends and our doctor who had saved Renee's life more than once.

Allen went back and chose the little town of Westfield, New York which is very close to Lake Erie. He told me he rented a really pretty house in a nice residential area. He said it was kind of big. We had very little furniture, but we were excited.

We said goodbye to Allen's family, and I thanked them very much for everything, even though they really kept us on hunger wages. I don't know what we would have done without my little students. I had met some lovely children and some wonderful adults who befriended me.

Alice Mae always tried to help me when I needed help with my children especially during the times that Renee got sick, and I needed help with Stephan.

I had to say goodbye to all my little students. That made us all sad. I had a little program for their parents in a school. They all had little tutus on and ballet slippers and small tiaras. They looked so pretty and were so happy. I was proud of them.

We had all our meager belongings packed up, and within three weeks, we were on our way to New York. As we headed down the road, we wondered what the future might bring.

CHAPTER SEVEN

NEW YORK HERE WE COME

It was a long trip from South Dakota to New York State. We had gotten a station wagon, which was Allen's business car, but it took us all the way to our new destination.

We had to leave Arco behind which made us so sad, but he had become overprotective and quite a responsibility. Allen gave him to his favorite farmer friend so Arco had lots and lots of space to run. We cried bitter tears when Allen took him to his farm.

Every change and every move, you have to give someone up and cry a lot of tears. But, we knew Arco had a much better life on a huge farm than in a small neighborhood.

It took us several days to get to New York State. We did not travel too many hours per day because of our small children. We got closer to the Northeast.

We bypassed Lake Erie and the city of Erie and turned up into the mountains. The hills were full of vineyards. That's where a lot of that New York wine grew and where the Welch's Grape Juice Company was who made that wonderful red and white sweet grape juice. We finally found our new little town, a very pictur-esque town of about three thousand people with pretty houses, pretty streets and hills. It was quite different compared to South Dakota.

We stopped for directions to the house of the people who rented their house to us because they built a brand new mansion, and moved into that as we would shortly see.

We found their house, and Allen went to the door. He got the key, and the young woman, who looked very friendly and waved at us, got into her car to show us the way.

She took us straight to a beautiful house on a quiet street with lots of oak trees. The houses were so different from South Dakota, where most houses were the new ranch-style houses. Here the houses were more stately, a little older, and had a lot of character. She opened the door for us, and we stepped into a little room which I realized in the winter was either the mudroom or the room for all the snow covered boots. Then we entered a hallway which led into a big living room, sunroom, and dining room. In the back was a large kitchen and pantry.

It was so much space; upstairs were four big bedrooms and two bathrooms. On the third floor was a big office. There was a big front yard, back yard, and a separate garage. We thought we had died and gone to heaven. Our few pieces of furniture would just disappear in this house.

The lady wished us luck, and said if we needed anything to let them know.

After having been in the car for so many days, the children and I started running through the house like crazy people, and Allen joined us.

The house was wonderful, and we loved it. How would we fill it with furniture? I had no idea. Stephan went right back to school, which was within walking distance. Renee and I walked with him the first few times, and then I let him walk with the neighbor children. I didn't have a snow-worthy car yet, and there was a lot of snow on the ground. One day Stephan came home with only one boot on, He said he lost the other one. I couldn't believe it. These boots were hard to get on and hard to take off. It was just an indication of things that would happen in the future. I dressed Renee, put different shoes on Stephan, bundled myself up, and we walked to the school, and searched everywhere the snow looked disturbed for boot number two.

We were almost at the school when we found it half-buried in the snow. Well, we were really glad when we pulled the boot out of the snow and turned to go home again. When we got there we made a fire in the fireplace. I fixed three cups of hot chocolate, and we sat down in front of the fire.

It had started to snow again. It did that a lot. As we sat there and watched out the window, I realized how much better life already looked after one week in our new home.

We had gotten Allen's first paycheck and rent deposit for our house plus the money for our movers. It was such a relief not to have to worry about where the next penny would come from. It was a new start, a new life, and we were ready for it. All the houses on our street were pretty large, a little older but beautifully kept up. The big trees were loaded down with snow. It was a beautiful sight.

Allen would be traveling from Tuesday to Friday. He would come home Friday afternoons until Tuesday morning. Three nights a week didn't seem so bad. Westfield was a pretty New York town with just one factory where they made Welch's Grape Juice. The town was surrounded by vineyards and hills. It was so beautiful. I could only guess how pretty all this was with the blossoms of spring. Lake Erie was only a few miles away. That's where all the "lake effect snow" came from. Canada was on the other side of the lake.

The people who owned our house had a party for us to introduce us to their friends.

Everybody seemed pretty well-to-do, and even though all our friends in Mitchell had been very wealthy, it didn't bother them that we were actually poor, but it seemed to bother this group.

There was one couple--he owned the local pharmacy--who had a darling wife and three nice children. They seemed to like us a lot, and we became friends. Allen seemed to be doing very well right from the start, and we were all invited to Ithaca to meet the big boss. We were very excited. Ithaca was famous for its university. I could not wait for this trip to come about.

Allen was very happy these days and seemed to blossom. He had started to get a really depressed look, but he already looked much brighter. One quiet evening, the children were sleeping in their beds upstairs, and Allen and I were sitting in front of the fire sipping a glass of wine and were talking. He told me that it was so bad for him that he did not make enough money to pay our bills. Even with my income and Renee's terrible hospital bills, we did not make enough money to make any progress. He told me how depressed he had gotten, and how bad he had felt that he had brought me there to live under such circumstances. I told him not to worry any more; things were already better, and I never blamed him for our situation. But I did blame his family for treating him so shabbily. Anyway, we had a better future to look forward to. We raised our glasses and smiled at each other and said, "To our future."

The next day when Stephan was in school, I bundled Renee

up, and she and I went to the YMCA. I asked for the director when we got there. She turned out to be a nice lady. I introduced myself and my little girl, and told her where I was from. I told her that I had been teaching ballet in Mitchell, and I would very much like to teach some classes for the YMCA. It was a very good meeting, and we came to an agreement. The YMCA was glad to have me there. We would offer a three-month course of beginner ballet for five years and up at one dollar a class once a week and renegotiate after three months. The YMCA would do all the advertising.

The classes were to start in four weeks; advertising would start immediately. By the time I started teaching, I had three classes of fifteen students, and the number was still growing as the children started to talk about it.

We joined the Presbyterian Church, and we joined the choir. Our children went to the nursery and didn't mind at all.

The next wonderful thing for me about the choir was that the choir director was a famous tenor himself and represented the United States in Bach Festivals in Salzburg. He was also the director of the music department at Fedonia College in New York. His music department was well known nationally.

I had come full circle, and my luck was just starting. He needed someone to take over the Youth Choir when he had to do concerts. He worked hard with me in music leadership, and he told me if I could attend a weekly class at his college, he would train my voice. You know one forgets about people from the past, and then all of a sudden you realize how they shaped your life and opened endless doors for you. I will never forget Dr. Paige Smith.

After my ballet classes got started and brought in some money,

Allen didn't mind at all for me to take classes at Fedonia College. I just took one private lesson at the school. It was one hour a week that Dr. Smith worked with me. He was awfully hard on me. He never told me that I was talented, so I struggled on and just swallowed his criticism and tried even harder. He would stop me in the middle of a word and make me start over if it was not perfect or if you could not understand every word.

He gave me the strictest schooling I ever had. Sometimes on the way home, I would cry and wanted to quit. When I told Allen, he told me not to quit. He said, "Maybe he sees something special in you."

With his encouragement, I kept learning, and I learned to do amazing things with my voice. I overcame my vibrato. My voice did not do what it wanted to do, but I was able to make my voice do what I wanted it to do. There was less yelling at me and actually some praise. I felt new born.

I had really good luck with the Youth Choir when Dr. Paige was out of town. It was a very productive time for me.

We loved our house and enjoyed the pharmacist and his wife, Don and Barbara.

Renee started getting sick again, and I went to Barbara's pediatrician. He took one look at Renee and said, "Those tonsils have to come out." He said he would wait about six more months, and then we take them out.

My father had another heart attack, and my brother wrote to me and suggested that I come soon if I wanted to see him once more. Allen arranged for the money for the trip, and we planned our trip for April. I was going to fly Icelandic Airlines because it was still flying propeller planes which were much slower but much cheaper. They flew from New York over Iceland to Luxemburg.

Flying time was thirty-six hours.

Allen got the money together. We bought our tickets, notified my mother and my father. My father lived in North Germany, and my mother still lived in Mannheim with her new husband. I was supposed to stay with my mother first, then take the train to visit my father, and then back to the United States.

The time passed rapidly. I was very nervous about this trip with two little children along. We flew to New York City, and left on Icelandic Airlines for Luxemburg. The first part of the trip, the children were very good, but the longer we flew, the more tired they got. We could not get comfortable in our two seats. A really nice young lady helped me for hours, holding one of my children so we could rock them to sleep. It was an ordeal.

When we finally got to Luxemburg, we had traveled more than thirty-six hours, and all three of us were miserable. I am sure my lovely travel companion was too. When we came into the airport my mother was not there yet, and I about panicked. My new friend said that if I had to stay there overnight, she would stay with me and the children. She was an angel, and I told her so.

At that moment, my mother arrived. When I saw her, I started to cry from gladness and exhaustion. My mother was not her typical self, and whispered in my ear, "Pull yourself together." I am sure she just wanted to make a good impression on her new husband. My mother was that way; appearances were very important to her. I like to make a good impression too, but appearances were never that important to me.

Well, her husband was a very nice man, good looking and good hearted. He soon had us tucked away in his car, and we were on our way to Mannheim, about one and a half hours from Luxemburg. When we finally got to her house, I fed my children, cleaned them up a little, and lay down on the bed in the room that was prepared for us, and fell asleep with both of them.

We didn't wake up until morning.

Once we got into a routine, things went much better at my mother's house. She was still quite rigid, but after a while she relaxed a little. They were good children, and we had been through a lot to get there, but that was just the beginning.

We had planned to stay for two weeks. We decided that we would stay with my mother for four days, and then take the train to Dusseldorf where my father lived. We would stay with him for three days, take the train back to my mother, stay for two days, and return to Luxemburg, catch the plane, and go home. I already could not wait to get home.

The trip to my father's home was easy. Stephan got a little restless, but that was to be expected. When we got to Dusseldorf, my father was standing on the platform waving his arms like crazy. He looked so good, and I was so glad to see him. From my brother, I had found out that he didn't smoke or drink any more since his heart attack. He just embraced me and the children. So did his new wife, and it was a really warm reunion especially after all we had been through.

We got to his condominium. Finally the children could get on the floor and play with their toys and talk all they wanted to.

We took some nice walks with my father, and the children went to sleep tired that night, but it was a good tired. The next morning when I got up and tiptoed out of our bedroom, my father was pacing around his apartment with a plate of orange slices and banana slices in his hand. He could hardly wait until my children woke up. When they finally woke up, he could not contain himself and had to feed them some of the fruit which they loved.

We had a wonderful time with my father. We went to the park, and he took them to the toy store and let each one pick out a toy for themselves. We had fun. Those days alone were worth the trip.

When it was time for us to go back to Mannheim, I was very sad. I knew that I was probably not going to see my father again. I cried very hard when we held each other to say goodbye.

"It will be all right," he whispered in my ear.

Now we were facing the train trip, then the trip to Luxemburg, and then the long flight home. I wished I could have clicked my feet together and said, "There is no place like home." But, we don't live in a magic world like the Wizard of Oz, and we had to face the long trip home.

When we were at my mother's, they had a late snow, and we got all bundled up, and walked and played in the snow right along the big River Rhine.

Then, disaster hit us, and Renee got sick. Before we had left home, the chicken pox were going around, I didn't think that she had been exposed, but it floats around in the air. She started running a fever, and I took her immediately to a pediatrician. We were supposed to leave the next day. I told him all of Renee's history with convulsions and all. He said that chicken pox was a mild children's disease. Her temperature was still low. He loaded her up with antibiotics and fever suppositories, and said she should really be all right.

I thanked him, and the next day at noon, we left for Luxemburg. My mother's husband, Richard was driving. The roads were slick, and it had started to snow again. Before we knew it, we got into fog. It gets very foggy in that area of Germany. We had to drive slowly. I noticed that Renee was getting hotter, and starting to moan a little. I touched her, and she was burning up. This was so scary for me that I can hardly write about it.

I said to Richard, "We have to stop at a hospital. I think Renee is getting ready to have a convulsion." Then I shouted, "She is getting stiff; my child could die."

Mutti shouted back, "We are trying."

Renee got stiff, and I put my finger into her mouth to hold her tongue down. I had given her a fever suppository before we left. She bit down hard on my finger. Richard shouted, "There is a hospital." I shouted back, "Get us there quick."

We pulled in, and I grabbed her, my finger still on her tongue, and ran into the hospital. They helped me immediately even though they had no pediatric ward. They took us into a room, examined her, and started bathing her to get the fever down. By then I was softly crying.

Richard, Mutti, and Stephan were waiting for us in the waiting room. They stabilized my baby, and as I am sitting here writing this forty years later, I am crying. Then they explained to Richard where the nearest hospital with a children's ward was located.

We headed straight to that hospital, and the kind people who had stabilized my baby had already called in. They were ready for us. They checked Renee out, and said that she had to be hospitalized, or she could die. So, Renee was carried into a room, and they put a hospital gown on her.

She cried the whole time. She wanted to be with me. They finally sent me out of the room, and I could only see her through a peephole. She was crying in the room, and I was crying on the outside. The doctor said she would be fine. He was going to watch over her, and they would take excellent care of her. I could come back the next day and see her through the peephole. They did not let the children see their parents. It upset them too much. I did not agree with him having spent so many nights already with Renee in the hospital by her side day and night. But I could not change his mind or their policy.

I left the hospital crying, and Mutti and Richard helped me find a nice little guest house and hotel to spend the night while they finally headed back to Mannheim. It was a very emotional goodbye. We had all been very upset.

The next morning after breakfast Stephan and I walked to the hospital to see how Renee was doing. The report on her was very good, but the doctor told me that she had to stay there until she was totally over the chicken pox. It was too dangerous in her case to discharge her any sooner. So it would take at least another week. I was very upset, but I was glad she was safe.

We went back to our hotel and called Allen. He could hardly believe the bad news. He said he was going to take care that they gave us a new flight time, and he was going to wire me some money for the hotel and food. When I had the figures of the money for the hospital, he would take care of that. I was so thankful that we were not in South Dakota anymore. Everything would have been such a problem. He told me that he was very successful, and his new bosses already liked him a lot. He had a bonus check coming. I shouldn't worry about the money. We were going to be just fine.

That was such a relief; I had to cry again. He told me to call him back in a couple of days and let him know how we all were and let him know when the money arrived. I thanked him so much and told him what a wonderful husband he was. He said, "You are such a good girl. Be brave, it is all under control."

He was sure that Renee was in good hands and would be fine. We both said, "The tonsils have to come out as soon as possible."

Stephan and I had lunch and took a short nap and walked back to the hospital to see Renee. This time we got to look through the peephole, and there she stood in her crib holding on to the side and crying with big tears rolling down her face. "Mommy, I want my mommy." It was heartbreaking. Stephan looked through the hole too, and when we left, we were both crying. We went for a walk through the town; and I let him buy a toy in a toy store. That helped him a little. Later on we had supper, and went to bed early. It had been a hard day.

We got into a routine, walks, walking to the hospital and buying an occasional toy. We also bought little toys for Renee that the nurse gave her. Her favorite was a little baby doll.

It was a long week. By the end of that week the doctor said that the next day we could safely fly. We were elated. We were in Luxemburg already, so we were allowed to pick her up by two in the afternoon and go straight to the airport just in time for the plane.

When we came to the hospital, they said to wait in the hall. After a few minutes, the nurse called from the end of the hall, "Here she comes." And there way down that hall she put my little girl down.

I called, "Renee Baby, come to Mommy." She looked up and started to run like I had never seen her run as fast as she could to my outstretched arms. I caught her when she got to me. She ran into my arms, and I flung her high, and then we held on to each other like we would never let go. And then Stephan had to get into that embrace too. It had been a long hard worrisome week.

We got her things from the nurse, medications, and instructions. She was pronounced well and off we went. I had a taxi waiting, and we swung by the hotel and picked up our luggage.

The rest of the journey was smooth until we got to Iceland. Just before Iceland, the heat in the plane went out so they landed there. To keep us busy until the plane was fixed, we stayed in the little airport which was nothing more than a barracks. But they fixed us breakfast. Then they loaded us into a bus and drove us all over Iceland in the pitch dark. What we saw was glistening snow, ice, and huge hot springs shooting out of the ground into the air and into the sky. The stars in the sky were so bright and so close you thought you could touch them and put them in your pocket. Like the song goes, "Catch a falling star and put it in your pocket, never, never let it go."

We were so worn out that we huddled under our blankets and actually slept until we got to New York. Guess who was there to surprise us in New York?-Allen!

We were stunned, and then we all wanted to get into his arms. He picked up Renee and then Stephan. I joined the embrace.

That was a happy moment. I could just relax and turn things over to him. I couldn't thank him enough. I said, "I'll make it up to you." And we smiled at each other.

After we had been home a couple of weeks, we took Renee to the pediatrician and set a date to have her tonsils removed. Allen was the one to take her to the hospital. I was a coward. After what she and I had already been through, I just couldn't leave her again, but I was there when she woke up. Renee was a healthy child from then on.

We had a happy time in Westfield. Allen did so well; he was a real success. The children loved it. My ballet classes did well, so did the youth choir under my leadership when Dr. Paige wasn't there. My voice lessons continued, and I could tell how much I had learned. I sang Bach and Mozart and anything I set my mind to. My teacher was still very strict, but he was much nicer than before.

When summer came, our friends took us out on a lake and taught me how to water ski. It was great fun. One time they took us on Lake Erie, and when I fell in, I thought I would instantly freeze to death.

Sometimes we all took our children along with life jackets for a nice little cruise. It was a good year.

When the year came to an end, Dr. Paige asked me to sing for his four year graduation class. I was stunned. I said, "But they had you so much longer than I did. I would be scared to death."

"I want them to hear how it is really supposed to be done."

I stood in front of him with my mouth hanging open. I said, "But, you were always so strict with me."

He said, "I knew we didn't have much time together, and I think you have a real talent, so I had to rush you. Now, I want you to sing for their graduation."

I was so happy and scared I could hardly believe it. I had a real collerator soprano, and he chose the song, "My Heart Ever Faithful," by Bach.

The big day came, and I drove myself to the college. They had the graduation in a big hall. When it was my turn to go on the stage, I was shaking in my shoes. I got up there, smiled, the pianist started to play, and I started to sing. It was just like my voice was taking flight. It was the perfect song for me. I lost all my fears, and at that moment all my dreams had come true.

My voice had just lifted and floated through that big hall.

When I stopped, and the last note drifted away, I took my little bow and received a standing ovation! I had made it. I was thirty years old. My teacher hugged me afterwards and told me, "I am so proud of you." I floated home like on "angel wings."

I could not wait to tell Allen about it. He was so proud. Of course, I tried to tell my children too. They said, "Mommy, you are happy."

It truly had been a great year with lots of excitement, but it all turned out so good for us.

Allen received notice that he was getting a promotion with a larger territory. So, we had to move closer to the Albany area. We got to pick the place. It was not so terribly far, so we picked a couple of days to get away, and took the children with us. We found a little town at the foot of the Adirondack Mountains very centrally located for Allen's new area. It was a cute old town with a couple of new residential areas. We found a house we really loved. It took some work to handle the financing, but Allen got the first mortgage, and I took out the second mortgage. It was so perfect because it was a nice three bedroom house with a full bath, large living room, large kitchen with dining area, and here comes the best part, a large room with separate entrances, where the former owner had had an accounting office. That was my very first real dance studio. I was hoping to take care of my part of the mortgage with my dance studio. All I had to do was put a huge mirror on the wall, install ballet bars, and I was in business. The house had a full basement big enough for the children to ride bicycles and tricycles down there. We couldn't believe our luck.

Not far from our house was the elementary school with a big football field and all kinds of places to play ball and run. We also had a nice big yard. It was a dream comes true. I met a really nice lady who lived right down the street, and I admired her so much. She had adopted four children. She befriended me and asked me over a lot, and my children got to play with hers and swim in her pool. I showed her my ballet studio, and she told everyone about the classes I planned to start in September. Her name was Dorothy, and her husband owned a really nice furniture store downtown.

Johnstown had an old fashioned downtown, and I loved it. There was also a wonderful delicatessen run by one family. They had the best stuff, and they prepared many wonderful things to eat and take home when you were in a hurry for supper. I don't even know if stores like that exist any more. As the summer came close to the end, people were starting to inquire about the ballet classes, and I already had three classes signed up before I ever started. My children got enrolled in elementary school which was three blocks from our house. Renee started kindergarten there. Things were moving so fast now, and we were so hopeful for the future. We had had a hard road.

My ballet classes got a really good start. The children loved school, and Allen was already having a lot of success in his bigger territory.

Fall was beautiful there, and we took some trips around into the mountains to see the beautiful fall colors. The Adirondacks have lots of small and big mountain lakes. We said the next summer we had to go into the mountains and swim in some of those lakes. They had even made sandy beaches for those lakes. It was a beautiful area.

Stephan started having difficulties in school. He had a real mean teacher who screamed at the children when they didn't know how to do something. Stephan was so terrified of school that he started to wet the bed again at night. I went to talk to the teacher and asked her to please be patient with Stephan. I told her that he was terrified of school and had started to wet the bed again. He didn't want to go to school. She was a very old hard woman and should not have been teaching little children any more. I also told her that I had taught Stephan German when he was little, and I thought that maybe had caused him some confusion. I found out that every year, several children got moved to other classrooms because they were terrified of her.

Winter came early in that area. One morning we woke up, and a thick blanket of snow was covering the ground, and it was still snowing. There is just nothing cozier than being in a nice warm house with your nose pressed to the window looking at the snow.

That day school was cancelled and the children and I got our sled out and pulled it to the school and sledded down the hills around the school with dozens of other children screaming as they were flying down those hills. We had a great time. That afternoon I met a young mother, my age, with blonde hair and the bluest eyes I've ever seen peeking out from under her cap smiling at me. She had a little girl to match her, and she was Renee's age. She was to become my best friend for years to come, and Renee and little Lynn also became best friends. I didn't know then, how she would influence my life. Her name was Kay, and her husband's name was Bob. He was the coach and principal at that school.

Allen and Bob befriended each other, and the next summer when Bob started a semi-pro football team, Allen played for him. I went to the games, and not knowing a thing about football,

I could never find my husband on the field. He was always on the bottom of the pileup. I would breathe a sign of relief when he appeared again unhurt.

We made a lot of really nice friends. The preacher of the Presbyterian Church lived right behind us with a lovely wife and a boy and a girl. It was a perfect neighborhood like you rarely find. We were happy there. Allen and I got along really well, and there were a lot of tender moments when we were alone at night.

I wrote my first ballet for my students, "Cinderella." There was going to be a mother dressed as a story teller. And then some simple lines for the main characters to speak. The mean and vain sisters had some lovely shrieking lines. The mean stepmother said plenty of cutting things too. Little Cinderella had some sad lines and tears. There was a fairy godmother, who spoke some kind words, and a handsome prince. Everybody got to dance, and there were group dances, solos, and duets. They were all very excited, and we worked on that the whole long first winter in Johnstown.

One day Kay asked me if we wanted to go with them to Albany to hear a concert by Peter, Paul, and Mary. I was not very familiar with their music. They were brand new. Of course, we wanted to go. We all got tickets, and the big night came nearer.

There was a really nice family living just down the street from us who had a sixteen year old daughter, Barbara, and a fourteen year old son, Bruce. They were wonderful babysitters. We hired Barbara for that evening so we could safely go out of town. We rode with Kay and Bob in their car. The concert was in some kind of technical college connected with the university. When we entered the auditorium I was amazed at the size of it.

I was not very familiar with folk music. It was new at that time, and it was just starting to get very popular. I was very excited.

Pretty soon they dimmed the lights three times, and it got very quiet. The spotlights came on and in walked two tall slender men and a beautiful young woman with light blond, shoulder length hair. They stood with her in the middle center stage when they were greeted with thundering applause. The two men, Peter and Paul were holding guitars, and the lady, Mary held a tambourine.

I cannot remember what their first song was, but it could have been something like, "I walk in the rain by your side, I cling to the warmth of your tiny hand. I'll do anything to help you understand. I love you more than anybody can."

They sang about love, they sang about the freight trains that men jumped on to get away from something quickly. They sang about travel; they sang about life. They sang about war and everything and anything you can think of. The melodies were simple, beautiful, and catching. I was in heaven, and I knew right then and there that this was the music I wanted to sing. I was so smitten; it was like having entered a new world of music, places, and stories.

What about the song, "Just a little rain, falling all around, the grass lifts its head to the heavenly sound, just a little rain, just a little rain, what have they done to the rain?" How much they already knew then. Folk music had gripped me with its simplicity, beautiful melodies, and truth of lyrics. That was going to be my new world.

We stayed through the long standing ovation. On our way home, I couldn't get over how these three singers, Peter, Paul, and Mary had turned my life around. Our new fiends were very excited about my reaction and Allen was totally excited too.

That was a Saturday night, and on Monday Allen left the house to run an errand. He came back about two hours later carrying a big guitar case. I just looked at him confused. The children were in school. He was grinning from ear to ear, and he asked me to follow him into the living room. I did with great curiosity. He put the guitar case on the couch and said, "Open it up."

I stepped to the couch, looked at him, and then opened the guitar case. There was the most beautiful guitar in that case, built out of shiny red rosewood with the picture of a humming bird on it. I looked at Allen not daring to believe what I saw.

He said, "It's a Gibson guitar called the 'Humming Bird,' and it is for you." I was so stunned I had to sit down. Then I started to cry and threw my arms around Allen's neck.

"For me, can we afford that?"

He said, "We can. Take it out and enjoy it."

"Thank you. Thank you." I was beside myself, I held the guitar like something very precious, and it was. Then I had to run to the phone to call Kay, she played the guitar, and tell her what had happened.

She was thrilled. She said, "I will teach you what I know."

My life really changed. Every free minute I had I practiced my guitar. Allen had also bought me a Beginner's Folksinger's Book.

Kay showed me some chords that we drew on a piece of paper. She dictated some lyrics for me, and I was on the way. The first two songs I played were, "Freight Train Going So Fast" and "If You Miss the Train I'm On, You Will Know That I Am Gone."

I wanted to sound like Peter, Paul, and Mary. So, I worked very hard to control my vibrato, and sound as clear and pure as possible. It was not so hard.

It was pretty tough playing the guitar. My fingers got really sore. But, I practiced daily, and I developed tough skin on the tips of my fingers. Then, it didn't hurt so much any more. I taught ballet classes three afternoons a week. My classes were 111, but I was not ready yet to start more classes. The money was enough for my second mortgage.

I spent a lot of time with my children on my free afternoons, and practiced a lot of guitar. My children were allowed to come into the studio when I taught, but they were not allowed to talk during that time. Renee wanted to join the classes pretty soon, and became my youngest ballerina. Stephan would play in the adjoining TV room. It all worked out great. I met another family whom I loved. Rosy, a widow, lived down the street from us with her three little girls and her mother, and old Italian lady. She fixed some really good Italian food. Rosy worked at the bank, and her mother helped her out a lot. She drove a little Subaru, and often took her girls to the mountains to go skiing.

About once a week, Kay invited me to her house when she had some other guitar playing friends over. I got the chance to hear some more new folk songs, and afterwards I would write down the words and draw the chords over the syllables. Of course, being so musical, I learned really quickly, and I had a wonderful time. Kay sang really good harmony, and pretty soon she and I sang and played a lot together.

Of course, we were surrounded by children, and it was not long before they wanted to sing with us. Pretty soon, we had a little group who all sang folk music with us, and would you believe it, we started to perform with them in the entire area. We sounded so good, and the children were so cute, that we became very popular.

I had to do a lot of work on my voice, but Dr. Paige had taught me so well that I could control my voice beautifully. What

I had to work on was to control the vibrato I had and keep my voice clear and straight. My voice sounded wonderful with folk music, very pure.

In the spring, it was time for our first ballet performance. We ordered tutus, leotards, ballet slippers, and some mothers made the costumes for the main characters. We practiced like crazy.

When the performance date came closer, everybody was very nervous. The school let us have the auditorium for our first show. The parents showed up, brothers and sister, uncles and aunts, and grandmas and grandpas.

The children looked so cute and threw themselves into their dancing and their performance with so much excitement that they got a standing ovation. And I got a bouquet of flowers. It was a wonderful success, and all the children hugged me at one time in front of the curtain. We were one big ball of love and happiness.

Allen and I were very happy with each other. That whole summer, we would drive to the mountains on weekends and swim in those beautiful lakes. We would pack a picnic and make a day of it with the children. It was a happy time.

We met another cool couple, Dick and Dee. He owned the Ford dealership. Dee was a lot of fun, and so was he. When she found out that I was learning the guitar, she wanted to learn too.

So her husband helped her to buy a guitar, and pretty soon we were practicing together. Dee was the school nurse, and she worked only part-time. She and I looked a lot alike, because we wore the same hairdo, kind of very short, "roaring twenties."

It wasn't long, and we started singing some Beatle songs too. "When I Find Myself in Times Of Troubles, Let It Be," or Michelle, My Belle," Yesterday, All My Troubles Seemed So Far

Away." We had a big time. They had two boys, eight and ten, and a three year old girl.

Allen enjoyed all that to-do and social life we had. The neat part was that we all had children about the same age. We included them in a lot of things. We also started to go camping together.

We did that in the Adirondack Mountains near a creek in a camping area. Most of our friends had "pop- up campers." We bought a Sears tent with cots and sleeping bags. It worked. When we went camping with our friends, after we fed the children supper, we would roast Italian sausages with onions and green peppers, and flush it down with beer. Guess what we did afterwards?

We would get the guitars out and sing until we were told it was time to let everybody sleep. I think that happened usually after 10:00. Then we would sit by the fire and talk way on into the night.

One night, Allen and I felt very romantic, and I climbed into his sleeping bag with him, and we made love. Afterwards, we just fell asleep in each other's arms. The children woke us up in the morning. "Mama, what are you doing in daddy's sleeping bag?"

"Mama was real cold last night." Allen said. We both grinned at each other.

Johnstown was probably one of the happiest times in our marriage. Life was as close to perfect as it can be. But, life goes on, and always changes as we change with it.

We decided to take a real summer vacation. Allen wanted to go to the coast. We picked Atlantic City, which was just a little resort town in those days. We found a camping place right by the ocean. It was very exciting when we pitched our tent. We had a little folding table now and folding chairs.

We had a little overhang, and that's where our cooking stove stood. We had windows and a screen door which could be zipped shut. It was all very primitive, but we had our cots and nice sleeping bags. It worked for us.

The first day it was very windy and a little bit rainy, but then the weather cleared up, and we really enjoyed the next few days on the beach. We dug in the sand, and we looked for seashells. We went swimming when the water was not rough. We got a great suntan and had a wonderful time.

We took long walks along the beach. Allen and the children did some fishing with not much luck. We walked along the boardwalk in the evenings and ate all kinds of wonderful junk food.

We watched people and listened to music. The time just flew, and before we knew it, it was time to go home again.

What a great time we had on our first real vacation.

After we got back to Johnstown, Allen had to go back to work. We really missed him. It was nice to have him around so much.

The children and I were back to our evenings alone. We would eat pretty early suppers, do their homework, and then we would settle in the living room, and either they would sit on the carpet and play, or we would watch TV together. I would have one in each arm, and we felt very cozy and happy.

Once a week, usually Wednesdays, Stephan and Renee would take an early bath, put pajamas and slippers on, and depending on the weather, bathrobes. We had a station wagon. I would make a really nice bed in the back, and put all the seats down so they could lie down if they wanted to. Then, we would stop at the Dairy Queen, and get wonderful junk food; hot dogs or hamburgers, French fries, and milk shakes. Then we would head for the drive-in and watch an appropriate movie. That was a nice break for us in the middle of the week.

Allen traveled a lot. His direct boss became a really good friend of his. He was the sales manager, and he traveled quite a bit with his sales people. The only thing I didn't like about him was that he drank quite a bit. When they were together, Allen started to drink more too.

Of course, I remembered my father too, and what alcohol can do to a relationship. My father and I had lost so many years because of alcohol. I just hoped that it would never become a problem. Allen and I talked about that, and he didn't think it would.

It was almost time for school and ballet lessons to start again. It was always hard to get back into the routine of all our obligations after the nice, long summer.

We had a great social life because we had met so many wonderful people. Allen and I decided that sometime in the winter, we had to have a party, and invite our friends.

We also were very active in our church. Our minister asked me if I wanted to teach music in the Sunday school for the children. I was happy to do that. So, he sent me from classs to class on Sunday mornings, and I practiced Christmas songs with them. We had close to 100 children in that church of different age groups. The older ones were more of a problem than the little ones.

There was only one really unruly boy, probably thirteen years old. He was a good looking boy, but nobody could handle him. One day, he told me that he played the drums at home, and had had some lessons. I told him to bring his drums to the church for Sunday school. I asked my minister if I could have all the classes together once. He agreed, but he was going to sit in with the

Sunday school teachers to see what I was doing.

We assembled all of them in the fellowship hall, and I was to have them all for a half hour.

The drums were set up right in the middle of a big half circle. We had 10 guitars and our pianist.

I cannot remember our drummer boy's name. We became such good friends. I will say his name was "Bobby." Bobby turned into an absolute angel since he was allowed to bring his drum.

He waited patiently until his turn came. Everybody was totally amazed. We started with "Go Tell It on the Mountain." The different classes sat together. I started with my strongest singers.

"Go tell it on the Mountain, over the hills and everywhere. Go tell it on the mountain that Jesus Christ is born." Of course that group was standing up, then the second group jumped up as group number one did, and group two shouted, "Hallelujah," and at the same time the drums came in.

It was very effective as Bobby did a great drum roll and kept on playing as they went on, "Go tell it on the mountain." Each time when a new group jumped up to join the others, the choir got louder. Anyway, we had lots of special effects like that and the children were so into it that, the music really grabbed you. Our minister and the teachers were so impressed that they gave us a big hand.

As we got closer to Christmas we rehearsed every Sunday. The congregation made capes for the shepherds. We had angel costumes. It turned out to be a big project. Everybody sang, even the kings. Mary and Joseph were a young couple in our church, and they had a little baby who was just a few weeks old.

We wove the songs into the Christmas story, which our minister told. Everything was shaping up great. We did the pageant two times before Christmas; Saturday night and Sunday morning. It was so beautiful, and the children sang their hearts out. I directed them, and played the guitar with my other guitar players, and don't forget the drums. The children sang as if their lives depended on it.

It was a beautiful experience, and the church was full both times. We ended with everyone singing, "Silent Night."

I will never forget that Christmas. Then, we went home to our Christmas. We were one happy, little family.

Naturally, we had a lot of snow that winter. The state of New York always had a lot of snow.

That was the year of the big blizzard. I was teaching ballet in my studio, and all of a sudden the lights went out. It was snowing outside, but it had only started less than an hour ago. The music stopped, and it was dark. I told the children to bundle up and hurry home. Luckily, that whole class lived in close walking distance from our house. They were on their way in no time at all. I called all the parents, and told them the children were on their way.

If I remember it right, this blizzard lasted three days. Many people in New York City, who had just gotten off work, it was right around 5:00, got trapped in elevators for hours. It must have been very scary.

We got out some canned beans and hot dogs, lit a fire in the fireplace, and had a lovely supper on the floor in front of the fireplace. We had a wood-burning fireplace, and it put out a lot of heat. We got our sleeping bags, and slept right in front of the fireplace. Before we went to sleep, we roasted marshmallows over the fire. The children thought it was marvelous.

When we woke up the next morning, our front door was

snowed in all the way to the little top window. The garage door was snowed in half way up to the top. Allen had to go into the garage and open the door all the way up so he could dig us all out. It took him several hours with lots of breaks to shovel one car out. It was important that he didn't overexert himself. Snow shoveling can be a dangerous thing

The next day he finished the garage and started on the front door. It was not nearly as much work as the garage, but it was pretty hard work too.

The third day we bundled the children up, and he took them outside to build a snowman. The snow was just perfect for a snowman. It really stuck perfectly. The snowman turned out huge.

We still have a picture with all of us in front of the seven-foot snowman.

It was a lot of fun. After three days, we had our electricity back, and slowly the people in New York City got their electricity restored. A year after this snowstorm, they reported a lot of births. I guess when you have no television, you have to find other entertainment.

Stephan still had trouble in school with that mean teacher, and we finally got him transferred to another school with a very sweet teacher who was extremely creative, and he did very well.

Stephan has been creative all his life, and that change was so good for him. Looking back now, we think that he might have had attention deficit syndrome. In those days, nobody knew what that was. He could not sit still nor could he pay attention very long. Nowadays, children get medication for that condition. Renee was a really healthy child now with no problems, and we were very grateful for that.

Allen was asked to come to Ithaca for a meeting, and I was supposed to come along. We had to get a babysitter, and travel to Ithaca. Kay was going to look in on the children and the sitter.

She was also going to be on emergency call.

I got to meet Mr. Babcock, the owner of the firm, and Allen's bosses. In the evening, we were invited to his sales manager's house for dinner. Bob and his wife fixed wonderful steaks, and we really enjoyed dinner. But, the two men and Bob's wife drank quite a bit, and before the evening was over, she had to go in the bushes and vomit. I encouraged Allen to leave with me shortly after. We thanked them very much, and left for our motel.

Allen had another meeting to which I was invited. They told me that he had done so well that they were thinking of the possibility of sending us back to Germany as international marketing director. They told me that Allen had been unbelievably successful, and they called him their "boy wonder." Allen flushed with pleasure when they said that. They asked me about his command of the German language. I said that he could make himself understood, but we could also work on that together. They encouraged us to do so, but all this was some time in the future.

We were pretty shocked and excited as we returned to Johnstown. But, it was just a thought that they were considering, nothing for sure.

We decided to have a party for all our friends in the dead of winter.

Kay and Dee and I were practicing Beatle songs for our party. We also bought Beatle wigs, big old curly things. Just planning this was crazy fun. The ladies were going to bring appetizers and some wine or beer. This house was perfect for a big party with the ballet studio, the adjoining TV room, and adjoining that the big living room, which opened into the kitchen. I think we had about thirty people there. I had a piano in the ballet studio and a record player. Our minister, Charles, used to play piano in night clubs to help pay for his college, and he knew about every tune there was. That evening the house filled up with people, laughter, and a lot of noise as the record player played popular tunes. When we got really rolling, Charles played the piano, everyone was singing and dancing. Later on Kay, Dee, and I went into a bedroom and put on our wigs. As we appeared in the midst of everyone, yelling a Beatle song, the party got even livelier. We were shaking our fake hair, and everyone was in a great mood. I think most of the ladies had a little crush on Charles, the minister.

His wife sat by his side on the piano bench protecting him from all of us females. I forgot to mention that we had sexy cocktail dresses on with our Beatle wigs. It was quite funny. We sang and danced until about two o'clock, and then slowly everybody left. It was fun.

The poor babysitter had fallen asleep with the children in Stephan's room. They were exhausted. Thank heavens the next day was Sunday. We could sleep in and get the house straightened out.

It was not long after that someone from the community theater asked me to come and audition for the musical, "Oh Kay."

Dee and I were going together, and Allen came along for the fun of it. To make a long story short, I was asked to sing the song, "There's a somebody I'm longing to see. I hope that he turns out to be someone to watch over me."

To make a long story short, I was asked to play the part of Kay. Allen got the second lead as the bachelor, and Dee had a twin sister in the play. It was a very funny comedy with beautiful music.

When I think back, I don't know how we did everything we did and were really good parents who spent a lot of time with their children. I think the explanation is that we were all in our late twenties--lots of energy.

The show was a huge success not only because it was a great show, but also because the cast had so much fun. In one sketch the bachelor had a fiancée, a very proper young lady, whose father was a judge. They had been invited to dinner for the judge to meet the bachelor (Allen).

Evidently the bachelor had changed his mind about the whole thing, and in addition Kay had quite a crush on the bachelor.

Stephan did so much better in school now, but if he was going to school nowadays, he would have been diagnosed with ADD. In those days, they did not know about this yet. Nowadays, they medicate children. How much easier his school years would have been for him. He often got punished for not sitting still and not paying attention. The poor child could not help it.

Spring had really come now, and the snow at Easter had been the last one for that year. Soon, the tiny green leaves came out, and the grass started to get green. The sun shown and the sky was blue. The awakening of nature was all around us. That was when we got the orders from Babcock that they wanted us in Germany by late fall or early winter. Allen was supposed to go to Germany with one of the sales managers and explore the opportunities in the Frankfurt area for offices. Frankfurt was an international city and almost every foreign company had their offices in Frankfurt or vicinity.

Allen felt that they should have their office on the outskirts of Frankfurt because the city itself was very expensive, and since they were just a small company, he thought offices would be cheaper. So they looked around in the Taunus Mountains which were only half an hour outside Frankfurt and a beautiful area. Many picturesque little villages were in the mountains and that was where most American and foreign business people had settled their families. There was also a wonderful "Frankfurt International School" where the main language was English, and the children learned German and French in addition. It was an area where foreign business people and their families could find everything they needed.

When Allen came back from that trip, he was so excited he could not stand it. His company praised him again, and said he should study German with me. We started doing that, and I must say Allen was not studious but very smart. And, even though his grammar was bad he could make himself understood.

We had brought a little Chihuahua mix doggie with us from South Dakota, and he was a cute, loving little dog. His name was "Jackie." We were all attached to him. In addition, we had purchased a black king-sized poodle in Johnstown, "Mark," and a beautiful yellow tiger cat had joined our family one cold winter day. We loved all three of them, and they were clean, well behaved, and much loved members of the family. Our children walked their dogs all the time.

And "Kitty" liked his house best, especially the big basement. Now we had to think also what we were going to do with our beloved pets.

We also had to tell our friends that we would be moving right around the holidays. Kay painted a huge sign that she erected in our front yard. It said, "Down with Babcock, fun wreckers." Babcock was the name of Allen's company.

Even though I was happy about being closer to my family in

Germany, I had a huge lump in my throat when I thought about leaving Johnstown, and I wondered if we would ever be received again with so much friendship wherever we went, and if our little family would ever be so happy again. After having moved so many times to such different places, I would say, if you are happy where you live, and if you feel you belong there, be happy and stay.

Our friends gave us a big party, and many tears were shed, and every one of us felt like we left a piece of our heart there, and never got it back.

We all had learned a lot in Johnstown. Allen had learned better German. Stephan had learned to play the ukulele, and I had started to sing and play with the guitar, and Renee had become the cutest little dancer. And, we had made friendships that would stay with us for a long, long time.

My mother had found us a bed and breakfast near the school, and the bus would bring the children right to the door. The owners of the bed and breakfast told her that we could bring the little dog, but because of their guests, they could not let us bring the big dog. Allen was terribly sad. He loved Mark. Whenever it thundered, Mark would jump on Allen's lap, and would not move until the bad weather had passed. We found a wonderful young family with one small child who wanted Mark very badly. We were all terribly sad when we had to drop him off. The family next door to our house wanted Kitty. Their children had often played with him, and given him treats. Our pets are so dependent on us, and give us so much love. I guess that is why I am sitting here so many years later, crying over our pets. The list of goodbyes gets longer and longer.

Jackie was going to fly on the airplane with us, and arrive at the same time. We found out that our furniture would be on the way in three months. We now started the process of sorting out things we didn't want to take. It is always a horrendous job.

Time just flies, and before we knew it, October was here, and we were doing a countdown.

Allen had had to go back to Europe and came back to Johnstown to pick us up. We had one more short evening with our friends, and then it was time to go.

Many hugs and wishes were exchanged, and hopes to see each other again.

Jackie had to go into his traveling case and fly separately from us, but he was on the same airline. He looked at us mournfully.

Up, up and away.

CHAPTER EIGHT

BACK IN GERMANY

THE JOYS AND TEARS OF THOSE YEARS

When we boarded the plane, I thought of my trip home, when my children were so small- Renee under a year, and Stephan not quite four years old.

I just knew this would be a whole lot easier and their daddy was with us. We had four seats next to each other. The children were equipped with books, writing material, colors, and anything else we could think of.

We were going to fly into Frankfurt, Germany. It was an overnight flight; we would get there about seven in the morning. There would be dinner and then a movie. We should all be tired enough by then to sleep a little. The time difference was six hours between the United States and Germany.

The stewardess woke us up with breakfast just as the sun was rising. We were over England and could see the channel as we crossed it. I was excited to see England from the air for the first time since I had lived there. I knew it would be about an hour and fifteen minutes before we got to Frankfurt. The plane circled over the Taunus Mountains and prepared to land. I was very emotional and pointed out places to the children that I recognized.

We landed and went through customs and got our luggage. We soon had a taxi which would take us to Oberursel in the mountains to get to our bed and breakfast. About 45 rninutes later we were there. They had breakfast waiting for us and to be polite, we ate for the second time. We had our little dog Jackie with us and took him for a little walk on his leash. Then he got a few bites from our breakfast, and we all went to bed trying to catch up on our sleep. It was ten o'clock in the morning there which would be four o'clock in the United States. We needed a good long snooze.

When we woke up, it was early afternoon. Allen had gotten up very quietly before us and arranged for two rental cars. We were going to see where the school was, and Allen also wanted to show us where his office was. The next day he had already set up some interviews for secretarial work.

I was going to take the children to school the next day and get them enrolled. We took Jackie for a nice walk. We found a wonderful restaurant for a great German supper, and of course, on the first day there, we had superb cream cake for dessert.

We made arrangements for an early breakfast and went to bed. In the morning, when we had our wakeup call, we hurried and left the house by 7:45 a.m. There was much traffic, but the children and I made it fine. Allen left about ten minutes before we did. At the school, we met the principal, a very nice very English lady. She took us around the school. We met several teachers who were English. We got to look into Renee's class and into Stephan's class. Most of the teachers were English and very friendly. They had a nice big gym and pretty grounds. Renee would be in kindergarten and Stephan in second or third grade depending on his previous schooling. This school was ahead of most schools. The children were pretty excited. Another good thing was that the classrooms were small, so the children got a lot of attention and help.

It also was very expensive. Allen worked for a good company now, and they were going to help with everything. It was new for Babcock to have representation in Europe, which was a very big step for all of us.

Allen was still their "boy wonder." We had to see how things worked out for him. He had to speak German now most of the day, and it was much harder work for him. He did ask me often to come along when he thought it would be very helpful for him if I could help translate if necessary.

I was pretty busy myself, driving the children to school and back.

Also, we had started to search for a small house with a back yard for the children and our little dog. Housing was still a tremendous problem in Germany, since there was not enough, and it was still very expensive. One morning, while we were having breakfast, I saw an ad in the paper for a three bedroom house for rent, with two baths, kitchen, and great room, located in Koenigstein in Taunus. I had heard about Koenigstein. It was supposed to be the prettiest little town in the Taunus, and the most desirable.

I called the number in the newspaper immediately. A young woman answered. When I told her why I was calling, she got very friendly, and told me that she could show me the house the next morning. I told her that I had to take my children to school first, but I could meet her by 10:00. She sounded as excited as I was.

The next morning, I took the children to school, and then

followed my directions to Koenigstein. Koenigstein was higher up in the mountains, and when I was about halfway, it started to snow. Several more curves and up a mountain, and there it was, almost white with snow. It almost looked like another world. And, the snow was still softly falling. I followed the signs to the center of town, and soon found the market place. The first thing I saw was a huge beautiful Christmas tree decorated by glistening snow. The marketplace was surrounded by old buildings with red tile roofs, stucco walls, cobblestone streets, little shops, stores, cafes, and a bank. Everything was very colorful and most charming.

In my dreams, I could not have thought of a prettier place. It was like a fairy tale. My directions said turn left, go down the hill, turn left again, second house on the right. It was a white stucco house with a red tile roof and black wooden shutters on the windows. I parked my car and walked up the driveway where a red wooden front door greeted me. I rang the bell, and I could hear it go 'ding dong' inside the house. After a while, the door opened, and a nice looking young woman answered the door. We introduced ourselves, and she asked me to come in.

The house was so different from American houses; not much open space, every room had a door. But they were glass doors, so that made it less confined looking. The house had a friendly feeling. It also had a nice size yard; it was big enough to play in, with a nice lawn, a rose garden, cherry trees, and a weeping willow. There were two very nice houses next to it. It was a miracle.

I was very excited. They needed six to eight weeks because they were building a house on the hill above, and it would not be ready before then. I said we would take it whenever they could move. It looked like it all would work out. I was so happy and excited.

As we turned to go inside again, I looked up and saw the ruins of an old proud castle on top of the mountain. The tower still reached for the sky. This was the stuff fairy tales were made of.

I couldn't wait to tell Allen and the children. The best part was that the rent was affordable.

On the way down the mountain to Oberursel, I took my time and just enjoyed the beautiful scenery and the snow white cover. I had no trouble though. It was just a very light layer of snow, but it was so pretty.

I will never forget what Koenigstein looked like when I first saw this beautiful town; the marketplace with the huge Christmas tree right in the center all decorated with glistening snow.

On Saturday, Allen and I and the children drove up to Koenigstein. I was so excited to show them what I had found. They just loved the trip with all the beautiful little towns, the mountains, and the hills. On the winding road, we saw three castles on the way up that I didn't see on the way up when it was snowing. The school was in Obersurel, and the trip to Koenigstein, depending on traffic was about twenty minutes. The Frankfurt International School also had school buses, but we didn't want the children to worry about when to get on and off until they were really used to it. Also, they were in a foreign country where people spoke a different language. I drove my children every day.

My mother lived in Wiesbaden, which is a beautiful resort city on the other side of the Taunus near Frankfurt. I visited her once a week, and she had us over for dinner once or twice.

That was more like an hour trip. I was very happy to see her and Grandpa Dick. The children were not so thrilled because she was not used to children, and she was very strict.

After five weeks of "bed and breakfast," we got the long

awaited call. Our house was ready.

"We will be out by the weekend, and you can move in on Monday."

We bought a beautiful dining room suit, and a beautiful bedroom suit. The children's bedrooms and the living room suit were nice enough. Now, we were waiting on the rest of the furniture. In an afterthought, we also bought a bunk bed, which came in very handy for sleepovers.

We had only one week to wait, but we could hardly stand it.

Toward the end of the week, we bought some kitchen dishes and a minimum of pots and pans. The furniture store held our dining room, master bedroom, and bunk beds. The dishes and blankets we were going to transport ourselves. It would probably be another five weeks before our things arrived from the United States. That Sunday, before we moved in, we took care of all financial matters, and got our keys. All our neighbors waved at us when we started moving some of our things in, and the neighbors to our right came over and introduced themselves, and brought us a beautiful and delicious homemade cake. It was great.

Jackie and our children ran around the yard and finally had a place to run. The neighbor children came over. They all spoke English because they learned it in high school. Michael was 16, Anne 15, Thomas 1 3, and Stephan was 10. They were all really good looking young people with great manners, friendly and smart. Our children were delighted. They had a great gym in their back yard, and Stephan and Renee both were soon hanging upside down on their gym set.

When I brought the children home after school, and Allen came home from work, I had beds ready for all of us, and everybody was very happy.

I had fresh bread from the baker around the comer, butter, cheese, some wonderful ham, and fruits for dessert. We were just as happy as could be.

The children and Jackie ran around the back yard, and soon the neighbor children came out and played with them on their gym. Soon two of the children from the next neighbor's house came over and introduced themselves-- Bettina, a cute girl two years older than Renee, and her brother Christian who was two years older than Stephan. Our yard was in the middle of the three houses so there was always a lot going on. I was so happy for them.

Allen liked the house too and sat at the dining table and went over some papers. He had a secretary now as well as a really good salesman. He was getting his staff together and did it slowly and carefully. This gentleman was Dutch, and I cannot remember his name. He had to move his family to Germany, but first he was on a three-month trial period.

We got along pretty well, and after two more weeks, we got a call that our furniture and my car would be arriving within five days. Now we really got excited. After my car came, Allen would give up my rental car, and he would keep his for a business car. The time went fast. The day came when I kept the children home, and we waited for the movers.

When the moving van came with a contraption behind it on which my Ford Falcon rode, I realized how big this really ordinary car was compared to German cars. When they took my car off the trailer and parked it on the street in front of our house, it looked as big as a battleship, and when the neighbor children came back from school, they all stood around it and said, "Boy, this is a huge car. Did you buy that in America?"

"Yes," I said, "but it didn't seem so big there. I guess the cars are bigger there than here, and the roads are wider."

It went like wildfire through the neighborhood how large the American's car was, and all the kids from the neighborhood came to inspect it. My children got a kick out of that and so did I.

I was really busy now. By the time Allen came home most everything was off the truck, they took the boxes into the house and opened them up. After that I told them they could stop now. We gave them a good tip, locked the house up, and went to a nice German pub in the town and celebrated by having a Wiener schnitzel again. The children drank grape juice. I drank some wonderful red wine, and Allen had some great dark beer. After dinner, I let them play in the yard with the neighbors, and Allen and I made the beds up and took some dishes out of the boxes. I told Allen that I thought I would get the children excused the next day and try to get most of this mess taken care of. He totally agreed with me. We were so tired. The children wanted to sleep in the bunk beds: Stephan on top, and Renee on the bottom. And I was so grateful when I could just cuddle in Allen's arms and pass out.

The next day it was time to go back to school again. I drove the children. They were going to eat lunch there, and I would pick them up again at the end of school. I went home and worked all day in the house trying to get things straightened out. I did the bedrooms and the kitchen first.

Then I tried to pick up the living room and get the boxes out of the way so we could function. I kept the dining room table picked up for homework and eating. It took me a week though to have the house halfway decent looking. My guitar was in the master bedroom so nothing could happen to it.

Allen brought papers home every night to get ready for the next day. He had an awf3 lot of planning to do and office equipment to buy. It was a very busy and exciting time for him. His sales manager came again from the states to help him and advise him on what to buy, etc.

Pretty soon, Allen and his sales manager, Gunther, started contacting prospective customers and told them about the chicken breeding stock his company had which was superior to almost any other chicken. They were planning to distribute those in as many countries as possible.

Talking to prospective customers was the time when he needed me the most for translating. But Allen was very smart and learned really quickly. Also his Dutch salesman, Helmut was his name, spoke good German and English. Most Europeans speak two to three languages. Also they were building a sales force who followed up on Allen's visits. His business and contacts grew by leaps and bounds.

Renee did great in school since she was just in kindergarten. Learning was no problem for her. Stephan, who was in third grade, had a harder time getting it all together. But he was managing. The children in the Frankfurt International School came from all different countries, all different backgrounds and languages. The classes were taught in English, but they all started them in the German language.

I was the one who had some loose ends. I had always taught, and I was just a little bored once I had my house straightened out. But I did get my guitar out daily and practiced and learned new songs. One afternoon, Micha, the oldest neighbor boy came over as I was practicing. He was so excited as he saw my guitar and told me that he was also learning to play and knew a lot of American folk songs. We became great friends and taught each other new songs. Folk music was becoming popular all over the world. Micha had a sixteen year old friend who also played the guitar so he joined us a lot. Then I met the art teacher at the school who played a fabulous jazz guitar. He would come and play with us and taught us a huge amount. As the months went by we had quite a group going. Several German students and students from my children's school had joined us and even several mothers, and we practiced officially now on Saturdays in our living room. We also had several more guitarists, and I had a few guitar students. All of a sudden, I was busy again teaching a little, and I was very happy. We bought Stephan a ukulele, and he learned that very quickly.

When summer came we would practice in our back yard, and the whole neighborhood would make it a point to come out on Saturday at three o'clock to listen to us sing and play the guitars.

It wasn't long before our group had grown to about 25, and our English guitar friend would play with us. He would play all kinds of fancy stuff while the rest of us kept it quite simple.

Together we sounded great. We now sang with harmonies, folk music style. We had a blast.

A newspaper reporter lived down the street from us. She heard about us and came to a rehearsal. She followed it up with a big article and pictures in the local paper. Soon after that we got requests to perform locally around the Taunus Mountains and even in Frankfurt. I sang quite a few solos, but the group sang a lot too. We took turns and backed each other up.

I also met the ballet teacher at my children's school. She was a beautiful slender woman about 60 and a fabulous dancer. She asked me if I would like to teach the little children, and then we would have a little program for everyone at the end of the year. All her students were high school age and danced on toes. It was an exciting time again.

My children loved all the excitement at school and at our house. Stephan learned to play the bongos. His father had bought him two bongos £tom a trip to Africa, and Stephan became a fabulous bongo player and was a star in our group. Now Renee wanted to learn the guitar. We bought her a guitar, and it was as big as our little girl. When she strummed that guitar and sang,

"When I was just a little bitty baby my mama would a-rock me in my cradle," and then the group would come in, "in them old cotton fields back home." The audience would go crazy. We had a lot of fun and soon became the center for the youth in Koenigstein.

Allen became extremely successful and his company encouraged him to test other markets in other countries. He had quite a few employees now: two secretaries and several salesmen. He was very excited and traveled a lot.

We had to fence our yard in because Jackie kept running away. He liked to travel, and he could smell female dogs in heat miles away.

Summer came, and the children had their first summer vacation. Allen wanted to show us something special and took us to Spain. We took the train. It was one of those extra fast ones that only stopped in the big cities. It was quite a trip. We traveled all through Germany, parts of Switzerland, and the southern part of France, and into the northern part of Spain to the Costa Brava.

We traveled through lots of mountains. It was a beautiful trip. We had a cabin that changed at night into four bunks. There was a very fancy dining car with good food all day long and late into the night. When we got to Spain, we were struck by the beauty of the beach. The water was aqua blue with mountains climbing up behind the beach, and rugged rock formations reaching out of the water.

We rented snorkels and goggles and put our faces into the water. It was amazing to see all the different fish swimming right around our feet in all different colors. I think I never saw a prettier beach or display of various fish in my life. The Costa Brava is very special.

We loved everything about Spain. The siesta time is the afternoon nap during the hottest part of the day. Even the stores closed. But busy life returned to the town and the beach after four o'clock until late into the night. We just went with the flow. At night there were the fiestas, guitar music, flamenco dancers, men with their dark tight pants and long sleeve fancy white shirts, and castanets which they clicked to the rhythm of the music and the rhythm of their feet.

We took the children to one nightclub where we ate a fabulous dinner, and then to our amazement the "glass roof' over our heads opened wide, and we sat under the dark starry sky of Spain as the music started to play, and the dancing began. We stayed in a beautiful beach hotel right across the street from where Stephan and Renee both learned to swim during our vacation.

We had such a good time. I will never forget Spain. The time went much too fast, and the two weeks just flew by.

The day before we went home, Allen took the train to Barcelona to see the bullfights. None of us wanted to go, but he was determined. When he came back, he was so excited he could hardly stand it, but after he gave us a detailed description, we were all glad that we spent the day on the beach. We felt so sorry for the bull; basically the bull did not have much of a chance.

The trip home was exciting again, over high mountains, through tunnels. It took us a little more than two days through Spain, France, Switzerland, and back into Germany. It was just fabulous. That's what memories are made of.

When we got back from our two week vacation, we still had four weeks before school started again. Jackie had to spend the two weeks at the vet's hospital in Spain. He almost went crazy when he saw us.

We just enjoyed the rest of the summer in Koenigstein. The time went quickly, and then it was back to school for the children, and back to teaching for me.

Allen was on the road a lot in Germany and other countries. His next trip was into Israel, and would you believe, the second day he was in Israel, Tel Aviv got bombed, and he had to stay three extra days until he could fly out again. What a restless world. We were so glad when we had him home again. He always came back with a bunch of contracts, and the Babcock Compay loved him.

That fall I went for the first time to the European dance teacher's meeting. I learned a lot of new things. I learned a whole new way of dancing. It was a combination of line dances with turns thrown into it and arm movements to popular music. I started a teenage dance group that got really popular, and they loved to perform.

I also took a dance course with Allen as my partner in Frankfurt at an Arthur Murray dance school. Everything I learned I used and soon choreographed my own dances for my teenage girls.

One of our prettiest performances that I remember was in the "Kurgarden" in Koenigstein.

Most little towns had a concert hall. Usually the concert hall was in a park-like setting, indoors and outdoors. There was usually also a very fine large restaurant which served lunch, afternoon cake, coffee or tea, and nighttime dinners. An orchestra played usually several times a week. In good weather, there was eating outdoors, in bad weather indoors. We sang in many of those places in the Taunus. I also was asked to bring either a ballet class or my teenage groups to perform. We had a beautiful park in Koenigstein right next to our restaurant. Also there was a place where people could go in the same area and drink the waters which came from underground natural wells. Insurance companies paid people money to go to one of these places for two to three weeks. It was a way to keep the population healthy. Healthy people can also do a better job. These facilities were carefully chosen and advertised. The Taunus Mountains had several places that were beneficial to people's health. People came from everywhere.

One Saturday night I was to bring my little ballerinas to the Koenigstein Park. Electricians had put up spotlights in the clearing right next to the Kurhouse. The lawn had been mowed. Seats were put up for many people. It had been advertised in the area paper. We had a record player and sound system so the music could be heard everywhere.

My little ballerinas were all dressed in pink; pink leotards, pink tights, and pink tutus. They all had a flower in their hair. They looked absolutely precious. When we came, there were some lights on outside. After the children lined up in their poses, the spotlights came on. There were several hundred people there, and they started to applaud, and the children started to dance. I was always visible to the children in case they got stuck, they could always see me with a hand motion ready to help. But, they did great. We usually did a forty-five minute program. The beautiful night, the lawn and trees surrounding us, and the beautiful music, and those little girls dancing so beautifully was like a "midsummer night's dream." When they were done, and did their bow, they got a standing ovation. We gave so much to others, but it was a wonderful dreamlike experience for us, too. The dancing and the singing kept me, my children, and my students busy. After that, we were invited to sing at Armed Forces Network, which was a great honor.

One summer, we went to Italy to the Mediterranean Coast on vacation. We stayed at a beautiful hotel again, right at the water. I brought my guitar along, and some evenings we would play the guitars outside, and play American and English folk music. It soon became a regular thing. We met an English TV producer from Anglia Television, and they flew me over to England several times to record songs with me, which they played on their magazine shows.

This school year, they tested the children Stephan's age for their IQ. Stephan usually tested really high one time, and very poorly the next. Nobody could figure it out. Today, we know that Stephan is very smart, but had A.D.D. Had we all known about this, Stephan would have been medicated, so his attention span was better. All these years in school would have been so much easier for him, and learning would have been so much more productive for him.

Allen traveled all the time. He went to South America next, and on some of these trips, he would be gone six weeks because they couldn't pay those flight costs and come back after a week or two. I could tell the stress on him from the long flights, and waiting at airports. It all took its toll. Then, when he was back in Germany, he would travel with his salesmen. He had really matured with all that responsibility, and had turned into a self assured, good-looking man. The bad part was that he started to drink more than he should have, and started to party with his salesmen after work. I got concerned about that and said, "Allen, don't forget, they are not your friends. They are your employees." But, it didn't change anything. He also started to neglect me.

At first, I didn't pay much attention to that, but it got to the point where he didn't make love to me anymore. I asked him if I was doing something wrong, and he said, "Maybe I just don't feel that way about you anymore." I was absolutely shocked. I just stared at him, and didn't say anything. Then, he started to come home later and later, and was often tipsy.

One night I sat in the living room waiting on him. When it was 2:00, I called his secretary's home to ask if she knew where he was. Her husband answered the phone, and he said that she wasn't at home either. I was shocked. I kept waiting up until 5:00 in the morning, when he staggered in the door, pretty drunk, saying, "You can be glad I made it home at all. I drove into the wall at my office." I didn't say anything, and just helped him into bed.

In the morning, I took my children to school, and when I returned, he was just getting ready for work. I asked him to please sit down with me; we had to talk. He didn't want to, but he did.

I told him that he was going to destroy everything he had worked so hard for. He shouldn't forget how hard it had been, and that he had hurt my feelings terribly. His answer was, "I want a divorce." He waked out the door. I had become close friends with Micha's mother, Mrs. Latsch. I ran over to her house. By then I was crying and told her what Allen had said. She was shocked.

I don't know what conversations went on that day in the office. I supposed that his secretary's husband had a few things to say too. The subject was never mentioned again in our house. I lived on pins and needles and just carried on, and he did treat me a little more attentively. We had now been married nine years, and the honeymoon was over. I kept myself good looking. I was still very pretty; took good care of my family; and tried really hard. I never quite trusted Allen again. I always wondered what he was up to. I shed quite a few tears when I was alone.

A big agricultural exhibition was going to happen in Munich, and Allen planned to take his secretary along plus some of his salesmen. I asked him to take me and Renee with him. He really fought it, but we finally agreed for me to take the train and spend three days. I could just imagine what would be going on if I didn't show up at all. I had no illusions anymore. Renee and I had a good time there, and he treated us well. I was pretty sure what would go on after we left.

I started to teach ballroom dancing, and I was well prepared. The young people in Koenigstein loved me, and the parents respected me. I talked to the minister of the Protestant church, and he offered me his youth building for the teenage classes which were mostly ballroom. I promised that in return, we would sing once a month for his youth service. All along I had taken more training and was able to teach my students more than most competitors. I now had a cleaning lady at home daily and 250 students. I used my best students to assist me, and all the teenage kids liked that, and so did I.

Each group of students had a dance every six weeks; one was just for them; and then a formal dance with their parents was like a formal coming-out dance.

We always had the same band. They were super. My ballet children would perform a couple of dances, and my teenage jazz group would do a couple of dances. My ballroom students would show off in a couple of dances that were choreographed, and I sang a couple of songs. It was fun for the kids and their parents. Allen always came to the formal dances and behaved very gentlemanly. He danced a great boogie.

We had one of our balls in a beautiful castle in the neighboring town. It had been turned into a hotel and conference center and was very elegant. It used to be the residence of the crown prince of Hessen. Hessen was our state.

It was getting close to Christmas, and Allen and I decided to invite the whole family. After all we had been gone for so long. We invited Aunt Pia and Uncle Fritz from Stuttgart, my mother and Grandpa Dick from Wiesbaden, and my brother and his wife Ulla from Dusseldorf.

I roasted a huge turkey, and stuffed it with meat loaf like we do in Germany. I cooked a big pot of red cabbage with lots of apples sliced into it, sugar, cinnamon, and some cloves. It was so delicious. We had mashed potatoes and gravy, German chocolate cake with whipped cream, and coffee with after dinner drinks. After that, one is so lazy that it is easy to sit and talk. All our company stayed in the Schloss Hotel (castle hotel) so they did not have to go far. Everybody went home the next day except my brother, Manfred and his wife, Ulla. I was so glad to be able to have some time with Manfred. I had not seen him in so long and loved him so much. The next day we just ate leftovers and talked and drank wine. Everybody had been so happy, and the children had received an abundance of Christmas gifts. We also took a long walk straight up the mountain through the vineyards. It was so pretty with a dusting of snow on the trees.

Allen and I never again spoke about our differences. I thought that maybe the alcohol influenced him still. We just tried to be nice to each other, and for a long time things were good again.

My brother called me and talked to Allen too. He wanted us to go skiing with him and Ulla in the Austrian Alps in March. He said that was the greatest time to go skiing because there was so much snow on the ground, and the sun was shining, and everybody got a great suntan. Allen and I had never gone on a skiing trip, and the more we thought about it, the more we wanted to go. We decided to invite Micha to come along as our babysitter at night, and everybody was very excited about the trip.

We stayed in the same hotel as my brother, a huge Alpine hotel with massive balconies all around the hotel. There were two big sauna areas inside with doors going to the outside; one for ladies and one for gentlemen.

They were protected from view but not from falling snow, so the custom was to go to the sauna, get really hot, and run out in the snow naked and roll in it. I tried my best to see some naked men rolling in the snow, but I never got lucky.

The children and I went to ski school and learned so much every day. We had the nicest ski teacher. He was about seventy, and as fit as a fiddle. He also had an alpine farm with cows. He took us up to the top of the mountain after a few days. Then he would take us down slowly, crisscrossing the mountain so we would stay safe. Allen only skied with us a few times, then he flew down that mountain as if there was no tomorrow.

I had one unfortunate incident. When I was supposed to get on the ski lift with my teacher, everybody followed us. Unfortunately, when I got on the lift on the bottom, I fell down and accidently kicked my teacher during the process and unfortunately I kicked him off the lift too.

We had to scramble really quickly out of the way of everyone else behind us. My teacher told me that had never happened to him before, and he had never been so embarrassed. He made sure not be anywhere near me when he got on the lift. It took a long time for me to live that down.

Micha went skiing with Allen now, and they had a good time. At night after supper, Allen and I had time to socialize a little while Micha got the children to bed. We had two bedrooms, one for Micha and the children, and one for Allen and me. Micha played lots of games with the children, and everybody loved the skiing. We were getting unbelievably brown and really looked healthy. The next thing that happened was an avalanche. They had to close the roads in and out of our little Austrian village and food was flown in by helicopter. We were very happy. It was a great vacation.

When we got back to Koenigstein, we all had to work hard again. My mother came to see me and stayed for lunch. She loved baked chicken with pineapple and a salad. We had a nice talk, then she went back to Wiesbaden, and I got ready to teach. I taught ballet Monday, Wednesday, and Friday from three to six o'clock, and Tuesday and Thursday from six to ten o'clock I taught ballroom dancing. The bookwork became a real burden for me with keeping up with who had and had not paid.

When we had the big dances, when the parents came, getting the tables right, and who wanted to sit with whom was always tricky. At those times, the phone rang all the time. Allen suggested we get an au pair girl for that part of the work. We had a huge basement, and it would be no trouble to finish one bedroom down there. That's what we did, and I got a really nice girl from Scotland. She was as skinny as Twiggy with a Scottish accent. She was really sweet, and the children loved her. She wanted to learn German. She got the children to bed at night when I was teaching and kept the books. I had approximately two hundred students and a waiting list, so I was always swamped.

Our life was running smoothly. I prepared dinner in the morning and answered the phone. I took an afternoon nap, and then I taught my classes. The children now took the bus to school. I often stopped to think how lucky we were and remembered my childhood. I knew how lucky my children were. I only worked two nights a week, and three afternoons, and I had a lot of help.

Allen was gone two to three nights a week, and when he traveled out of the country, he was sometimes gone several weeks in a row. Our au pair was heaven sent. She was lovely to the children and happy with us.

I remembered when after the war, there was hardly any housing and how people had taken us in. Two families in one small apartment, and I felt I had to do something too to help someone.

We had an orphanage in Koenigstein. It was run by nuns. I called them, and asked if I could come by and talk to them. When I got there, I introduced myself. I told them that after the war, when we were so needy, people helped us and now that we had so much, I wanted to help someone. My children needed to learn to help and share. If they had an especially needy child, I would like to invite him or her to come and visit us, and if it worked out well, I wanted to pick that child up maybe every other weekend.

They told me that they had one little boy who never had company. He was the child of a black American soldier, and his mother had a drinking problem and was not allowed to take him home with her. He also was a very good little boy and would I like to meet him. I was very excited, and they called him to the office for us to meet. It turned out that he was the most darling child, and he and I talked for a while. I asked him if he would like to come and visit us sometime, and he was very excited. I told him I was going to be back to pick him up on Saturday, and he could stay overnight. He was a beautiful little boy with the most wonderful smile. He had the most beautiful big eyes. I gave him a hug and told him and the head nun, if it was all right with her we would be back on Saturday about ten o'clock. His name was Volker, and he was about six years old.

I discussed this with Allen, and since he had spent two or three years in Boys Town, Nebraska, when he was very little he was very much for it. Our children were excited. Allen was not a bad person. Sometimes good people do something bad, and bad people do something good.

I think with Allen a lot of it was being alone on those big trips and drinking too much alcohol. Of course, the deal with his secretary was bad and hard to handle for me. Saturday we went to get Volker, all four of us. Everybody was very excited. We brought Volker home. He liked our house, the back yard, and the neighbor children. He was supposed to sleep with Stephan in the bunk bed.

I had told my neighbors about Volker and everybody was very nice to him. He was the only black child in our town. I learned more about his mother also. The nuns had told me that his mother had tried to escape from Communist Germany with her family when she was seventeen.

They tried to sneak across the border at night. The guards

saw them as they ran across the border and shot at them. She was the only survivor. She got away into Germany. She was seventeen with nowhere to go. I don't know all the details, but she ended up working in a G.I. club. A black soldier befriended her, and she lived with him. She was supposed to have been very pretty. He took care of her, and after he left, she found out she was pregnant. It was Volker.

When the black soldier was sent back to the United States, she was alone again, but at least she still had her job. Her drinking problem got quite a bit worse, and she had no one helping her when she went to work so Social Services placed Volker in the Catholic orphanage.

The nuns were very nice to the children, but they were totally overworked. Each nun was responsible for eight children. They had those children from morning until night, getting them ready for school, feeding them supper by six o'clock, and having them in bed by seven o'clock.

For some children, that was just too early, so they lay in their beds, and kept beating their heads into the mattresses until they were asleep.

Volker, who had that annoying habit, just about drove Stephan crazy, even when he got to go to bed much later. So, there were some things that were difficult. One time Volker disappeared.

He had gotten upset over something. No one knew what it was or where he was. We started spreading out all over the neighborhood, looking for him everywhere. And we told everyone we saw that he had disappeared. After two hours, we were getting very upset. After about three hours, he came walking up the street very leisurely. We had to call the troops back, and tell them that he had been found. When I took him in the house with me, and sat down to talk with him, he told me in the orphange, they didn't keep track of him that closely. He took a walk in the woods often, when he had to think about something.

He was such a good, little boy though, and made no trouble at all. Volker actually was a little closer to Renee, since they were closer in age, but Stephan had to put up with him in his bedroom. That took a little getting used to, but basically they were all three very good. The first thing we did was buy Volker his own bicycle. He was so thrilled. We had a great road for bicycle riding, with no thru traffic. There were always a bunch of kids riding bikes. It was a great place to live. All the kids watched out for each other. Renee was the youngest.

We got Volker every weekend now, except when we went on a trip. My brother came to visit with his wife on weekends a lot. I was always glad to see him and my sister-in-law, Ulla.

We kept up with our singing rehearsals on Saturday unless we went out of town. Volker came every Saturday, and he enjoyed his weekends. We often took long hikes on Sunday into the mountains and either ate somewhere or packed a picnic lunch in a knapsack.

We had the yard fenced in, but Jackie still dug out, and we kept getting phone calls telling us where he was. One really nice old man called us and told us that he really liked our little dog and would love to have him. We loved our little Jackie too, but our fence didn't keep him in but that old man's fence evidently did. He was holding Jackie when we came to pick him up, and he looked like he didn't want to part from him. He had traveled about five miles, and these were all busy highways, so we decided to let him stay there. That old man was so thrilled, he almost cried. We came back to check on Jackie about six weeks later. The old man was working in his vegetable garden, and Jackie sat in the fresh dirt watching him. Jackie already looked real roly-poly, and the old gentleman said with pride, "I really like him, and he has not run away, and when I buy a bratwurst for me, I buy one for Jackie too."

Well, if Jackie gained two more pounds, he wouldn't get out of anybody's yard anymore.

Jackie looked really content. Maybe the bratwursts would make him forget girls.

We missed having a dog, and Allen missed his poodle so he gave us some money and told us to buy a big poodle again. We took off to the pet shop. They didn't have big standard-sized poodles, and for the money we could only get a dachshund. Well, I took my chances with the children's support, and we brought the dachshund home. If you have never owned a dachshund, you have really missed something. The little long haired dachshund has his own idea about life, what he needs, and in this case what she needs and what she wants. She would sit in front of us and tell us with little groans, that she needed something a- bad. It was our job to guess what it was. When we guessed, she would turn circles around herself, and bark and wag her tail like crazy. She was really entertaining, and even my husband, who had his heart set on a poodle, could not escape this little dog's charm. We were all crazy about her.

Renee loved her the most because "Peanuts," that's what we called her, liked to be dressed and lay in her doll buggy with a little baby cap on and her back on a pillow and a blanket over her. Renee took her for long walks on our sidewalk, and Peanuts loved all the adoration from the other children.

Peanuts liked to sleep with me at night, but she went with

the children and slept with them until she heard me going to my bedroom, then she sat and looked at me groaning, until I picked her up and put her on the foot of my bed. She waited until she knew that I was asleep, then she evidently carefully got under my covers, crawled all the way down to my feet, did a turn, and came up to my pillow, where I saw her every morning, her face facing my face sound asleep.

She was truly dear to us. We all loved her so much. Peanuts loved all the children and young people who came to our house, but she hated the mailman, and when he delivered something to our door, one of us had to hang on to her. She also hated an old neighbor who was a very cranky man and tried to her hurt by sticking his umbrella through our fence trying to poke her. She went almost insane when she saw him, and once or twice she got a hold of his umbrella and tore it up.

We did not replace it because he stuck it in our fence and tried to hurt her. All in all, she was the most popular dog in the whole neighborhood.

I had two more opportunities for fame and fortune. I entered two contests, one with BASF, a large record company. They invited me to come to Hamburg and audition for them. They had an English producer who loved my voice. They signed me to a two-year contract. As I found out, that didn't mean anything because when the English producer went back to England, they recorded two records with me and did nothing with them. I was just too old in the German producer's opinion. I was in my late thirties. It cost a lot of money to promote a new singer and a new record. Most of my competition was under twenty. The same thing happened one more time.

The most famous German songwriter wrote two songs for

me and could not get a producer to promote me or the record because I was getting too close to forty. But later my dream came true.

The next summer Allen bought a huge camping trailer, and we took it to Austria then to Italy and back. I have to tell you this story. It was a beautiful big camper, and Allen drove the biggest Opel GMC that they made in Germany. We were heading for Austria and invited Micha along.

We took our little Peanuts too. The camper had a master bedroom in the very back, bunks, a couch, and an eating table in front by the kitchen.

We were going to cross the Alps by the St. Gotthard Pass. First, we went through a tunnel and then over the pass. Our car and camper were loaded on a train along with other cars. We sat inside the car with the trailer behind us as the train rushed through the tunnel. All of a sudden, we noticed these Italian-looking people standing next to their car behind us waving at us jumping up and down and looking panicky. Evidently the vibrations of the train brought our trailer closer and closer to those people, and we couldn't do anything about it. When we came out on the other side of the mountain, there were maybe ten inches between our trailer and their car. No wonder they looked a little panicky. But we made it okay.

From where we got out of the tunnel, it went straight into the snow covered road up to the St. Gotthard Pass. The snow was deep, and Allen asked me if I wanted to drive a little way. He was really tired.

I said, "Sure." We started upwards on this road. The snow had piled into walls on both sides and left very little room for driving. Soon we saw the sign, "St. Gotthard Pass two miles." I looked at Allen and he was asleep. I said, "Allen, Allen, we are on the pass, and I am scared."

He said, "There is no place to turn. You will have to take us across." Can you imagine yourself being on an alpine pass? When you look down, you see nothing but snow, high mountains, and deep valleys. I was frozen in fear.

Allen said, "Relax you are doing fine. Just go slow and don't panic." When Allen said relax, there was always something to worry about. He was a daredevil. Somehow we made it, and as soon as there was a place to stop, I asked him to take the wheel. It was an unbelievable trip, the glaciers above us, and the setting sun painting everything with a golden glow.

We came into a little mountain village, and a sign said, "Camping five miles." We decided we had had enough adventure and pulled into the camping place. We put something into the frying pan, a hamburger and some vegetables. We had German bread and fruit for dessert and each had a big glass of milk and cheese.

We were very satisfied and ready to take a walk in the snow. We were still at a very high altitude. When we got chilly, we went into the trailer. The beds were made up. We washed up, brushed our teeth, and crashed into bed. It had been a very eventful trip.

The camper was very comfortable. We had heating, cooling, and a bathroom. We called goodnight to each other, and it got quiet very quickly in our camper. Peanuts really dug in under the blanket right by my feet. As usual, I found her facing me on my pillow in the morning.

We couldn't wait to eat our breakfast and get outside in the snow and look around. It was truly beautiful. I assume that the snow never melted at that altitude. After we had taken quite a walk and bombarded each other with snowballs, we were ready to go on and see what was going on a little further down. The next two days, we headed toward the Adriatic Sea We found a beautiful camping place really close to the ocean. The evening of the second day we spent at the Adriatic Sea. It was beautiful there. There were lots of Germans there trying to catch some sunshine and some waves. Allen told me that he had to fly back to Germany to do some work, and he would pick us up in one week. I always wonder now, what else he was up to, but I didn't say anything.

We had a great time, even though sometimes I did feel sad because I was lonely for my husband. We made a lot of friends, and we played the guitar every night. People from all over the camp brought their chairs and sang popular American folk music with us. You can make so many friends with American folk music, any music actually. It was a beautiful time to live in.

Everywhere we went people came and wanted to sing with us. Micha had gotten very good with singing harmony, and of course Renee and Stephan were good children and loved their music.

Usually by ten o'clock we all went to bed. All day, we played by the ocean and we were turning brown. By the time Allen came back, we had made a lot of friends and had telephone numbers and addresses.

We were so happy to see Allen and hung on him and didn't want to let him go. He should have felt very loved. We went on to Italy where our next destination was Venice.

Venice was absolutely beautiful like a fairy tale of a world gone by. All the channels and the palaces along the water told of a splendor and riches that we would probably be unable to imagine. The gondoliers paddled the gondolas through all these channels and told us all about the gorgeous old palaces. We went under little bridges, and the gondoliers sang Italian songs all the while.

It had gotten dark, and the stores were closing when Renee saw a beautiful doll in the window of a toy store. It had beautiful silk clothes on with a porcelain face. She could close her eyes. Her name was "Bella" which means beautiful in Italian. The store was closed.

Renee was so upset. She thought the doll was the prettiest one we had ever seen, and I agreed. Well, daddy finally agreed and even though we had other plans, he said that he could come back in the morning and get "Bella." Renee dried her tears and looked forward to the next day. Now we had to look for a camp ground. Allen was driving, and I could relax for a little bit.

It didn't take us too long to find a camp ground.

We were all pretty tired. Every day we saw so much. It was an interesting time. It seemed that we had just gone to sleep when we heard Renee, "Everybody wake up. It is morning."

We got dressed and found a place for breakfast. Then we headed straight to Venice. It took us a while to find that store again. And there was beautiful Bella still sitting in the window still smiling. We bought Bella and gave her to Renee. We bought Stephan some fishing stuff, parked our camper, and walked to St. March Square to look at the church, the many pigeons, and the many people. It was quite a sight.

Now we had done what we planned for Venice, and we left Venice for Lake Garda. I cannot remember how long it took us to get there. It is south of the Alps. Lake Garda is a beautiful lake surrounded by mountains.

We found a nice hotel. That night we were going to live in

luxury. Micha and the children were going to dine in this beautiful hotel, and then go to the room, bathe or shower, then watch TV for as long as they wanted to.

Allen was combining business with pleasure because we were supposed to meet some business people he wanted to talk to at a very famous place where he invited them to dinner. The place we were going to was the villa of Mussolini's lover, who after the war was killed just like Mussolini. The villa was in a park like setting and now had a famous restaurant in it. The whole park had tables set under trees with islands of light. It was so beautiful and romantic. It is sad, that in our world, beauty and romance live side by side with tragedy.

We had a fabulous Italian dinner there. The Italian business people were very charming and nice to talk to, and Allen got a lot of information that he needed. Evidently, the whole getting to know each other meeting turned out really well for him. I learned a little bit about how big business gets conducted.

It was very interesting. After our visit at Lake Garda, we headed through Switzerland, one of the most beautiful countries in the world. Soon, we were in South Germany, and not long after, at home. It had been a marvelous trip, and everybody enjoyed it so much, Micha too.

Micha was the perfect babysitter. Our children loved him, and he enjoyed himself. We are still close friends with Micha, and he always told me that we awoke his love for travel. He said that we showed him how large the world was, and he continued to travel more extensively than we did.

It was nice to be home again. There were also great reunions with the kids in the neighborhood. That weekend, we went to get Volker, and he was one happy little kid.

I believe he had missed us, and we were also happy to see him. Allen and I talked about taking him along sometime, when it was not such a huge trip.

Soon, we were back in our routine; getting ready for school, getting ready for my dance teaching, and getting our singing group sharpened up again. We now had a group of 30. We had guitars, tambourines, bongos, and other rhythm instruments. Some of the mothers of our children sang with us, too, and they were a great addition to the group.

It was also time to get the children's school clothes. So that I could give each one plenty of attention, I took only one at a time. I started with Renee. We went off the mountain, down to the beginning of Frankfurt. There was a large shopping center. Renee always loved to shop first, and then we would have a really nice lunch at a fine restaurant. It was fun to shop with Renee. She knew what she liked, and she understood what we needed to buy. She also liked to look cute.

That made it fun for her mama, too. Renee picked out two books.

Then, I took Volker. It was a first for him. Volker loved to hold my hand and to talk nonstop. I will never forget Volker's little hand in mine, and his beautiful dark eyes, with long lashes looking up at me. He was kind of a dainty boy, but he was cute, and so smart. He loved to call me mama, and he always talked a little loud. I got the once -over from many people, but he was too precious to me not to be proud of him. He was thrilled to pick out his own clothes, but he was very good about suggestions from me. We also had a fancy lunch when we were done shopping. Then I picked out two books to read.

Stephan was my last project. He knew exactly what he wanted.

I had to rein him in once or twice, but he did a good job, and he ate the biggest lunch when he was through. It was a good time to shop with each one. Stephan loved books, so I bought him a couple of books to read also.

Allen traveled all over the world, even to Pakistan, where a big dinner in his honor was prepared. He had to eat some Pakistani delicacies. One of them was sheep eyes. Of course, as the guest of honor, he couldn't turn down anything to eat, and had to eat it with a show of enjoyment. He said the sheep eyes had been the worst, but he flushed them down with a healthy drink of scotch. He brought all of us great gifts. I had a wonderful jewelry collection. Most of it was handmade in heavy silver with many semi-precious stones.

Allen told me this story of when he had gone to Kenya, Africa and sold these Caucasian landowners lots of chicken stock, and four days after he left there was some sort of uprising, and the wealthy white owners of this unbelievably huge farm had their throats slit in the night. Many of his customers were dead.

He said that Kenya to him was the most beautiful country he had ever seen. He loved the wild animals you saw everywhere; giraffes, elephants, zebras, lions, and all kinds of exotic birds.

He had a fascinating life, but he was getting tired of traveling though, and always being alone. One day he decided to start his own business. He bought some land in North Germany, built some big chicken houses, and started buying breeding stock from his own company. I don't know the details. He did very well the first two years, and then it got tough. The borders around Europe were opened, the Dutch, and the Belgiums. Many other agricultural countries exported into Germany, and they were terrible competition since they could produce so much cheaper than

Germany. Allen saw his business slowly going down the drain. He ended up having to look for a job, and started selling for a Dutch company.

He was very unhappy and sad. He could not keep his dream. I felt so sorry for him. I still had my dance school. Allen was very resourceful and well known. He made a good living, but he was pretty heart broken.

He would stay out late many nights, and come home pretty tipsy when he finally did come home. One day I got a call from Holland. Allen had been picked up for drunk driving, and lost his driver's license. He came home on the train and had to take a taxi from the station. When he came home, I had to tell him that it was his fault that he lost his license, and I did not have time to drive him around, and that he had to rely on trains and taxis.

One evening on a Friday, I was waiting for Allen, and he didn't come home. He finally arrived three hours late. He had come right by our town, but he was so busy talking to a Dutch singer that he forgot to get off the train. I was pretty upset with him. I was actually wearing out a little bit. Sometimes his wild streak was a little much for me, and I wished I wasn't married to him anymore.

Volker was at that age now where children either got promoted into high school or went on in elementary school and programmed to learn a trade. He was so smart that it would have been a waste, so we talked with social services and got permission to let him live with us and go on into high school so he could later go to the university. Volker was thrilled. I had to give him this big talk now that he had to work harder than his classmates, and because of his color, he had to make better grades than all the others so he could go on to the university. I told him I didn't think that it was fair, but he needed to work really hard so that he could have the same opportunities as the others. He looked up at me and said, "I understand. I will always work really hard." He did and became a very successful man.

That spring vacation, we drove up to the Belgium coast. We all enjoyed that very much. We just packed the children up and drove to the coast with Allen. Our little dachshund got to come with us. Belgium is a charming country. The food had a touch of the French influence. The people are very friendly. We went to Knokke at the North Sea. It was a really beautiful resort town with lots going on. We stayed in a small hotel half a block from the beach. They had wonderful food, and I constantly ate fillet do Sole. It was a wonderful delicate white fish that you only get from the North Atlantic.

Knokke had long, high sand dunes all along the coast, and almost every day we rented bikes and bicycled on the paths on top of the dunes for miles on end. The wind was constantly blowing, and it gave you a really clean, good feeling. We got really brown.

Volker was hilarious, when we put on suntan lotion, he wanted some too. I am sure that it was good for his skin, but the funny thing was, he then wanted to lie out in the sun to get a deeper tan. He had never been on a vacation and enjoyed it so much. The children built sand castles and had such a good time. The most fun for them was when they had built a castle, and the waves came in to flood their castle, and how they tried to save it from the water.

The kids also went fishing off the pier with Allen, and what a victory when they pulled something out of the water that was big enough to eat. It was immediately taken to the hotel kitchen which was only a block from the beach. There it got trimmed and presented at suppertime.

It was really sad, after having been married sixteen years, Allen in my mind had become a liability. I never knew where he really was. I didn't trust him any more, and as young as we were, I did not sleep in the same bed with him any more. I realized that I had stopped loving him the way you need to love your husband. I was still very attached to him; it was like he was still my lover. I think drop by drop the love spilled out of my cup until it was empty.

He now got a really good offer from his Dutch company, especially since he no longer had a driver's license. They asked him to work for one of their subsidiaries in the United States, at least until he had his driver's license back. The pay was good, but nothing like it had been before.

When I thought about that, I had a hard time not to show him my anger. Neither the children nor I wanted to go back to the United States. We were happy, we were settled, and the children's German was good, so Stephan and Renee were going to German school now.

Stephan had been to four schools now, and Renee to three. I had my teaching, and was making good money, even though it was not enough to be able to pay for all the expenses, but together we still did fine. And what about Volker? I was so upset. I felt like I was going to have a nervous breakdown. My poor mother knew what I had to think about. My brother was upset. Were we going to lose everybody again; our whole family, the many wonderful friends, adults and young people? I had to tell Allen that I didn't know if I could get us uprooted like that again. At night in bed, when I was alone, I cried many a bitter tear, now knowing what I needed to do. I also knew that our marriage was on the rocks. How could I trust Allen again with all our lives?

On the other hand, I did not make quite enough money to make ends meet. I did not know if Allen would help us, if we did not go back with him. What finally helped me make a decision was when Allen said, with tears in his eyes, "Please don't put the ocean between me and my children."

I finally decided that we had to go with him. We couldn't be a charity case, and burden my family, and break Allen's heart. We talked to Allen's company, and they told us that they had a pretty good position for him in the Charlotte, North Carolina area. Later on, we could, when his problems were over, probably return to Europe.

It was a bitter pill to swallow. Since we would be living in the south, it would not be good for our family to bring Volker along. That was another terrible upset. One of my close girlfriends from school days and her husband were both pharmacists, had a drug store in a small town not far from us, offered to help with Volker if we could get him into a good boarding school. She and her family would take him on vacation days, and make sure he was all right. She had three boys and a girl of her own. How was I going to tell Volker what was going on? I spoke with the people from social services, and they told me to let him pick out any boarding school of his liking. He had done so well. He deserved the best of schools.

I don't remember how I told Volker that we were going to move again. Everybody was crying--me included. Why can't we stay here? Well, daddy got a new job. Maybe we can come back in a year. What else could we do? Because it was the South, we could not take Volker with us and live in a good neighborhood. But my good fiends would take care of him. And to Volker I had to say that he could pick out the school. I got a list of schools, and we took day trips and looked at a lot of them. We finally found a school just north of Frankfurt in the mountains. The school was in a beautiful castle. Everything was big and rich. Volker and I were both impressed.

The fact remains that he did not quite understand that we were really moving. I was so upset.

I could not quite get it either. My children were numb. Nobody wanted to leave but Allen. He wanted to have a new beginning. He couldn't really function without a driver's license. The sad thing was that he had brought it all on himself. And it changed everybody's else's life forever.

We decided to leave after the next ball, which would be the beginning of vacation. Our house sold so quickly it was unbelievable. It was such a great little house. We probably would have never found a nice house like this for the price again in Koenigstein.

The next three months went like we were in a fog. A month before we left, we bought a black and white Newfoundland. He was eight weeks old and was to be sailing with us on the last trip of the SS France to America. He was the most beautiful dog, and we were all crazy about him.

I planned the ball lavishly and as a really big goodbye from me. The program was planned in detail; we had our band and 450 guests. The news had trickled out that we were leaving.

Every seat was sold in that ballroom. When we were through with part of the program, Micha walked up to me. When I saw him, I started to cry. He was the fm person I had met when we moved in, and here he actually was the last I talked to. I asked him to please drop my guitar, records, and equipment afterwards at my house and to please announce over the sound system that I had left because I was too sad to say goodbye.

Micha said, "But we have such beautiful flowers for you and a great speech."

I was crying in earnest then. I gave Micha the check for the band and walked out with my children and Allen behind me, after I had given him a long hard hug. We were so sad.

Myra came the next morning to say goodbye. She now had a German boyfriend, very seriously. She had a great job in an optic shop with friends of mine. She had done great. She spoke fluent German now and had stayed with us for two years. We were going to miss her too.

CHAPTER NINE

REMEMBERING

Now, looking back, I remember some of Stephan, Renee, and Volker's adventures. Two blocks below our house was a huge pasture which connected Koenigstein and the next little bitty town, Scheidhain. That big huge field supplied my children and their friends with lots of adventures.

One day the children played somewhere probably in the field, when Volker came running home totally out of breath. He could barely talk. "Renee is in trouble. She is stuck in that big tree in the middle of the field and can't make it down. You need to come and help her."

Allen was home, so we both jumped up and ran to the field. There was a big tree, right in the center of the field and Stephan and Volker always climbed that huge tree. I guess Renee had to try that too. She was sitting pretty far up crying her heart out.

"Mama, Daddy, please help me down. I can't do it."

I called, and I was so scared, "Don't cry, Dolly. Calm down. We will have you right down."

Well it wasn't so easy. Stephan had to climb up, and Allen had to give h a step by step directions as Stephan took one step after the other. At times, she got really scared. We had to tell her not to look down and to take only one step at a time. Then Allen climbed up a little ways and helped her and finally lifted her down. She sobbed on his shoulder and then on mine. I don't think she ever tried that again.

Stephan got into trouble very easily. To make it worse, he had a friend, the son of a doctor, who was even worse than Stephan. They had a great talent for doing extraordinary things. Their favorite thing was to go to our grocer's around the corner from our house. They also had a nice delicatessen.

Once in a while I sent Stephan to this little store to pick something for supper: chicken, vegetables, or fresh bread. Something simple. With all the activity in our house, it was sometimes hard to be organized.

I found out by accident that I had a bill there with items that Stephan had charged. He had bought chickens, bread, butter, cheese, beer, and cigarettes. I would never have noticed if the bill had not been quite a bit.

I had a little talk with Stephan and found out that he and his friend made fires by the creek and roasted chickens, drank a little beer, and smoked a few cigarettes for dessert. They had great fun, but after I talked to them and the grocer, there was no more charging.

One time they took Renee, Volker, and the two little neighbor boys along. They were all fishing in the creek which was against the law at that particular spot. At the same time they had a fire burning. They did not notice that the fire got out of hand while they were fishing. When they noticed that the fire had spread, it was too far gone to contain it. They took their coats off and were beating the fire out with their jackets, but they couldn't contain it. I heard a fire truck, and shortly after they all showed up at my front door. Their jackets had holes in them, and their faces and hands were black. They were lucky that they didn't get hurt. They were totally out of breath and scared.

They got another long lecture, and Stephan, Renee and Volker were punished by not being allowed to see their friends for a week. They did not like that, but it made a strong impression on them. To this day, forty years later, they still like to talk about their adventures in the field.

Another thing Stephan and his friend liked to do was to climb to the castle with shovel and bucket and start digging for treasures. They found some items that must have come from the kitchen of the castle a long time ago.

When I think about their childhood in Germany, I think just like they do, that it was perfect.

After the terrible things that happened in my childhood, the new Germany was just so wonderful, and life was very romantic and exciting. We never felt like we belonged anywhere else. It sounds glamorous when people live in many different places, but the other side of it is that you don't ever feel like you belong.

We had taken many trips, and usually Allen spent one week out of two with us, then he would return to his work and come back to pick us up.

The children and I took one more memorable trip together. This one was to Lake Geneva.

Lake Geneva is a huge, wild lake in Switzerland, surrounded by the Alps. There were three languages spoken around this lake; German, French, and either Austrian or Swiss.

Storms could come up suddenly at this lake. We witnessed one. We were having afternoon cake, sitting outside right by the lake, when a sudden wind came up and got really strong. The help from the hotel came running out and dragged the chairs, umbrellas, etc. into the hotel.

Within minutes the wind was so strong that the waves had gotten really high and blew over the embankment. Big tourist boats tried to tie up at our pier, but couldn't because the waves were too high. It was really scary. Everyone watched from inside the hotel. We couldn't help anybody.

They just had to stay on the lake until it blew over and stay as close to the shore as they could. It blew over fast, and as violently as it had come it was gone. It was very scary. On the opposite side of the lake in the French area, a boat capsized and 30 some people drowned. We never forgot that.

We showed our children eleven different European countries.

From our hotel, we could see a great big castle built into the lake. A political prisoner spent years chained to a big pillar. His prison was below lake level, and when we went to see it we could hear the waves licking against the walls of the castle. The prisoner was released and wrote a whole book about his thoughts when he was imprisoned. The castle was close to Montreux, and the book was called, The Prisoner of the Chateau de Chillon.

Now it was time to leave again, and the thought was almost unbearable to us all. Volker was the saddest.

"Auf Wiedersehen." Goodbye. I had to take Volker to his school, and he and I had to say goodbye. He was such a little man already and was so brave. It just tore me up. To this day, I wished we hadn't had to go.

The day we left, we stopped at my mother's house in Wiesbaden, and a lot of tears were flowing. When would I see her again?

244

Allen had bought a Volkswagen Bus for the journey. We bought an orange VW. We had to take the bus with children and dogs to Cannes, France, where many of the big boats stopped on their journey to the United States. The ship was so big that it could not fit into the harbor so they picked the new passengers up by a smaller boat and took us out to the SS France.

Our huge brand new Newfoundland puppy was still easily scared, so we gave him a couple of tranquilizers the vet had given us, just to get him on the boat especially up that steep ladder.

Sammy did not cooperate too much, so a sailor was pulling and Allen was pushing his big fanny up the stairs with Sammy's rear end right in his face. Once we were on board, there were no more problems. We got to walk him to the special deck, about one third down from the top which had huge clean kennels.

We looked at today's menu: filet de boef, vegetables, etc. Peanuts got to go into a small run.

Everybody had blankets, and we could walk them as often as we wanted to.

We were then shown to our four bed cabin, and soon after that we were on our way. It was exciting, but a huge sadness was in my heart.

The crossing was to take five days, but about halfway across we got into an uncomfortable storm. The ship rocked quite a bit, and a lot of people stayed in their cabins. The dining room was quiet. I had spent most of the day in the library with a double brandy and my guitar. Allen ate a nice big breakfast and showed up very pale in the library also. He had already lost his breakfast. The children had cokes and did not get sick. I only had some brandy and some crackers and got queasy but not sick. By evening, things were better, and people dressed up and tried a little nutrition. The next day was sunny and beautiful.

We met a lot of interesting people and were sorry to say goodbye to them. When we had gotten off the boat, we had to stand in line for the customs officers. As we stood there for our turn, a man with a huge fully grown St. Bernard came pretty close to us, and as the St. Bernard saw our younger and smaller Newfoundland, he promptly attacked Sammy. That was some huge noisy dog fight, and Allen got bitten in the hand. Allen had them wrap something around his hand and off we went.

We headed straight out of the city, south toward North Carolina. It was a long journey, and I remember the great beauty of the Shenandoah Valley. Allen had bought a house in Mooresville at the lake, and it was beautiful but oh so lonely.

I would get everybody up and fix breakfast; Allen would drop the children off at school, and go on to work. I would make four beds, and then sit and cry most of the day. I was lost, no friends, no children to teach. I had my two dogs, and I walked with them.

We had two neighbors. One was a very young family who had us over for a barbeque and a trailer that belonged to people from Winston-Salem who came about every other weekend. It was just too lonely for me. Everyone I loved was gone, my whole support system. Men had bought a small boat with life jackets for the children, and as soon as they got back from school they would get into their boat and visit classmates right across from us on the lake. They didn't return until suppertime. They started to take the school bus soon, and I didn't see them much at all. After supper, they did their homework, and that was it for that day.

After crying for about a month, I made a very selfish move. I took the VW bus and drove to Statesville and looked all over that town. It was very different from Mooresville. I found several nice residential neighborhoods, and I got to know the town really well.

Allen knew how lonely I was at that uninhabited lake, and so I told him about Statesville. So on the weekend we told the children we wanted to show them Statesville. They didn't like the idea, but they were very understanding.

We found a really nice neighborhood with pretty houses and families about all our ages. The next day I found a realtor, and started the process of selling our house and finding a new one. We had lots of problems. We were kind of shell shocked. We had been so involved in so many nice things in Germany, and we could not quite find our way. The children were so far ahead because of the German schools that they neglected doing their schoolwork here and regressed. But we all slowly started to make friends. At first, they made the wrong friends. We were in a society that was strange to us.

But after a while we got a little better adjusted. Allen and I made some nice friends at the country club who introduced us around.

The war at home continued. Allen drank quite a bit in the evenings. I am sure he had his own depressing thoughts. The children were unhappy, and so was I. I finally was teaching dancing again in a really cute studio in town. I also met some really nice adults who liked folk music, and we sang together in a couple of churches. They were a fun group.

By the time spring came, I was ready to do something else for the summer. We all went to Myrtle Beach for a weekend to look around. There was a big hotel, the Sheraton, just about ready to open up. We went in and asked for the hotel manager. He was very friendly. I told him that I had just arrived this year from Europe, and I was looking for a singing job. I had brought my portable record player and some recordings of mine. I played several for him and sang along with my record. I was hired for most of the summer to sing five nights a week, four hours a night. It turned out to be forty-six songs a night.

When we got back to Statesville, I had my work cut out. I practiced daily with my guitar to build a repertoire. We rented a house for the summer for us and our two doggies, and the children looked forward to the summer. They didn't have their family and friends, but they were going to have the beach.

Allen had a great job offer with a company in the Catskill Mountains. It was again in the chicken business. These people wanted him to be part owner. It was a really good offer, and I thought that maybe this was the right time to part. We just had nothing left except our children, whom we both adored, How irresponsible of us to take them away from their roots at that time in their life.

It took them several years to get adjusted. We went to Myrtle Beach, and Allen invited them for a trip across country. From Myrtle Beach they went all the way out to South Dakota and back again. Before they left I had a long te& night with Allen, where we talked about getting separated. He wanted to patch things up, and we both cried, but I didn't think there was enough left between us. So after seventeen years we both brokenheartedly decided to get a divorce. I didn't have enough strength to keep the marriage together. It was the hardest thing I ever did!

Allen took the children to Washington, Chicago, and South Dakota on a trip. By the end of the summer, the children were back with Allen. He had gotten so upset, that he cancelled his job offer. He had stopped smoking, he had stopped drinking, and he had turned in the opposite direction. He was going to go to Bible College to become a preacher. The college was in Pensacola, Florida, Stephan could go with him, and Renee could stay with me.

I realized how hurt we all were, but now we had to make it through it. What a mess our wonderful life had turned into. Our house in Statesville was for sale, our furniture stored, and we felt like gypsies. This was as bad as after the war.

Renee started school in Myrtle Beach, SC and I stayed busy singing.

Slowly, I started to feel free, like a huge load had been taken off my shoulder. What pressure I had been under these last few years.

I had made a nice friend, the hostess at the Sheraton, who owned a little house, and had two teenagers, a girl and a boy. Renee spent the evenings at my friend's house. That worked out well.

Some business people from Hickory heard me sing at the Sheraton. The place where I sang was always packed night after night. They came back several times, and finally asked me if I already had a winter contract. I told them that I didn't. They told me that they owned several furniture factories plus the Ramada Inn, which was at that time the best hotel in Hickory. They offered me a singing job in the Ramada Inn for the winter, and a furnished apartment. They owned those also, and offered the same pay as the Sheraton. I was to sing from 5 p.m. to 8 p.m., then the band came in.

I didn't much want to leave the beach, and Renee and I cried bitter tears again. But, it was my only option until I had more of a name. But, we already knew that we were coming back in the spring. I was booked through the whole next summer between the Sheraton and the Hilton. We had our apartment reserved, and the next summer was all set. That was some consolation.

When Renee and I had to say goodbye, and leave the beach, we were very sad, but knowing that we were going back in three months helped a lot. I felt so sorry for Renee with all that upheaval, but right now, it was survival again. It sounded familiar.

Renee and I took one more walk on that beach where we had spent so many hours, days, and weeks. We looked at the waves rolling in. We felt one more time the sand between our toes, and felt the wind tugging on our hair. We had learned one thing, that in the closeness of the mighty ocean, the mighty creation of our God, our problems, even though huge to us, were small compared to what we saw and felt here. We let our dogs off the leash one more time, and ran as fast as we could, laughing, yelling, and screaming, "We will be back."

Then we embraced and squeezed each other hard. We called the dogs, put them on the leash, and walked them to the car. We all got in, and I wept.

I had a big station wagon, and with all our stuff it was tightly packed. Peanuts sat on Renee's lap, and looked out the window. Sammy sat in the back seat, and the rest was packed to the ceiling.

Before we closed the doors, we looked up at the sea gulls one more time, swooping up and down, sailing on the wind, calling to each other, "Don't worry, and look at us. We are free; sailing on the wind. Have faith! Have faith!" Why did it take me so long to learn that? Things would be all right. We were on the way to North Carolina.

CHAPTER TEN

JOHN

We flew down that road and talked about the wonderful time we had had in Myrtle Beach, and how we could not wait to return there. The trip was about five hours. We were to meet our new friends at the Ramada Inn. When we got there, a whole group was there to welcome us.

Poor Renee was the only teenager. They had a nice double room for us, and the next morning they showed us a nice almost brand new apartment. We could have our doggies there, and everybody was really nice to us.

They gave us kitchen utensils, towels, everything we needed. They also furnished the apartment with furniture from their factories. They took such good care of us. Within two days, I was ready to start singing, and since it was from five to eight, Renee could come with me. She would do her homework or eat supper. It was very hard for her at first, but once she knew some kids, it was a little better. It was still far from perfect for a young teenager.

We befriended some people, and one day a young man said I want you to meet some nice people. So he invited some people to our apartment. It was kind of unconventional, but it was a start.

They all brought food, wine, and soft drinks. We played music, and we danced. Renee had a good time too because she got to dance, and she danced better than anybody.

It was a fun time. There were two young lawyers there who were friends and seemed to kind of like me. It was John whom I liked. We danced together like we had danced together for many years. He held me tight, and swung me around the room. He was barely taller than I was. He had kind brown eyes, and a salt and pepper moustache. I liked him a lot. He had been a government appointed judge, and he had opened his own law office. Well, most everybody left at a decent hour. Renee and I crawled into my bed and fell asleep.

The next morning we got up, and I fixed her breakfast, and we left for school. I know these were the toughest days of her young life, and I felt so bad for her.

We had become gypsies. It was harder on Renee than it was on me. She was so young, and the only constant she had now was me. I really did not know how Stephan was doing. It must have been hard for him too, maybe even harder because I always had been the parent who was always there. But Stephan really had gotten too hard for me to handle.

I called Stephan and talked to his dad. He was going to school and did a paper route early in the morning. Life had surely changed for us. What I am writing here sounds like a bad novel to me. It was a nightmare, but things did get better slowly.

We got into a routine: get up and take Renee to school, do things around the house, learn some more music, pick Renee up from school, rest for an hour, and sing from 5 p.m. to 8 p.m.

I had supper with Renee, took a walk with the dogs, watched TV, and went to bed John came over a lot of evenings. Either I invited him for supper or we went out, but I spent a lot of time with Renee.

When I think back today, I think it was all much harder for her than I thought at that time.

Renee and I were going to Myrtle Beach for Thanksgiving, but something bad happened. It was a lousy day, raining, gray, cold, and the roads were very busy. We were driving down Hwy.64-70 when all of a sudden we must have hit black ice. Our car spun around and took us straight into that big cemetery next to the highway. Then the car spun around some more and took us back onto the busy highway after I left deep tracks on several graves. We stopped right in the middle of a busy highway.

There were a lot of squealing brakes, but thank heaven no one collided. It was just a lot of noise. Renee and I were both scared to death and went home to our nice little apartment.

I fixed us a really nice Thanksgiving dinner and invited a couple of really nice people including John who also could not make it home for Thanksgiving. We played a lot of music and had a big beautiful dinner. Thanksgiving felt right even though we did not have our family together. Peanuts and Sammy got a lot of attention, and everyone seemed content and happy.

I kept thinking a lot about Stephan, and how I could have handled this better. I talked to Stephan and asked him to do his best, and when we went back to the beach, we could look into the situation again. But I told him he had to be good and not run wild. Maybe we could find another solution for the summer. To be honest, I did not know how to handle him.

We got into a routine, and Renee often came with me when I sang. She made friends with young ladies and people that I befriended. She was so mature, and she really did try with her school work. She had tested way out of her grade level, maybe she could graduate sooner. She spoke three languages: German, English, and French. She also had a couple of girlfriends now in school. We had to get through this winter and find a better solution next year.

John was such a great guy, and we started falling deeply in love. He was legally separated from his wife and could soon get his divorce. I was ready to make my separation legal too. Those were unstable times, and I would never want to go through all that again. If we had done this in Germany at least my children would still have friends and family. John tried so hard to help us, but he really couldn't.

Renee did her homework at night at home while I learned new music.

Christmas was near, and we did Christmas shopping. Stephan was going to spend Christmas with us.

John took us to the mountains to ski, and while everyone went on the mountain I skated in the skating rink on Beech Mountain, N.C. They were playing cheerful Christmas music, and I skated to the beloved songs. I looked at the mountains, and the snow covered trees all around me.

It was so beautiful.

That's where I met my long time friends, Bill and Evelyn. They were friends of John's, and we became good friends too. My children loved Bill and Evelyn. Evelyn was strikingly beautiful with long blonde hair and very blue eyes. They invited us to their A-frame house, and we had hot chocolate and cookies and visited for a while.

That had been a great weekend. The days flew and soon Christmas was here. One of our new friends, Ted, took us into the woods, and we cut our own Christmas tree. We thanked Ted, and the three of us went and bought some decorations just enough to make it festive. It helped. We put the tree right in the window so you could see it from the outside.

We didn't have many gifts, but we each had something nice, so we could put a new outfit together. It was not like it used to be, but we were okay. We couldn't help it though to reminisce.

I kept saying, "Next year will be a whole lot better." I felt sorry for Allen, but the good part was, it was really peaceful.

Even the children made a statement that what happened to us was sad, but it was so nice that no one was fighting. To this day, my children tell me that we should never have left Germany.

Life would have been so much better for the three of us. But, I did not make quite enough money to carry the whole load. And now America was our home.

We had a really nice Christmas dinner at night and invited some people again who did not have family here. We ate and drank wine and sang Christmas songs in English and in German.

We had made friends.

On New Year's Eve we got all dressed up, and the four of us came along for my singing, and then we stayed and danced to the band and drank champagne at midnight. The children had Coke. Stephan and Renee both were fabulous dancers because they had danced in my school in Germany. John was also a good dancer, so we had a wonderful time dancing in the New Year.

We had one little surprise. Allen called and said that a friend of his would come to Hickory for one day because she wanted to meet Renee and Stephan. We were not too happy, and I told Allen that I did not want to meet her. She would have to go to a hotel. Well, the children were not too pleased, but they did meet her. She was about twenty-five years old and was after Allen. I was not going to get in the middle of this. Evidently he met her in Bible College. The children told me she was not pretty, but very young and pretty nice. Later Allen married her and started a whole new family.

My children really liked John. He was the kindest man I ever knew and was very well liked in the community. He had been a judge before he opened his law practice, and now he had this little law office right by the railroad tracks. When a train came by, and he was on the phone, he had to excuse himself. He told me that he had lost everything "in the war" with his ex-wife.

Christmas vacation was over, and Stephan had to leave. He hugged our two dogs, little Peanuts and big Sam.

We were all sad when we took him to the little airport in Hickory. Before he left, Stephan took me in his arms, and whispered in my ear, "Mom, if you let me come back to you, I will never try to run away like I did when we lived in Statesville. I promise."

I said, "We will talk about it. I love you."

We all shouted, "See you in the summer. See you in the summer," as he boarded the plane.

That night, we all felt very blue. The holidays were over, Stephan had left, and John and I felt like everything was temporary. Renee went to bed early, and John stayed late. We sat on the couch, he held me in his arms, and we whispered to each other. When I thought about us leaving, in not too long a time, I really got so sad that I started to cry.

John said, "We can always see each other on the weekends."

I was so sad. I was just sure it would all be over with us.

John was just so sure we would last forever, and we almost

did. That night we made love, and I felt as if I had always belonged to John, and that was where I needed to be. John said,

"When we both have our divorces, I want you to marry me and be my wife." We held each other for a long time until John and I went to bed.

The next morning, I took care of Renee, and went back home and headed straight for the bed for a little extra rest. I had just fallen asleep again when my doorbell rang. I tried to ignore it, but whoever it was would not go away, so I stuck my head out the upstairs window, and there stood John.

"This is not fair," he called up to me. "I have to go to work, and you get to sleep."

I just laughed and said, "You can come up."

"No, I can't," he said. "I have to go to court, but I would like to take you and Renee to dinner tonight. Is that okay?"

"With pleasure," I said. "So, that's a date. See you at 8:15."

"Bye," I shouted, and again went back to sleep.

John was at the Ramada Inn at eight o'clock. Renee and I were very excited. He said, "I am taking you to the best steak house in town."

"Wow," we said. "Did you win the lottery?"

"I got a really good case in," he answered.

We had a wonderful dinner, and talked and laughed a lot. Renee was very cheerful too because spring was quickly approaching, and all she could thing of was going back to the beach.

I was supposed to be back at the Sheraton in mid-March. Renee and I had planned to go back to the beach during Easter weekend, and check to see if our condo was still being held for us. Money was tight because in March I had to pay for the Hickory apartment, and start paying for Myrtle Beach. I got a raise from the Sheraton. That would really help.

The snow on the mountains was getting less, and Evelyn and Bill called us to see if we wanted to come up to the mountains before it was all gone. They invited us up, and one Sunday we went up and spent the day there. We left just before dark because John wanted to show us the "brown mountain lights." The story went that in a certain area on the way back from Beech Mountain, you could see these lights when you looked down from the highway over the rolling hills and valleys. Quite a number of them would move all over, and it looked like they were being carried. People had tried to catch up with them, but they could never reach them. No one ever found out where they came from. The story was that they had something to do with slaves of the olden days.

As we came out of the mountains, it was just getting dark, and we parked the car and waited a while. Then we saw some lights way in the distance as if they were walking away from us. I felt the hairs on my arms stand up. Renee and I wished that Stephan could have seen them because he loved spooky things.

Soon it was time to pack our few things. This time we took a little U-Haul. We got ready to leave for the beach. The night before we left, we took the dogs for a huge walk because they had to sit in the car for many hours the next day.

When John and I said goodbye, we could barely let go of each other. Renee gave him a big hug too. And then we were on the road again. "See you next weekend."

It was a long trip, but everyone was good and patient and full of anticipation. I tell you; dogs are so smart. They just knew that we were making a big change. Sammy looked out the window almost all the way. When we got to Myrtle Beach, they could smell the ocean, and we opened the windows so we could smell the ocean breeze too.

That's when we got really excited. Everyone was sniffing the wonderful ocean air.

We went straight to the agency and got our house key. I had already paid the whole month.

(John had helped me.) He had said, "Let me pay the last months here in Hickory. I lived there too."

I already missed him, but as soon as we drove up in front of our little two-story townhouse, we got excited again. We got out of the car, and we could hear the ocean. We were three blocks from the beach and could hear the waves and wind. We put the doggies on the leash, locked our car, and headed for the beach. I asked Renee to take Sammy. He pulled her forcefully toward the beach, and Peanuts and I were going pretty fast too. The closer we got to the ocean, the faster we went until our feet touched the sand. Our shoes went sailing through the air, and we raced to the water with our doggies.

Oh, the wind and the air. We had been liberated and felt free again. There is no place, no place at all like the mighty ocean. Better than a church, the greatest place of all creation. Thank you, God.

I gulped deep breaths, and felt like I was newborn full of life and happiness. To this day, I feel this way about the beach, but I am staying near my children and grandchild now.

We took everything into the house and straightened up for the rest of the day. The only thing that needed to be taken care of now was my music equipment, which was still in the car and had to be taken to the Sheraton and set up on the little stage in the bar.

I had three days off now: Saturday, Sunday, and Monday.

Renee had Saturday and Sunday off. We decided to spend as much time on the beach as we could. It was so good to be back, and John was supposed to arrive Saturday morning. We needed John to help us set up the beds.

We had big low pillows to sit on in the living room, and a low round table. I was going to buy a pull-out couch for the living room within the next two weeks.

It was so great to have John there. Sunday, the three of us took our dogs to the beach with their leashes, and we settled down to some serious digging to build a castle and a deep moat around it so the waves couldn't get into it so easily.

We kept putting lotion on each other's back as we got redder and redder. You call that a suntan, not a sunburn, even though it could hurt some.

It had been a glorious day. The doggies were totally exhausted when we got back into the townhouse. The dogs drank tons of water and were fed and curled up and went to sleep. And we went to eat something small, came home, showered, watched a little TV, and went to bed and slept like logs. What a great day it had been. This was one of the many wonderful weekends we enjoyed at the beach.

I was singing now from eight o'clock to 12 o'clock at night. Four times I sang for forty minutes; then I had a twenty minute break and then I sang forty minutes again. That came to forty-five songs a night. I had excellent sound equipment, and used my microphone with skill so I didn't get hoarse too easily. I talked a lot to my audience, and they loved that. They really loved my German accent, and paid close attention to what I had to say and what I sang. I asked people what they wanted to hear and passed a list of one hundred and fifty songs around from which they picked their favorites. We did a lot of sing-a-longs, and when people are involved, they have such a good time. People would come up at the end of an evening, and thank me. They told me that I made their vacation. It was a hard job but a fun job.

Stephan was supposed to join us for the summer. Renee had made fiends with the hostess's children, Pam and Doug. They were right around Stephan and Renee's age. They spent a lot of time on the beach together either at their house or at our house. Once in a while, they would go to the movies. I liked their mother very much. Her name was Connie. She was a real pretty blonde.

One afternoon after I had taken a rest, since I had to sing until midnight, I went out to the beach to check on my teenagers. I saw all these people standing on the beach and pointing out to sea. The tide was just coming in. It was a rough tide, and the waves were very high.

I asked someone what was going on, and they pointed out to sea and said, "Way out there is a small sailboat, and there are two teenagers on it, It has tipped over, and they are hanging on the outside." Someone had already gone out there but couldn't help them. The water was too rough.

Now, they called the Coast Guard. I saw someone I knew, and they thought it was Renee and Connie's son out there. I thought 1 was going to pass out.

I asked where Connie was, and they said she was on the roof of the hotel watching. I was going crazy with worry. I didn't want to go to the top of the hotel. I wanted to be by the water to see when the Coast Guard was coming. We could see how they were trying to right the boat.

Then a young man took his motor boat out with a friend and went to see if they could help.

They both had swim vests on. They went way out there in that rough ocean. One of them stayed in the boat while the other one jumped into the water and swam over to Renee and her friend.

They tried several times to right the boat, and about the third or fourth time, they had it up. A big cheer went up along the beach. I started to cry, and Connie showed up from the rooftop. She was crying too.

Then the Coast Guard showed up, and accompanied both boats to shore. Renee and her friend were exhausted and half frozen. We bundled our children up and took them home. Not going to work was not an option in my job. Stephan fixed supper, and Renee got bundled up on the couch. I got ready to sing. The lounge was already almost full with people waiting for me.

They had to open the folding doors to the dining room, which was crowded too.

First, I told everybody about our scare on the beach, and when we were done talking about that, I started to sing. It was a very emotional evening. In my mind, I kept thinking, thank you God for saving my little girl and her friend.

At the end of the evening, I sang, "Amazing grace, through many dangers, toil and snares, I have already come. 'Tis grace that brought me safe thus far, and grace will lead me home."

I hurried home to my children.

We had stricter rules for the kids now, about how far out they were allowed to go, and they must always wear life jackets. You had to let one of the parents know when you went on the water. They had to always watch the tides, coming in and going out, and they must check how strong the wind was. Life is just one big risk.

Stephan liked to go crabbing, and often supplied us with

buckets full of crabs. He cleaned them, and cooked them to perfection, with hot butter. They were yummy.

Stephan did not want to go back to school, so he was studying for his G.E.D. My children had been so far ahead anyway, that Stephan's plan way okay with me. Stephan had a lot of talents. He was an artist, and painted well. He was a good musician too, and he expressed a desire to become a hairdresser. He was also a very good cook. Renee had three more years to go.

I had some recordings made, and used them for promotions, and I also sold many of them at the end of the evening, which helped us financially.

Every morning, I walked my dogs on the beach before it got too hot. Peanuts, who was 11 years old now, got tired when I walked my miles, and she would stop by the lifeguard, who had an umbrella. We tied her up under the umbrella, in the shade, with a dish of water, and she gladly stayed with him, and rested in the shade, all the while looking for me and Sammy. When we got back, I would take them home, and that was their walk for the day. My Newfoundland didn't get tired, and loved to swim, so I always made sure that he had a big swim before he had to go in the house. He would swim right along with me, always watching, but beyond the big breakers.

People would stop on the beach and point at him as he happily swam. One time, he saw some dolphins swimming beyond the breakers also, and he was so fascinated with them that I had trouble getting him out of the water. My dog and I were real beach bums. My children had a great time too. It was a wonderful way of life.

The time just went by so quickly, and the summer seemed to get shorter and shorter. Every weekend John made the trip to the beach. We were so in love. He was the most patient man I had ever met with me and my children. He also was so generous and loving. He had one flaw though, and it was a bad one. He was very forgetful. Every night before I went to work, I took my dogs outside on their leash so they could go potty. Every night, I said, especially to John, "Please don't let the dogs out. They have done their business. I will take care of them when I get back." I was always worried about my animals. We did not have a yard there, so I'd rather do it myself.

I went off to work. It was a Saturday night, and the whole bar and the dining room were full with people. All the doors were open, and everyone was waiting for me.

I greeted several people, plugged my guitar in, and was ready to go. I turned my microphone on, and got on my stool. I looked at everyone with a big happy smile, and they all smiled back at me. I would say some friendly things like, "Did you all go on the beach today? I see some really pretty suntans." People liked a little talk, and they would talk back to me, and actually tell me about their day.

Then it was time for me to do some serious singing. I would sing all kinds of different songs, and mix them up: something with a Jamaican rhythm, something more serious, and some well known folk songs which almost everyone could sing along. It was a lot of fun for everyone. I handed out my list of 150 songs for my audience to choose from. I knew all these songs by heart.

John came in a little later and sat down in front of me with my friends. My girlfriend from High Point, looked a little serious that night, and I smiled at her. The evening went by quickly, and I was getting tired. At twelve o'clock, I thanked everyone, sang one of my favorite songs, and got ready to go home.

It always took some time to get out of there, because I had to say goodnight to so many people. Some wanted to buy some tapes, and I autographed those. Then I could finally go. I said goodbye to my friends, and John and I went to the cars. We had to drive home in separate cars.

When we got home, he took me in his arms and held me for a second, and then sat me down on the couch. He said, "I have to tell you something terribly sad."

I got very scared.

"The children are okay, but something bad happened to Peanuts."

"Where is she," I said. John said, "She wanted to go outside, so I let her out for a minute.

One of your neighbors backed their car out of the parking lot and backed over her. She was instantly dead." I let out a scream, and then I couldn't catch my breath. Then I yelled, "Where is my Peanuts?" I loved our doggie. We had brought her from Germany. She slept in my bed every night. She would lie down on top of the blanket next to me, and after I went to sleep she would go under the cover, crawl all the way down to my feet, and come up. So, when I woke in the morning, her head would be right next to mine on my pillow, facing me.

There was a little box standing near the front door. I looked at it, and John said, "That's where she is." John looked so sad and told me how sorry he was.

I said, "I told you not to let her out and without a leash in the night." I started to sob, and John didn't know how to console me.

"I want to go and bury her," I said. John carried the box to the car, and we drove to the beach. We parked the car, and I picked up the box and carried my doggie to the beach. I opened the box, and Peanuts was all rolled up in a big towel. I put my hands on her beloved familiar body, but she was still and cool. I dug her grave with my own hands.

Then I touched her again. I prayed over her, and thanked God for her. I asked him to please take her to a place where she could be happy, and where I could see her again.

We put her box in the grave, and covered her up with lots and lots of sand. I didn't want to leave her there all alone, but I had to. It was a beautiful night, and the moon was up.

I did not mark the grave. I did not want anyone to mess with it, so I left her. I cried all the way home and for the next two days. I stayed in my room. I just asked the children to take care of Sammy, and I asked John not to take care of our dog, the children and I were doing that. I know he must have felt terrible, because he was such a kindhearted man, but I couldn't talk about it. I did not have to sing on Mondays, so I had that extra day at home. When John left on Sunday, I hugged him and kissed him and told him I loved him.

Tuesday morning, I talked to my children and asked them to forgive me that I had not paid more attention to them. I know they must have mourned Peanuts too. Every one of us spent a lot of time with her. And she loved the rides that Renee gave her in her doll buggy.

We now talked about her and mourned her together. We talked about when I had her bred to the beautiful red and black long-haired Dachshund down the street, so my children could see a birth. Well, Peanuts got pregnant, and we waited with great anticipation for the birth of the babies. Well, the day came, and our vet stayed on the phone with me, but something was wrong, the babies did not come out. We rushed to his office, and she had to have surgery to have her babies. No natural birth. They were all healthy though, and Peanuts healed well and was such a good mother. All the babies went to neighbors who all bought one. It was a great joy. Once we talked about her beautiful babies, we were much happier with that wonderful memory. Now thirty years later, her picture is still hanging on the wall in my bedroom.

We went back to our routine and enjoyed the last days of summer. This time I went to Charleston, South Carolina to find a winter job. There were three really nice Holiday Inns. I called them and got to talk to the main man. We made an appointment, and they gave me a contract all the way through the winter. I finished in Myrtle Beach at the Hilton Hotel, and then it was time to get the children into school. Stephan went to the Community College and did his G.E.D. And Renee went back to high school.

We rented a three bedroom house across the river in Hickory in a nice, modest, one family neighborhood. The children made friends immediately, and they seemed to fit right in.

John moved in with us and kept his eye on them. They both had jobs now after school, and that kept them out of trouble. They both had a little car too. Things went pretty smooth for quite a while. I came home every Sunday morning and left on Tuesdays. I bought the food and wrote out daily menus. We had a cleaning lady, and everyone was very organized.

Stephan still wanted to go to hairdresser school. I think, mainly because he hated school so much.

John had his divorce now, and I would have mine in the spring. We were still totally in love.

We lived a modest lifestyle, but everyone was making progress. Everyone had friends and seemed to be happy.

During that time, I was the one who commuted home to see my family. Another year and we could probably leave them alone some on weekends. Stephan passed his G.E.D. and was ready to start cosmetology school. But as always with Stephan, it took him, altogether, I think, three different schools to graduate.

When school started again, Renee and I went to Hilton Head Island. I made a wonderful girlfriend, Margret, and we still are very close. She needed a roommate, and I stayed with her and shared the expense of her condo.

She and I had a lot of fun together. Once a week we would go to the Island Club on Saturday nights. All our friends would be there too. We had two days off, and everybody danced. When John was in town, he would go dancing too.

We met a lot of nice people there. A bunch of them were Germans, and they had the best restaurants. We got so many phone calls that sometimes we fell asleep with a phone in our hand, and did not remember who we had talked to. That happened especially often to Margret. I loved John so much; I didn't even flirt, even though I was a master in that subject.

Renee had a bunch of friends through school, and they all hung out around the pool of the Hilton Head Inn, where I sang.

Stephan had a lot of studying to do, and John worked with him, and drilled all these rules into Stephan's head by reading them to him with a German accent.

Spring came, and I got my uncontested divorce. I had no anger against Allen, but he sure messed up my life and the children's. It would take us a long time to recover. The only really good thing that came out of that was that I had such a wonderful, giving man. He helped us to stay sane and to adjust.

John proposed to me, and asked me if I wanted to go to Germany with him so my parents could meet him, and he could meet them and my brother. I was so excited. We saved our money for the trip. We got married in John's office. One of his lawyer fiends had a certificate that worked when he needed to be a magistrate. He read some words out of the bible, we said I do, we slipped the rings on, and were married.

My children were there, and Bill and Evelyn were there. We had sweet rolls and coffee, and we were off. Bill and Evelyn gave us the keys to their mountain house, and that's where we spent the night. On our way up we passed Sugar Mountain. We parked the car, and climbed the ski slope all the way up. We sat down and just looked at the scenery around us. We sat in the prettiest green field with mountain flowers growing all around us.

We said, "Let's always remember that we sat on this mountain the day we got married." We were so happy, and we were holding hands, and we never wanted to forget this.

After that, we went down the mountain to our car, and drove on to Beech Mountain. It took us a little while to find Bill and Evelyn's house. "There it is," I shouted-the cute little A-frame house. We unlocked the door and stepped in. It smelled so good, like freshly chopped wood, and the fire was laid in the fireplace.

We put our things in the master bedroom downstairs. We hugged and kissed, and somehow couldn't stop.

We had a very late supper. Evelyn had all kinds of goodies in her refrigerator which she told us to use and enjoy. They had also sent a bottle of champagne with us. It was a little chilly at night, so we lit the fire, and we were toasty warm in no time at all. It was a wonderful place.

We held each other and whispered half the night, and then we fixed the fire again and went to bed. When we woke in the morning, we woke to wonderful sunshine.

We got ready, packed, and checked the house one more time. Everything was neat and clean, and we slowly wound our car down this steep mountain.

I had to get ready to go back to Charleston the next morning to sing. I had to be there by the afternoon. All the way down the interstate, I was happy and sad. I was happy because I was married to the most wonderful and kindest man in the world, and I was sad because I already had to leave him again.

We decided to go to Germany in the fall. We had so much to look forward to.

We built an A-Frame house in a development right by the lake in Hickory. The development was called Bethlehem. It was very pretty but very lonesome. The time flew by. And I was back again on Hilton Head Island. I made a lot of money there singing and still had my friend, Margret.

We were so close, almost like sisters, and since she had lived so long in Switzerland with her first husband, she saw things a lot like I did.

Margret met someone, and they both fell in love, and a year later, they were married too. The great thing was that John and Tom liked each other too. We had so much fun together.

I got an engagement with the Grove Park Inn for a summer of singing in Asheville, N.C., which I really enjoyed. This famous and gorgeous inn was really wonderful to sing in. I always had a great view over the mountains.

John and I decided it was a good time for us to take our trip to Germany. We got passports and scraped our money together. Per telephone with my mother, we planned our trip for October. Finally, we had some quality time together.

We so looked forward to our trip. We flew out one day before my birthday. I would see my mother on my birthday. Mutti and her husband, Richard picked us up at the Frankfurt Airport, and took us home to her condominium in Wiesbaden.

When we approached Frankfurt, I thought we had come a long way. It was a struggle, but we had done it.

Renee graduated and wanted to go to Balder Fashion School in Miami. We both traveled with our own cars to get all her things to the school. Two months later, she was home again. She was too homesick. I had to go back to Charleston, and while I was there, she signed up with the Air Force. I thought I would die. My beautiful, smart little girl was in the Air Force. She simply said, "Mom, I have to do this because they will make me stick it out," and she was right.

Stephan had finally graduated from cosmetology school, and he had a really good job as a hairdresser on Hilton Head Island.

Our house was empty without the children, and John had to come and see me a lot because I couldn't stand the quiet in our lonely house.

My dog, Sammy, was always with me. Every morning, after breakfast, I would drive out to Sullivan's Island to walk on the beach for three to five miles. While I walked, Sammy took his morning swim. He was a powerful swimmer.

Every morning, we had to cross the Cooper River Bridge. Sammy would look out the window when we crossed the bridge, and I would have my eyes only on the lanes. In a cold sweat, I wondered if we would make it. The bridge hung on steel ropes, and when it was pretty windy, the bridge would swing back and forth.

One morning, it was very foggy when we got to the beach, and you couldn't see much. There were no people out, and it was very spooky. Usually at this time, the fog would already be gone, but not that day. It was very thick, and you could see no sky. I was just walking along with my big dog, Sammy, when suddenly I saw a black shadow come out of the water, noiselessly. I just stopped walking, and grabbed my dog by the collar, and we both looked, standing really still. It was a submarine.

It just passed us, close to the shoreline, no noise at all. It headed for the Charleston Harbor, and it was gone soon. Sammy and I just stood there mesmerized. That was a really spooky experience.

Renee finally got to call me once a week from boot camp. She had to stand in line, and when she finally got her turn to call me, she was so upset that she sobbed through the whole conversation. I was crying too.

Through time, that got a little better, and after a while we could talk halfway through the call, and cried the other half of the time. After her boot camp, she got to come home for about a week.

When we picked her up at the airport, she had her Air Force uniform on with her little cap. She walked so straight and had this self-assured look. I was so proud, and I could have cried. She had definitely gone through quite a change. She had grown up.

She was now in an Air Traffic Control School. They started with 100 students. After three weeks, they were down to 25. I don't remember the exact figures any more. This was 30 years ago. She graduated after grueling work with fifteen other students. She was transferred to Pope Air Force Base which is quite close to us, and she started to work there. I went to see her often, whenever I was home.

It was time for us to make preparations for our trip to Germany. We had to pack summer and fall clothes. It could get chilly there quite early. When we landed in Frankfurt, I saw all the old familiar landmarks and got very excited.

We had to go through customs, and then we saw Mutti and her husband. He had been the youngest professional colonel in the German army and fought under Rommel in Africa He was such a nice guy and now worked for General Motors in Germany. He had a great job. He was a very honorable man and was never a political person. We were so happy to see each other.

We took several little trips while we were there. We took the train to Dusseldorf to see my father, who worked in research for a pharmaceutical company. We saw the world famous cathedral in Cologne, and my brother and his wife Ulla. We took the train to South Germany, to Stuttgart, and to see Uncle Fritz and Aunt Pia. They loved John too, and he loved them.

This was a very strange story, and there are many like them. All around the cathedral in Cologne, everything was bombed, and you hardly could see a wall standing, but the cathedral rose out of the rubble, and reached straight for the sky, practically un-harmed. A few of the stained glass windows were blown out, but you could see the steeple, reaching for the clouds. Even in a war as cruel as the Second World War, there were still miracles.

I heard people telling how everything around the cathedral had burned except "God's house."

They said it had taken people almost five hundred years to build this cathedral with all the art work in it; paintings on the walls, the ceilings, the stained glass windows. One generation after the other added the art work. It was a masterpiece. Now, a lot of these had to be repaired. It was a work of love and faith, and showed again what faith and devotion can do.

When we finally left Germany, after we had visited some of John's old army friends, most of them Germans, we had rekindled love, friendships, and memories, and my love for my family.

By the way, I almost forgot about John's dance teacher. He had told me about her. She had light blond hair, which she wore in a bun, beautiful blue eyes, and a lovely personality. She laughed easily, and she spent hours trying to teach him the waltz. She had also rather big bosoms, and I am sure that really helped with all the turns you have to do in the waltz. I loved to tease him, but he always had a good time, and danced a great waltz.

We stopped in Frankfurt to visit my old friend, Micha. We stayed at their house, and he took us to the airport the next morning. The plane took off, circled over Frankfurt, and did another circle over Koenigstein. It always does that, and then we were headed for England. Goodbye my sweet home again.

When we got home, and settled in again, and Sammy was home from the vet, the dreams started. Having been back in Germany again must have brought back many memories, because I started having scary dreams. They were all about the war. The dreams came quite often now.

I dreamed about hearing the artillery, the planes, and getting shot at. My husband had to wake me because I made scared noises. He had to calm me down, and hold me until I could sleep again. I always dreamed about a little town with very hilly streets. On top of one of those hills was a house looking like a black forest house. I always tried to walk to the house, but I couldn't find my family.

I dreamed that I was at the ocean, and all of a sudden, paratroopers came from the sky, and tried to take the people on the beach prisoner. I dreamed that I tried to fly away from the soldiers, but I could never fly well enough to be safe. I dreamed about our house being on fire. It was one nightmare after another. Then, it would stop for a while, and months later, start again.

Renee got married while in the Air Force. She had just been transferred to Louisville, Kentucky to work as an Air Traffic Controller. Her young husband was a really nice young man, but they were not compatible, and neither one was mature enough for marriage. The next thing that happened was she got pregnant, and all she wanted to do was come home.

I was still singing, and John was keeping our love alive by taking turns with me, to come see me, or my coming home. We still were as much in love as we had been the first day. We never had a fight. John didn't fight. He let me complain, and then it was over.

I was pretty much stressed out by all the years of traveling, twelve in all, and I really wanted to be able to do something where I could stay home. Everyone always followed me to where I was singing, so I asked John's opinion. "How do you think a small German restaurant would work in Hickory, like on the square?"

We thought about it and asked fiends and acquaintances, and the feedback was always good.

Well, I talked to some of my wealthy friends and found two wonderful partners. We remodeled an old shoe store right on the square and built a lovely pub type restaurant like the Germans like it.

When it was finished, it looked totally German, and at first it was a huge success. We had a stage, and we always had entertainment. I found myself hosting, singing, and trying to run a restaurant. John had his law practice, and we still didn't see each other much. We both worked harder than ever.

We ran the restaurant for a little over a year, and then we sold it to someone else. That is one of the hardest businesses anyone can go into.

Renee took maternity leave and came home to have her baby. Dr. Boyd in Statesville was our doctor. One night Renee stood in front of our bed and said, "My water just broke." I never saw

John move so fast. "Get dressed, Renee. Get your suitcase." I was dressed in no time, and we were on our way to Davis Hospital. They had called the doctor, and everyone was ready for her when we got there. Our doctor was on vacation, and Dr. Fulghum delivered my grandson, who to this day is the light of my life.

Watching my grandson being born was one of the greatest experiences of my life. When his beautiful little face came out, it was the most touching thing I had ever seen. When the actual birth started, neither Renee nor I wanted to look, but Dr. Fulghum made us. I will always be grateful.

John bought us a small condo, so I could sing some in Myrtle Beach, but not to the extent as I did before. I sang there off and on until Matthew was kindergarten age, and that last summer Matthew and I spent fourteen weeks there. I felt like the ocean was my home. I had to play so many mini-golf games with Matthew that I could not count them all.

Renee had been invited to sing and play the piano with a famous band, and she traveled all over the world with them. Matthew stayed with me, and he went everywhere I went. He was totally spoiled by John and me. He was such a good little boy, who was maturing fast, and he was great fun for us.

When he was school age, we bought a house in Conover, North Carolina around the corner from a great elementary school. The first day Matthew went to school with his little lunch box.

His grandmother was allowed to stay for a while, and then she had to sneak out because she was crying. Matthew did just fine.

Uncle Fritz and Aunt Pia passed away in their mid-eighties. I was so sad; they had always been such kind, loving people. I will always miss them. They left me enough money to fulfill another lifelong dream to have some land and animals on it.

I bought five acres of farm land, fenced it in, put a barn on it, and built the first wing of a little horseshoe-shaped house. Renee came to visit us often. She was now singing in Atlanta, and we took Matthew to visit her often. We always made these little trips fun.

I had also started to volunteer music at Matthew's school. They had a great need for that, and I met one of my dearest friends there, Les, the minister of Trinity Church in Conover. I told him that I would like to start an after-school program in the fellowship hall of his church, that the regular after school program was not good enough for the children. He talked it over with me.

I hired a gymnastics teacher, a piano teacher, and an art teacher. I taught ballet and children's theater. We hired two assistants from their school and the minister's son, and we had a great program. The parents paid for the babysitting part, and extra for any lessons the children wanted to participate in. We paid for the electricity for the fellowship hall, and for cleaning up.

Everybody got paid.

We did a ballet the first year, a play, and a circus. By then, we had big and little horses on our farm, and brought some to our plays. The children almost went crazy with excitement when a horse stuck his head into the fellowship hall.

We made many wonderful friends, and all those children did fantastic in school. We served 35 children from kindergarten to fifth grade for three years. Our minister remained one of our dearest friends.

John built all the stage settings, lanterns, and whatever we needed.

We had one sad thing happen. Our pastor relocated to Naples, Florida, and we have missed him ever since. After losing him, we joined another good friend's church, a Presbyterian Church.

We got to listen to this great preacher, Ron. I also became choir director. It was just a small country church, and the minister there became very important in the growth of my faith.

One day, he told me that he had to go to the prison camp in Taylorsville to do the Sunday morning service. I immediately offered to come along if he wanted me to sing a hymn for them.

He was very happy about that, so the next Sunday I had my guitar and a song all picked out, and John and I went with him and a couple of friends who had wanted to come along. I was kind of scared, because I saw no guards around.

But, Ron started his service, I sang a song, and we all joined together on another hymn, a prayer, and it was over.

A few days later, I got a call from the prison chaplain. He asked me if I would come back on a Sunday afternoon, and sing for the men. He said he would come along, and several guys from our church would come also. I agreed, and two weeks later, we met at the prison on Sunday afternoon.

The little church was packed with men. About 80% of the

men were black. After introductions, I started talking to them, and entertaining them. I was a singer entertainer, and I had been asked to do just that. I played calypso tunes, and everbody started singing along and clapping. I had some tambourines and marocas, and handed them out. Pretty soon the whole place was rocking, and there were lots of smiles, and everyone was having a good time.

All of a sudden, a strange thing happened. I stopped playing and singing, and looked straight at the prisoners. I said, "You know, have you really thought about why you are here? Do you feel that circumstances have brought you here? Do you think that you didn't have the same opportunities as others? Maybe you have a chip on your shoulder. I want to tell you something.

You can be whoever you want to be. Everyone can make their own choices, and follow their own goals. You probably think that I had a great youth. My husband is here with me. He is a lawyer.

You probably think our road was easy. I grew up during World War Two in Berlin, Germany. We starved, we got shot at, we were in our house when it got bombed, one nightmare after the other. We were such scared children. You can't even imagine, and it lasted for six years. We ran away from Russian soldiers, and we finally got taken in to other people's homes. It took us children years to get over these things. We were like our soldiers who fought in Vietnam, scarred on the inside. People who hadn't lived in the cities, like we did, the people who lived in the country, did not know what we had been through. But, we followed our dreams. I wanted to be a singer, and I followed my dream, and I did become a singer. You make your own fate, and if you pray, you will find how much strength you have. Pray a lot; pray for strength."

Some of my friends from my church, who had been young soldiers when I was a child, told some of their stories and openly cried.

It was a very emotional scene, and it was good for all of us. I cried also while I was telling these things. I had never told my best friends what we had been through, and here I told it all. It was such a relief for every one of us.

I had always believed in God, you see his works everywhere. I always had believed in Jesus.

We knew his life, his suffering, his healing, and so many great stories. But I had never known what to do about the Holy Spirit. Now I knew. It happened to me one or two more times. One time I was supposed to speak to a gathering for especially gifted seniors in high school. There were close to 100 of them. I was supposed to give them an inspirational talk. I thought and thought I could not think how to start this talk to reach them. They were young, smart and usually would take everything with a grain of salt. For days beforehand I wracked my brain how to go about this. I went up to the podium and looked at them, and I started to talk. Everything flowed out of me; clear, sure, perfectly strong, and everything made perfect sense. "It's your life.

If you have a dream, follow it. Don't get discouraged, don't give up, and it will happen. Pray for strength!" The whole time, their eyes were riveted on me, and when I was done, I got a standing ovation. I was so happy because I felt I had inspired them. The Holy Spirit had put the words in my mouth.

Now I know there is God, there is Jesus, and there is the Holy Spirit.

My pastor, Ron, talked to me about these things, and he said he felt that I should do inspirational speaking. He had been so surprised about my speaking because I had not told him any of this before. He wrote me up a pamphlet, and it was beautiful. We had a picture on the front of the pamphlet of me and my brother. He was seven years old, and I was four, when the war started. We mailed some pamphlets out, and the calls started coming in.

Over the next few years, I must have talked and sang in several hundred churches. People still recognize me, and I barely recognize all the churches.

John always came with me. He loaded up my car with my sound system, and listened to all the inspirational speeches. John was changing though, his business had changed a lot, and it was harder and harder to get insurance companies to pay his clients what they deserved for injury on the job or in accidents.

He had to let some people go, and he got even more depressed. He went to a psychiatrist and a psychologist, and he was on medication.

Thank heavens we had our farm and our horses. He often said, "This farm is saving my life."

We spent a lot of time on our f m working and enjoying the animals. We rode the big horses.

We rode a lot on weekends until Renee and Matthew moved into town. Matthew was into sports.

He was a fine athlete. Renee divorced her first husband and married a fine young local man who loved Renee and Matthew a lot.

Renee's father, Allen, and John walked her together down the aisle on their wedding day. It was very sweet.

I was learning a lot about miniature horses. I learned to breed them, and I learned to help them give birth. I always called the vet when they went into labor, but often I had already helped the mare to give birth by the time the vet arrived. We had some really sad things happen too.

Miniature horses have a lot of trouble giving birth.

I lost two of my favorite mares and two babies through the years. We cried bitter tears over them. These little horses were like dogs. They knew their names. When I called them, they came running as fast as they could. We loved them.

These little horses make great cart horses, and they can pull a small cart with a grown man in a race. Children can easily handle them to pull a cart when they are well trained. These are sweet and amazing little creatures.

Matthew still enjoyed bringing his best friend out, and riding his pony, who was the only one who would tolerate two boys on his back. He patiently rode them around on the farm. When Matthew rode alone, he would ride his mother's big Arabian. But, they didn't come to ride much any more. Their lives and their interests had changed.

John kept getting more and more depressed, and nothing seemed to help. One day, he called me from his office and told me to take him to the family doctor. He told the doctor there that he had suicidal thoughts, and needed to go to the hospital. They called the hospital and told them that I was coming with him. People who have not had clinical depression don't even comprehend what a terrible sickness this is. I had no idea, and I could not understand why he couldn't pull himself up from this. I couldn't understand why he didn't want to be outdoors anymore, which always made him feel so good. We were both so unhappy, he for feeling so bad, and me for seeing him like that.

One day he just didn't come home at the usual time, and as

I worked outside, and took care of the horses, it started getting dark. I got more and more scared. I finally called his secretary, and asked her if she knew of anywhere he had to go after work.

She said she would call around. Another hour or so went by, and I was going crazy. Then I saw a truck come to the gate. It was the truck of his private investigator and his secretary. Behind them was a police car. I went to meet them. They were both crying and said, "He is gone."

The police car pulled up and said to me, "Your husband has committed suicide, Mrs. Ingle." I just stared at everybody and did not comprehend. I asked if I could see my husband, and the policeman advised me not to.

I just stood there and looked across my pasture, and in my head it went over and over. "He left me, he left me." I couldn't even cry. I asked the police officer, "When can I cry?"

He said, "You are in shock. That can take weeks."

I went to the phone and called my daughter, my son, and my closest friends, Bill and Evelyn.

They were all with me within minutes. My son had to come from Atlanta.

My daughter called my minister who was there within a short time and stayed late. I was disoriented and did not know what to do.

It was the most horrible incident in my life. My John. The day of his funeral, I started to cry quietly. The tears just started to flow and would not stop.

I wrote his eulogy. I told about his happy childhood; how the whole family would drive on Sundays to his grandparent's house. How he played with many of his cousins. How he loved that. I often said, "Just think, John, how I could have turned out if I could have had your childhood."

Then I thought of the struggle my children had had, and I cried for them. At the end of John's eulogy, I said, "John was a strong believer, and he knew where he was going. God is with him!"

And I said, "This song is going through my head over and over. Michael Bolton sang, "How am I supposed to live with out you, after loving you so long." Over and over it played in my head. Love, Meg

My pastor friend read this for me. Everyone cried with me. His ashes were buried in the church cemetery on Old Mountain Road. All the country folk were there.

When we had the memorial service at Trinity Church in Conover, the church was packed.

They had come from everywhere.

John had been such a lovely person, so smart, and so well liked, and in his time, he had been a wonderful judge. That's what he liked the best.

Many people had been at my house, and afterwards, I was just hiding out. I couldn't even think.

My son stayed with me for two weeks. That was a big help. Stephan was really good to me.

We worked on the farm together and sat and talked at night. The third night that he was there, we decided to go to bed about eleven o'clock. He had gone to the big guest room, and I was in my bathroom, when Stephan came out of his room and looked white as a ghost and said that there was a sound like Morse code in that guitar case that was leaning against the corner in his bedroom. I said, "Oh Stephan, you must have imagined that, that can't be." I stayed in his room with him for a while, and we didn't hear anything else.

We went to bed and slept soundly. We had three farm dogs at the time, and they were never allowed in the wing where the bedrooms were, but since John had died, I let them sleep wherever they wanted to and that was right around my bed.

When Stephan had to leave, I was very sad, and I felt very much alone. Matthew and Renee lived with Rodney now, and I just had to get used to my situation. I did not hear much from my friends. I guess the stigma of a suicide was too much for them. Maybe they didn't know what to say to me. My minister talked to me almost daily, and sometimes I drove to the church just to talk to him for a short time. The people from that church were very good to me especially during that time. The minister counseled me all the time. It helped.

I got an invitation to sing for an evening at Rock Barn Country Club. I accepted, and it was several weeks away. Also the Trinity Baptist Church in Hickory called me, and asked if I could do my inspirational program for them now that I had to cancel. I booked with them and gave myself four more weeks. I was afraid that if I cancelled everything, I might get totally out of the picture and not get asked any more.

I did the inspirational speaking at First Baptist first. I just made up my mind that I would only concentrate on what I had planned to say. It was hard, but I made it.

Then I got a call from the Hickory Little Theater. They did their yearly fundraiser, it was a really big deal, and it was done on three levels in their theater. They handed out programs when people came in the door where they announced all the different programs on each level at the theater, and at what time.

The firemen's kitchen was a very popular room with a big stage downstairs, and the last show was there with really well-known soloists and groups. I cannot remember if I was the last or next to the last. The longer I waited, the more nervous I got. Most of the soloists either had great pianists, or duos accompanying them. The lady before me, an accomplished singer, had a pianist, and on her last song she had a harmonica. It was beautiful. And then it was my turn.

I was pretty nervous. I went on stage, and did what I had learned through all the years I had entertained people. I put my guitar around my neck, looked at everyone around the room, there was standing room only, smiled at everyone and said, "I am pretty intimidated, everyone had the most beautiful accompaniment, and here I am all alone, just me and my guitar."

I strummed my guitar once, and belted out, "Summertime." It was totally quiet in that room.

You could have heard a pin drop. After thundering applause, I sang several more songs, and finished with, "Oh Danny boy, the pipes, the pipes are calling, from glen to glen, and down the Mountainside. The summer's gone and all the flowers are dying. 'Tis you, 'tis you, must go and I must bide." It was the goodbye song from a father to his son, who had to go away to war.

After the first few notes, I heard a harmonica playing from the very back of the room, and then the people parted, and down the center came the young man who had helped the other singer, walking toward me playing his harmonica while I was singing. I smiled at him, and so did everyone else. It was so pretty.

He stopped right in front of me, in front of the stage, and we finished the song together. I bowed, holding my guitar, and then I shook his hand and smiled at him and pointed at him for acknowledgement, and the people applauded for a long time, and gave us a standing ovation.

I was very happy about this evening, and got many beautiful letters because of it.

CHAPTER ELEVEN

YOU CAN LOVE AGAIN

When my date with Rock Barn Country Club came closer, I decided to call some friends to give me support. A bunch of people came from Hickory, several came from Newton, and Conover. I had heard that one of my friends from our singing group in Statesville, our friend whom I had not seen in over thirty years, was a widower, too. I called him, and reintroduced myself, and told him that I was singing at Rock Barn Country Club, if he would like to come by.

He did want to come by, and I saw him again after all those years.

It was late in the evening when he came in, and if he had not told me on the phone that his hair was snow white, I probably would not have recognized him. But, he was still very handsome.

After I was done singing, I introduced him to some of my friends. Rock Barn Country Club was getting ready to close, and he asked where we could talk a little bit. There was nothing around that didn't close by ten o'clock. I told him my farm was just around the corner from the club. I told him we could go to my farm and talk a little.

He agreed, and followed me to my place. At that time, I had a really pretty farm right on Highway 16. We went there, and after we had unpacked my equipment and carried it into the house, we sat down and talked. We talked about so many things, especially about our spouses, and how they died. It was a sad subject, but it is something one wants to talk about. To me, it was such a sad subject, I didn't want to have to talk about it again.

Alex said, "It is good that you can tell me about this."

We talked about how society pretty much ignores you, when all of a sudden you are single again, even your good friends go through periods when they ignore you. "It is a very painful time," Alex said. He went through the same thing.

It was good for both of us to be able to unburden ourselves. It had really gotten late. I invited him for supper for the weekend. We hugged each other, and Alex left. I really liked him, and looked forward to seeing him again.

He called me the next morning, and thanked me for the visit. We both said that we looked forward to seeing each other on the weekend.

We started to date regularly. He took me out, and I invited him over. He loved my tiny horses, and he's a real dog lover.

I had some construction done in my house. I enclosed a covered porch, took part of the wall out, and opened it up to my large living room. I ended up with a whole row of windows, and a room with indoor/outdoor green carpet, and a small palm tree under each window. The white wicker furniture made a nice contrast with the green.

I had taken my job on again as choir director in my little church. The friendship many of the people offered me there really helped.

On the way to church, John had always held my hand, and I missed him everywhere I went.

I would cry and say, "Please, John, tell me and show me where you are, just once. Please hold my hand."

I would hold my hand out, but I never felt his. I asked him, "Where are you now?" and I remembered what he said once, "In another dimension."

One night Alex and I were sitting on the couch after supper, and he had his arm around me.

All of a sudden, with a terrible crash, two framed pictures fell off of the top of the bookshelf, a portrait of John, and a portrait of me. They had been standing side by side on the top shelf.

"Whoa," said Alex. "Maybe I better get out of here." And he smiled.

That night I woke up out of a sound sleep, and saw John's face real close to mine, looking into my eyes. "John," I said, "It is about time that you came to see me." I was petting his face, and he said to me, "You have to be very strong now," and he faded away.

I never saw him again, but I felt like he was near me all the time, and it gave me a lot of strength.

Matthew visited me the next day with Renee, and we played with the horses all day. In the evening, we cleaned all the stalls, and put fresh bedding in, fed and watered them, and everybody was happily tucked away. It had been a great day.

I was waiting on Alex to have supper with me. I glanced out the window, and saw this tall, handsome man walking up my driveway with a beautiful smile on his face.

His blue eyes were sparkling, and his snow white hair glistened in the setting sun. I went to meet him, returning his smile.

When I got to him, I rose on my tiptoes, put my arms around his neck, and kissed him. His arms went around my middle, holding me firmly, and smiling down at me he said, "What a wonderful way to be welcomed." My heart just went out to this giant.

Later on, we had supper by candlelight in my Florida room, at the back of the house.

It was a very warm room with the white, soft wicker furniture, thick green carpet, and tropical plants along the windows. With the candlelight, it was a very romantic setting. After sitting and talking to each other, we got up, and our eyes met and locked. He took me in his arms and kissed me, first softly, and then passionately. It was as if the world had stood still, and we were young again, a magic moment.

And then the rain came falling softly against the windows. Alex and I looked at each other, and held each other for a long time.

And we knew: "You can love again."

EPILOGUE

When I look over my life today, I think it was pretty rough, and sometimes it was. But I was so blessed in so many ways. God had given me so many talents which rescued my children and me whenever it was necessary, whenever the need arose.

First, I was a mother and a dance teacher. I didn't have to leave my children when I worked. I did this for years, and kept studying dance while I taught. I took children's stories and set them to dance. My children, my students, and I had a lot of fun wherever we lived.

Then I became a professional singer. I sang in Germany, England, and the southern part of the United States in the popular resort areas. I recorded and also taught what I had learned, and my students turned into very talented musicians and performers. Renee sang and played the piano. Later she joined the Air Force, married, and had a wonderful baby, my grandson. He is my pride and joy.

My daughter is a beautiful lady with long blond hair and big brown eyes. She is a beauty inside and out. She is a successful business person, and my best friend. After she toured half the world singing with a well known band, she still sings at least two nights a week. She saves dogs, one at a time.

My son is fifty years old and just went back to college. He has really gotten interested in computer science and sings occasionally in Atlanta. He saves people one at a time.

My grandson is now a successful business man with a six-figure income. He at one time had a promising baseball career but had to make other choices because of injury. While Renee traveled and sang, my husband John and I raised Matthew and lived like young parents. Matthew made our life so sweet and gave us so much love. We helped children and saved dogs.

Those years were beautiful. They were the years where we had our farm first with miniature horses and later full sized animals. Those years were like a dream come true. We also helped a boy from an orphanage here until he was married and independent. He was a very sweet young man with a very rough past. Volker whom we had to leave in Germany grew up with my dear girlfriend and did so well with school and University that he became a well known doctor. He married a beautiful German girl. We went to see him for the third time, and I was so happy at how successful and happy he was with his wife and two beautiful children. We stayed in touch through the years. He had come to see us, and we had gone to see him.

The tapestry of my life tells many stories. Life is always full of gifts and also full of losses.

My first husband Allen had remarried a much younger wife and had two children, but he died relatively young from kidney failure. He and I became very good friends after we got divorced, and we all mourned him deeply after he died.

My father passed away next from a heart attack at age 65. My mother died at 93 and was ready to leave this world and go home.

Alex and I had kind of a stormy relationship, but we had gotten so used to being together that even today I could not imaging living without him. We have now been married for five years.

Two years ago, Alex took me to Germany to visit my brother. He flew me first class, which was a first for me. What a luxury that was! My brother had had a liver transplant, which worked for him for ten years. Now his health was getting bad, and he did not want to live anymore. I was so glad I got to see him. We held hands for three days, then Alex and I continued our trip through Germany, visiting everyone we had close ties to. It was a wonderful trip down memory lane. My brother died three months later, one week before Christmas. I miss him. I believe more and more that we will see each other again in heaven, and even my beloved animal friends.

When I look at the tapestries of my life, I see in the background ghostly ruins of cities, fire, and smoke. I see faces coming and going, smiling at me. And I see a thread winding through the landscape of my life, and I know that the golden thread winding through light and shadow is all the love I have received from the people and creatures whom I loved so much.

My husbands, my children, my grandson, they are the sun on the horizon when a new wonderful day is born, and the smiles in the shadows when the evening star appears, and we contentedly lay down our heads to sleep.

I thank you, God, for every day with a gold thread of love winding through it, and every night where we can sleep in peace.

LaVergne, TN USA
17 January 2011
212814LV00004B/4/P

9 781432 761622